Computer Programming in C for Beginners

Avelino J. Gonzalez

Computer Programming in C for Beginners

 Springer

Avelino J. Gonzalez
Department of Computer Science
University of Central Florida
Orlando, FL, USA

ISBN 978-3-030-50752-7   ISBN 978-3-030-50750-3   (eBook)
https://doi.org/10.1007/978-3-030-50750-3

This Springer imprint is published by the registered company Springer Nature Switzerland AG
The registered company address is: Gewerbestrasse 11, 6330 Cham, Switzerland

Preface

It is universally accepted that computers have radically changed the way we live. In the not-too-distant past, computers were only for scientists, engineers, and tinkerers. No longer. The devices we carry in our pockets and handbags to which we casually refer as "smartphones" are nothing but pocket computers that just happen to make phone calls, among many other things. This has forced most people to become computer savvy in ways that were unimaginable even 15 years ago.

However, being savvy with computers these days generally means being able to use apps, write email, and manipulate websites. These apps and websites are generally preprogrammed to work in a point-and-click fashion, with a limited menu of things that can be done by the user. The intent, of course, is to make them easy and intuitive to use, as well as to ensure that the common user cannot do any damage to the system. The programmers of the app or the website take on the responsibility of making the user's life as simple (and as secure) as possible. That is, the user need not know how the app works … just how to use it.

The truly valuable skills, therefore, come from being able to program a computer to do interesting and useful things. This can only be done by being able to write programs that tell the computer what to do and how to do it. This is where this book comes in.

Modern computers are highly complex electronic devices. It can take several years of university-level studies to truly understand how one works. This is what computer scientists and computer engineers typically do, although it is also very possible to self-learn most, if not all of that. Nevertheless, to program a computer, a programmer need not fully understand the computing device. This is true even for writing relatively complex programs. Therefore, we believe that self-learning computer programming is not only possible but also done commonly.

From my many years of teaching engineering and computer science at the university level, I fully believe in the concept of hands-on guided learning. The guided hands-on approach espoused by this book was found by college students to be very helpful in their learning computer programming. Therefore, this book naturally represents a hands-on, self-teaching tool for learning computer programming ... in C. It is specifically designed for those with little or no prior programming experience. One could say that it is like a participatory narrative – a story, if you will – in which the reader must participate in the plot by implementing the exercises as they are presented and discussed, from the first to the last page.

It can also be used as a laboratory manual in an academic setting, which is how it was used and tested for several years before being enhanced to become this self-contained textbook. Alternatively, it can be used as part of a professional course in C programming.

So, the question then is why C?

Since its introduction in 1972, the C language has been one of the most widely used high-level programming languages. Its heavily typed nature (this will be explained later) and its ability to offer the programmer low-level functionality such as direct access to memory (through pointers) and bit-level operations have set it apart from other high-level computing languages. As a result, C is often called a mid-level language. These very features, on one hand, have made it a difficult language to learn for most beginning programmers; on the other hand, these same features provide an excellent opportunity to learn more about how computers work.

We warn the prospective learner that this book was not designed to be merely read. The programs included herein are not examples, but rather working exercises that demonstrate the features (and also foibles) of programming in C. Therefore, success in using this book requires that the learner follow along by programming the progressively more complex exercise programs presented in this book. Merely reading the book without doing the exercise simultaneously will reduce its effectiveness.

Furthermore, the book adheres to the just-in-time-learning philosophy. That is, concepts are introduced just before they are needed. Therefore, it is not likely to work well as a reference book.

Problems at the end of each chapter will challenge the learner to explore the concepts learned in the chapter in an independent fashion.

The course and book employ an *integrated development environment* (IDE), to be used by the learner to implement the programs that exemplify the concepts and programming features being learned on the spot. We should note that other authors recommend against using the IDEs in favor of a generic text editor and a compiler invoked through a command line prompt. While there is some merit to that approach and I do not disagree with their basic premise, I do think that for beginning programmers to learn quickly, using an IDE is preferable.

The open access IDE called **Code::Blocks** is recommended, but any other IDE that has the basic functionality of IDEs can be used. The process of following the text step-by-step and implementing the code found in the text is the key to quick and effective learning in this book and represents its main distinguishing feature from most other basic programming books.

One thing to note is that computer programming lingo can be overwhelming to beginners. Terms that programmers use regularly can be befuddling. Rather than define them at the beginning of the course and by following our just-in-time learning philosophy, we introduce them and discuss them in context, exactly when it first becomes necessary to do so.

It should also be noted that this text does not cover advanced concepts of C programming. It is designed to treat basic programming concepts in a straight-forward manner, and without the many programming shortcuts that are so common in C.

Orlando, FL USA   Avelino J. Gonzalez

Contents

1 Creating a Simple C Program, Compiling, and Executing It 1
   1   Downloading and Installing Code::Blocks 2
   2   Compiling and Executing Your First C Program 6
   3   Anatomy of a C Program 7
       3.1   The `main()` Function 7
       3.2   Pre-processor Directives 8
       3.3   Comments 9
   4   Creating Your First Program 9
   5   Summary 13
   6   Problems 14

2 Variables, Memory, and Operators 15
   1   Variables – A Brief Introduction 15
   2   Some Operations on Simple Variables 16
       2.1   Data Typing in Variables 18
       2.2   Defining and Initializing Variables 18
       2.3   Setting and Reading the Values of Variables 20
       2.4   Mixing up Data Types 22
   3   Working with Variables and Operators 23
       3.1   Addition, Subtraction, and Multiplication 23
       3.2   Division 24
       3.3   Increment/Decrement Operators 26
       3.4   Boolean Operators 27
       3.5   Embedded Operations in C 29
   4   Input/Output Functions 30
   5   Constants 32
   6   Summary 33
   7   Problems 33

3 Selection Structures 35
   1   Selection Structures – A Short Introduction 35
   2   Single-Selection Structures 36
       2.1   Exactly What Is Defined as the "Designated Code"? 37
       2.2   How Does One Handle the "Otherwise" Case? 38
   3   Double-Selection Structures 39
   4   Multiple-Selection Structures 40
   5   The `break;` and the `return;` Statements 42

	6	The `switch` Structure	43
	7	Summary	45
	8	Problems	45

4 Repetition Structures 47
	1	Repetition Structures – A Short Introduction	47
	2	`for` Loops	49
	3	The `while` Loop	55
	4	The `do-while` Loop	57
	5	Generating Random Numbers in C	58
	6	Alternative Ways to Work with the Repetition Constructs	60
	7	Nested Loops	62
	8	Summary	63
	9	Problems	63

5 Defining and Calling Functions 65
	1	Defining and Calling Functions – A Short Introduction	65
	2	Defining Functions	67
	3	Calling Functions	70
	4	Returning Values	73
	5	Passing Values of Variables to Functions	75
	6	Scope of Variables	75
		6.1 Global Variables	76
		6.2 Local Variables	77
		6.3 Static Variables	79
	7	Summary and Conclusion	79
	8	Problems	79

6 Pointer Variables 83
	1	Pointers – A Short Introduction	83
	2	Declaring and Initializing Pointers	84
	3	Input/Output with Pointers	86
	4	Calling Functions by Reference with Pointers	88
	5	Pointer Math	90
	6	Double Pointers	93
	7	Summary and Conclusion	95
	8	Problems	95

7 Arrays 97
	1	Arrays – A Short Introduction	97
	2	Defining and Initializing Arrays	99
	3	Arrays, Pointers and Pointer Math	101
	4	Arrays and Loops	102
	5	Passing Arrays to Functions	104
	6	Character Arrays – Strings	106
		6.1 Inputting Strings with `scanf()`	107
		6.2 Printing Strings with `printf()`	108
	7	Multi-dimensional Arrays	108
	8	Summary and Conclusion	111
	9	Problems	111

8   Structures..113
   1   Structures – A Brief Introduction.................................113
   2   Instantiating Structure Variables 114
       2.1   Instantiating within the Body of the `struct` Definition 114
       2.2   Instantiating Structure Variables Using the Structure Tag.............115
       2.3   Defining New Structure Data Types with `typedef`....................116
   3   Member Access Operators: The Dot and the Arrow Operators.............117
   4   Passing Structures to Functions.................................120
   5   Structures, Arrays, and Loops 123
   6   Summary and Conclusion 124
   7   Problems 125

9   Strings and Advanced I/O 127
   1   Strings – A Deeper Treatment 127
       1.1   Initializing Strings 127
       1.2   Setting Values to String Variables 128
       1.3   The Length of a String......................................129
       1.4   Comparing Strings...129
       1.5   Concatenating Strings 130
   2   Other Input/Output Functions in C for Characters and Strings 131
       2.1   The `puts()` Function......................................131
       2.2   The `putchar()` Function 132
       2.3   The `gets()` Function......................................132
       2.4   The `getchar()` Function 133
   3   Optional Formatting Features of `printf()` 133
       3.1   The `width` Specifier......................................134
       3.2   The `.precision` Specifier 136
       3.3   The `flag` Specifier 137
       3.4   Really Long Strings in `printf()` 138
   4   Escape Characters 138
   5   External File I/O 139
       5.1   Writing to External Files 139
       5.2   Reading from External Files 141
       5.3   What About That Thing Where `fopen()` Returns `NULL`? 143
   6   Summary and Conclusion 143
   7   Problems 144

10   Multi-file Programs...147
   1   Programming Considerations When Building Multi-file Programs 147
       1.1   The Obvious Ones 147
       1.2   Scope of Variables 148
       1.3   Scope of User-Defined Functions 148
   2   Our Example Program 149
   3   Case 1: Simple Split with Local Variables..........................150
   4   Case 2: More Complex Version Using Local Variables.....................150
   5   Case 3: Introducing Global Variables into the Equation 151
   6   Case 4: Complicating the Issue with More Global Variables 153
   7   Case 5: More Complex Still – Functions That Are Not Seen 154
   8   Case 6: The Use of `static` for Functions..........................155

    9   Summary and Conclusion 155
    10   Problems 156

11 Dynamically-Allocated Memory and Linked Lists 157
    1   An Introduction to Defining Variables During Run Time 157
    2   How to Allocate Memory Dynamically for Variables 158
    3   Linked Structures – A Brief Introduction 160
    4   How to Link Together Dynamically-Allocated Memory 162
    5   Traversing a Linked List 167
    6   Inserting Nodes into an Existing Linked List 168
         6.1   Inserting New Nodes at the Front of the Linked List 168
         6.2   Inserting New Nodes at the Tail of the Linked List 169
         6.3   Inserting a New Node Somewhere in Between 170
    7   Deleting Nodes from the List 172
    8   Doubly-Linked Lists 172
    9   Summary and Conclusion 172
    10   Problems 173

12 Searching and Sorting 175
    1   Searching – A Brief Introduction 175
    2   The Sequential Search 176
         2.1   Sequential Search of an Array for the First Appearance of a Key 177
         2.2   Sequential Search of an Array for Multiple Appearances of a Key 178
         2.3   Sequential Search of a Linked List 180
         2.4   Thoughts on Advanced Search Techniques 182
    3   Sorting a List 182
         3.1   SelectionSort Algorithm 183
         3.2   BubbleSort Algorithm 186
         3.3   Thoughts on Advanced Sorting Algorithms 188
    4   Summary and Conclusion 188
    5   Problems 188

Glossary 189

Index 191

Creating a Simple C Program, Compiling, and Executing It

1

Writing a computer *program*, in its most basic sense, is the process of putting together a set of *instructions* in a correct and meaningful sequence for the computer to execute, to achieve some desired result. These instructions tell the computer what to do and how to do it. Instructions that a computer is capable of executing are pre-defined in the computer's *instruction set* - only these instructions can be included in a program. Such instructions are (possibly long) strings of 1's and 0's, where 1's represent a certain level of voltage (e.g., 5 volts DC), and 0's represent a lower level of voltage (possibly 0 volts). These strings of 1's and 0's form what is called *machine language*, and it is the only thing a computer's processor can understand. (Actually, it is the voltage levels that the processor is able to understand, but that is a topic for a different book.)

Certainly a computer program can be written directly in machine language, as they were in the very early days of computing. However, as one can imagine, writing programs composed of very long strings of 0's and 1's is an extremely difficult and tedious process, and subject to many errors. To address this problem, computer languages were developed where pseudo-English text statements represent one (or more) machine language instruction(s). A sequence of such text statements comprises the program *source code,* and is placed in a text file called the *source file*. (Source files in C typically have a `.c` extension.) C is one of these so-called *high-level programming languages*, as are Python, Java, Basic, Pascal, Lisp, Prolog, Fortran and many, many others. From this point forward in our discussion, you should assume that we are referring to C when we mention a high-level programming language, unless otherwise specifically stated.

However, as we said above, processors don't understand text – only 0's and 1's. These high-level C language statements in the source code must be translated from text into machine language in order for the processor to understand them. This translation process is called *compilation*. So, the source file is sent to a C *compiler* that will "translate" the C language text statements in the source code into machine language instructions that the processor can understand. Then, if successfully compiled (i.e., no errors) and *linked* to other program files specified in the program (e.g., standard libraries), the program becomes *executable* – that is, able to execute. The executable file (usually with the file extension `.exe`) will run, and if correct, it will provide the results sought by the programmer.

The difficulty in programming a computer comes from ensuring that appropriate program statements are used, that they are written correctly, set in the correct sequence, and presented with the proper data. This can be bewildering and frustrating to beginner programmers, but rest assured that as one gains experience, it becomes much easier ... and much more fun.

© Springer Nature Switzerland AG 2020
A. J. Gonzalez, *Computer Programming in C for Beginners*,
https://doi.org/10.1007/978-3-030-50750-3_1

Going forward, the process of building the source file, saving it with a .c file extension, compiling it, linking it and executing it can be done through more than one means. In this book we will make use of an *Integrated Development Environment* (IDE) specifically designed to facilitate the building, compiling, debugging and running the C programs you write. The specific IDE recommended for this book is called Code::Blocks. It is a public domain (i.e., free) system, downloadable from the internet. However, any IDE can be used as long as it has a well-accepted C compiler associated with it. Nevertheless, it is possible that some of the C statements discussed in this book may not work, or at least not exactly in the same manner.

In this chapter, we will show how to download the Code::Blocks IDE, install it, and then compile and execute the iconic first program "Hello, World!" in C, that comes as default with Code::Blocks. We will then modify it to display something different to get you used to working with the Code::Blocks tool. We will also purposely put some errors in the program to gently introduce you to errors – something you will unfortunately have to get used to – all programmers do! We will cause two types of errors for your learning experience – *compilation errors* and *logic errors*. In the process, we will learn what some of the C statements used mean.

We continue by downloading Code::Blocks so we can start writing very simple programs.

1   Downloading and Installing Code::Blocks

Code::Blocks has many features, most of which you will NOT need for the exercises in this course. This IDE was originally designed for Windows, and not MacOS. So, if you have a Windows computer, it should be easy to install. Unfortunately, if you have an Apple product, it may not be quite so easy. It will work … ultimately, but it may take some extra effort to get it to work properly. For Mac users, you can watch the following Youtube video that will teach you how to install Code::Blocks on your Mac. Note that the video refers to a C++ program, but don't worry about that.

The link is: https://www.youtube.com/watch?v=4JPSt7ZIF4M

For the first step in downloading and installing Code::Blocks on a Windows computer, visit the website http://www.codeblocks.org

Go to the "Downloads" link found in the overhead menu and click on it.

In the Downloads page, click on "Download the binary release". If you are more experienced and want to download the source code, feel free to do so, but you will be on your own.

In the subsequent page you will find several choices. The main classification of choices involves whether your platform is Windows, Linux or Mac OS. We will assume here that it is Windows. So, click on the latest version of Code::Blocks available (at the time of this writing, it is v17.12, so the file you will download is `codeblocks-17.12mingw-setup.exe`), and choose `Sourceforge.net` as the source. The source you select doesn't matter – both are good – but you have to choose one, so make it this one.

The setup wizard will ask a few (very few) questions. Use your intuition to answer them properly. The system will then download the file, and when done will ask you if you wish to install the file. Of course, say yes. Once the installation is complete, double click on the Code::Blocks icon to launch the system. The screen should look as follows (or probably very similar if it is a more recent version of Code::Blocks):

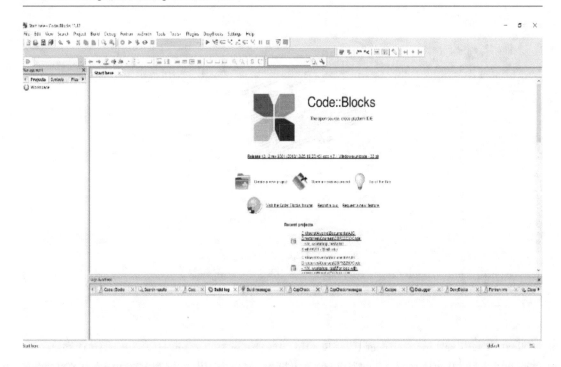

In this page, the only two meaningful links as far as this book is concerned are:

```
Create a new project
```

and

```
Open an existing project
```

Given that this is likely to be your first time seeing this screen, go ahead and click on

```
Create a new project
```

The next screen is called the "New form template" (see below). It has several choices.

The only one you will need in this page is the top right one – `Console application`. (It may be in different locations in the same screen in more recent versions.) Please double click on it.

Next it asks whether you want C or C++. It's a simple question, so there is no need to show a screen shot for this one. Put the blue highlight on `C` and click on `next >` at the bottom of the page. Note that the highlight will by default be placed on `C++`, so please be sure to actively move the highlight to `C`.

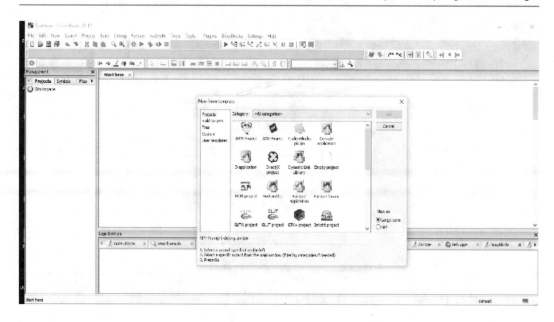

Next, it will ask for a project title. For this chapter exercise, give it the title of the relevant chapter. So, call it Chap-1. Code::Blocks will automatically fill in the other entries. If you prefer to save your program in a specific directory, then you should specify that on the second line titled "Folder to create project in:" See below:

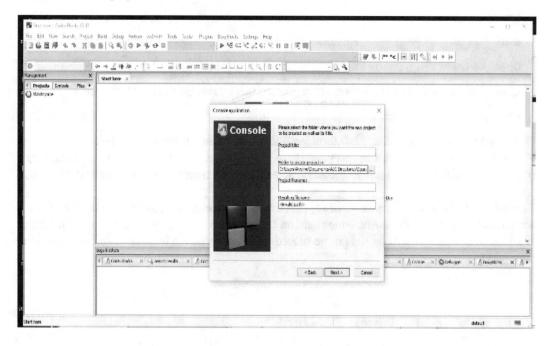

Lastly, the succeeding page will ask you some questions about compilers, debug configuration and release configuration. Just use their default answers and hit the button titled "Finish" (not shown here).

After that, it takes you to a screen with four windows (well, really three useful ones). See below:

The largest window is your editor space, where you will be writing your program. This will be your most important window. The smaller window below the editor page is where all messages from the system to you will be posted. Any errors or warnings generated during the compilation process will be shown here. Unfortunately, this will be your second most important window.

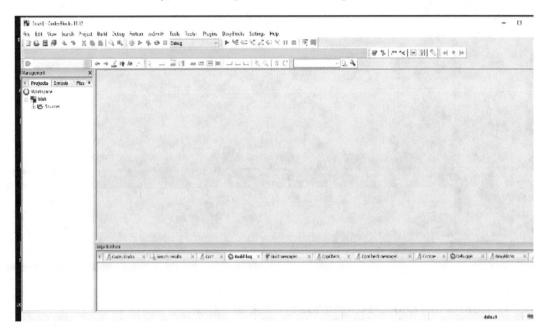

The vertical window on the left shows the structure of your program. It is titled "Workspace". For complex programs, this is an important thing to know, as it shows the structure of the files that make up your program. However, for the relatively simple programs you will be writing here and for the next few chapters, it is not that important. Nevertheless, you will need it once at the beginning, as you will notice that the screen editor is dark gray-colored and inaccessible. To enable access to it, go to "Sources" on the left-side vertical screen and click on the + sign on its immediate left. A sub-branch in the tree called `main.c` will appear. This file will be your main program source code file, or simply, the source file. In C, source files traditionally have a `.c` extension, although that is not an absolute requirement. For this book, however, assume that it is an absolute requirement. You will later be able to change the name of the source file to whatever name you want (e.g., `Joe - chap-1.c`), while still keeping the `.c` extension.

For now, click twice on `main.c` and the editor screen will turn to white and display some C code statements. See the screen shot below. This happens to be the first program that you will run. It is traditionally a beginner's first program in C and it is aptly called "Hello World!".

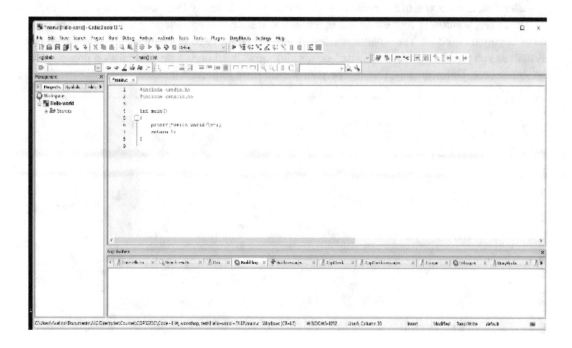

2   Compiling and Executing Your First C Program

Let's now look at the program that appears by default in the *main ( ) function* in Code::Blocks – the iconic "Hello World!" program. It is about as simple as it can get. It is re-printed below for your benefit, but note that we added a *comment line* at the top (explained later). We will work with this program to start with.

```c
// Our first program
#include <stdio.h>
#include <stdlib.h>

int main()
  {
    printf("Hello world!\n");
    return 0;
  }
```

With the source code for the Hello World! Program being displayed in the editor box, let's turn our attention to the fourth window located along the top of the Code::Blocks display. Well, it is not a window per se – it is actually three lines of icon-based menus. (In earlier or later versions, the arrangement may be slightly different.) You won't need most of these icons for the exercises in this book, but you will need two of them (or three) very frequently. Refer specifically to the line that begins with a brown/yellow gear icon on the extreme left, followed by a green arrow head that points to its right. To the right of these, there is a combined gear and arrow, indicating the combination of the two previous functions.

The yellow gear activates the compiler to compile whatever code is in the editor box. Click on it. After a few moments of thinking, it will write some messages on the lower window. Most of it is talking to itself, but at the end it will print out the results of the compilation. In our case here, there are no errors and no warnings, as is indicated by the statement at the end of the process (often in blue or red font). This means that the compilation was successful and the program is now ready to execute. You are good to go! On the other hand, if there had been any errors, it would show them here, as we will see later.

So, now click on the green arrow icon to execute the program. A black, small window will appear on your screen and will display Hello World! at the top. This is followed by a line indicating how long the execution took. Hit return and the window will disappear from your screen. You have now (probably) run your first C program. This is the routine you will be following in this book to create, compile and execute programs.

We next want to make changes to the Hello World! program. But before we do that, we need to explain some things about what we just did. Bear with us here.

3   Anatomy of a C Program

Before continuing with the use of Code::Blocks, we need to discuss the anatomy of a C program so that we can understand the very simple program that we ran and those that we are about to write/ compile/run. There are some special requirements in terms of the overall structure of a C program that we need to discuss at this time. Refer to the set of *pseudo-statements* shown below (they are not actual C code!).

```
//Comment lines (if any)
Pre-processor Directives: Header files
Pre-processor Directives: Macros (if any)
Function prototypes (if any)
Global variable declarations (if any)
main() function (required)
    C statements that make up the program
```

Let's skip the first few lines for the time being and go right to the second line from the bottom to discuss the main() function. This is the most important part of the C program, and it is essential.

3.1   The main() Function

Every C program contains one *main () function* where the C source code statements that make up the program will go. The label *main* is a *reserved keyword* and so has special meaning (we discuss reserved keywords further in Chap. 2). The processor will always execute this function first. When it finishes executing main(), the program ends. By *function*, we mean a program per se – one that performs some functionality. For simple programs such as those we will be writing in the first few chapters of this book, the main() function is the only function that we will need to populate with C statements. We refer to this process as *defining* the main() function. So, that means that all the C statements that we will be writing will be placed inside this main() function. This makes things easy for us at first. Larger and more complex programs will use several different functions in addition to main(), and *pass* inputs and results back and forth between them. This is more efficient for larger programs, but can also complicate the task of programming. We will cover how to define other functions later in Chap. 5, but for now, we'll only use `main()` for our programs.

In the scope of this book, `main()` will be defined simply as.

```
main()
    {
                    .
                    .
            body of code (composed of C statements)
                    .
                    .

    }
```

The source code statements that make up the *body of code* of the `main()` function are enclosed by what we call *curly brackets* { }.   (They are called *braces* in other texts, but that has a connotation we don't like.) This is generically called a *block of code*. We will see this concept of blocking off code many times in future chapters.

3.2   Pre-processor Directives

Another important element of a C program is the *pre-processor directives*. You can find these in the pseudo-code right under the comment lines. These directives are special types of statements in C that generally appear right at or near the top of a program, above the definition of the `main()` function. They are identified by the # symbol in front of them. There are two types of pre-processor directives of interest to us here, the `#include` and the `#define`. (There are others, but they are outside the scope of this book.) The notable feature of these directives is that they are executed prior to compilation, and typically involve making some changes or additions to the source code. When the compiler comes across one or more of these directives, it processes them by adding to or changing the source code before compiling it.

The first of these directives is the `#include` directive. It has an *argument* (the label that follows the name of the directive) in the form of a file name. It tells the compiler that the code in the argument file is to be included in the compilation process. The file identified in the argument should be a text file containing C statements. Standard C libraries can be used with C programs with the help of *header* files, typically identified by a `.h` identifier. The header files contain the *prototypes* of the functions found in the standard C libraries. We will see later (in Chap. 5) what these prototypes are and why they are necessary, but for now just take our word that they must be included in the compilation process. The `.h` extension (stands for *header*, of course) is used to indicate such standard files, but any other extension can be used for other files that may need to be included.

If the file to be included is in the same directory as the program, the file name is placed within double quotes, as in

```
#include "filename"
```

However, if the file to be included is not in the same directory but is found elsewhere (e.g., standard library depository), then < > brackets are used to enclose the file name instead of the double quotes, as in:

```
#include <filename>
```

For now, assume that the standard library files stdio.h and stdlib.h will be included in all of our programs. In fact, you should <u>always</u> have these two files included in all your programs, plus possibly others about which we will learn later.

The second pre-processor directive of interest is the #define directive. It has two arguments. It causes all instances of the first argument found in the source code to be replaced by the second argument. For example,

```
#define A 29.25
```

This directive will replace all instances of A in the source code by 29.25 <u>right in the source code</u> and before it is compiled. There are some exceptions to this universality that will be discussed later when it is more appropriate. This pre-processor directive is very advantageous for defining variables in the code that can be easily changed by the programmer. We discuss constants in more depth later in this book. The #define directive can be used to define more complex expressions, such as macros, but we will not use those here.

Next, let's discuss *comment lines*.

3.3   Comments

Refer to the first line of the pseudo-statements above. *Comments* are statements that the programmer wants the compiler to ignore because they are written for the programmer's own benefit. More specifically, comments are used to document the purpose of a statement or have some other useful information in the source code for the benefit of the original programmer at a later date (when she might have forgotten what she did), or for another subsequent programmer who may be trying to figure out the original programmer's code. It is good software engineering practice to produce properly commented code. Comments are indicated by a double forward slash // at the start of the text that is to be ignored by the compiler. This will tell the compiler to ignore everything from the double forward slashes to the end of the line. There are other more flexible ways to incorporate comments in the source code, but let's keep things simple for now and only do them this way. There is no limit to the number of commented statements one can add to the C program; however, keep in mind that too many can become distracting to the programmer and make the source code cumbersome to read.

Now let's modify the Hello World! program and introduce some errors on purpose.

4   Creating Your First Program

For example, say that you would like to change the output message to state something more useful than "Hello World!", such as:

```
My name is John Smith.
I'm a computer science student at UCF.
I am learning C programming
```

Let's write a program to do this. We will use the already existing Hello World! source code to help us get started.

Begin by placing a comment line indicating the name of the program and the date; maybe also your name. Then add another comment line (or two) explaining in your own words, what this program does. For example,

```
// Modified Hello World Program - John Smith Nov 1, 2021
// This program is for learning to write, compile and run basic C programs.
```

The source file is saved automatically when you compile it in Code::Blocks, but it is a good idea to get in the habit of explicitly saving your code, in case you someday work with an IDE (or an editor) that does not automatically save when you compile. To save the source file, go to the save icon under "View" (in our version of Code::Blocks) and click on it. Now your source file is saved.

Next, compile and run the code as you did before. It should give you the same output as you had when you executed the default `Hello World!` program, as the commented lines have no effect on the program execution. This is exactly the point of comments. Hit return to make the black window disappear. Be certain that it really does close, as you will not be able to modify the program source code while the window is active (open), even though it may disappear from the computer screen. If you re-direct your screen pointer elsewhere in the screen (before hitting return), the black window will cease to display, but it will still be open.

Now let's we proceed to make some changes to the C statements in `main()`. Delete the line that starts with `printf(...)` and replace it with the following line exactly as it is below:

```
printf("My name is John Smith")
```

Leave the `return 0;` line as is. We will explain `return` later.

Now hit the yellow gear and invoke the compiler. Look now on the lower window. After some lines, it states under the **Message** column:

```
In function 'main':
error: expected ';' before 'return'
=== Build finished: 1 errors, 0 warnings  ====
```

You have experienced your first <u>compilation error</u>. That is, the source code statements made no sense to the compiler and it was not able to translate them into a meaningful set of machine language instructions. So, it punted the ball right back to the programmer, so to speak. We now have to fix the source code to repair this "bug".

You will also notice that the debugger makes an effort to indicate the location of the error, in our case, specifically on line 7 of the source code. However, the debugger is not always exact. It only identifies the <u>vicinity</u> of where the errors are. As it turns out, the error in our code is not in line 7 as suggested by our debugger, but rather in line 6. Our error was that we (purposely) omitted the semicolon; at the end of the `printf(...)` statement in line 7. In C, every compilable statement needs to end with a semicolon. This is not exactly true for some of the more complex constructs we will see later, but that is for later. For now, assume all C statements (but <u>not</u> blocks of code!) must end with a `;`. That tells the compiler that the statement ends here. In our program, the compiler thought that lines 6 and 7 were one statement because there was no semicolon to end line 6, and that didn't make any sense to it.

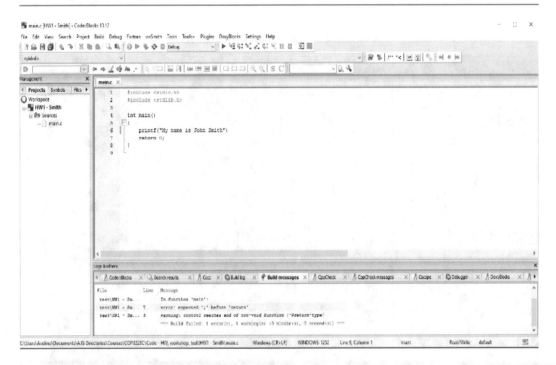

We now add the *;* at the end of line 6 and voilà, it now works.

Note that *warnings* are also identified in the debugger messages in the lower window (in addition to errors) when the compiler notices that something is amiss in the code, but not serious enough to abort the compilation process (as would an error). The program will compile and the program can be run with warnings, but the compiler wants you to be aware of what it found to be uncommon. It is good practice to fix any errors first, as warnings often disappear by themselves when the errors are resolved. The compiler sometimes lists multiple errors that are caused by only one mistake in one code statement. Nonetheless, when all errors have been resolved, if warnings still persist, a good programmer will always resolve all warnings before executing the program (or at least try to understand them). Otherwise, the issues identified by these warnings will often lead to some incorrect result later on.

As one can surmise, the `printf(...)`; statement is an output statement used to print to screen. Now let's add `printf(..)` statements for the other two lines we want to display to the body of the `main()` function.

```
printf("I'm a computer science student at UCF");
printf("I am learning C programming");
```

Compile it (yellow gear), and it compiles successfully. Good! Execute the program (green arrow) and it executes just fine. So far, so good! See the figure below. You have successfully modified, compiled and executed the program.

However, note that the three sentences in the output are running on to each other. That is not exactly what we wanted. You have now experienced your first <u>logic error</u>. The computer understood your instructions (compiled properly) and went ahead and did exactly what you told it to do. Unfortunately, what you told it to do was not exactly what you wanted: everything not on the same line, and not running into each other. We now need to modify the `printf()` statements to go to a new line when it prints the words within the quotation marks " ". This we do through the *newline control character*, just as in the `Hello World!` statement. We add a `\n` after the words to be displayed. (This will be further explained in later chapters; for now we just want to run these simple programs.) See below:

```
printf("My name is John Smith \n");
printf("I'm a computer science student at UCF \n");
printf("I am learning C programming \n");
```

This gives us the desired output.

```
"C:\Users\Avelino\Documents\AJG Directories\Courses\CO...    —    □    ✕

My name is John Smith
I'm a computer science student at UCF
I am learning C programming

Process returned 0 (0x0)   execution time : 0.004 s
Press any key to continue.
```

We have not yet seen the third type of error: **run-time errors**. We will see those later when we have more interesting things to compute that will cause such errors.

---

5   Summary

This chapter covered the very basic processes in computer programming: writing statements (in our case, modifying an existing program), compiling the source code, and executing the executable program. In the process, the learner downloaded and installed an IDE (Code::Blocks) and learned to do some very basic things with it. These basic steps are important because all C programs that we will write will follow these same basic steps. Secondly, the basic anatomy of a C program was discussed as a way to understand the simple program being discussed. Lastly, we introduced some common errors to expose the learner to the bane of computer programmers – errors in the code. One type of error was a compilation error – typically the easiest type of error to fix because the compiler provides some help in identifying the specific error, as well as (more or less) where the error is located in the code. The second type of error experienced was a logic error, where the program compiles and runs successfully, but provides an incorrect (or undesired) output. Logic errors are generally much harder to find and fix because there may be no indication in the execution or the output that the result is wrong (or undesirable). Undesired results are often far from obvious, as they may not always appear. A rigorous validation process is typically required of commercial programs to identify these bugs. In our specific exercise, however, the error was rather obvious.

6   Problems

1) Use the `printf(..)` statement to add new outputs to be printed in the `Hello  World!` program.

2) Omit one (either one, or both) of the quotation marks (") inside the `printf()` statement in the `Hello World!` program to see what error is provoked.

3) Place a double slash // <u>after</u> the end of one of the `printf();` statement (on the same line), and add whatever you want to say in your comment.

4) Remove one of the forward slashes (/) from one of the commented lines to see what kind of error is provoked.

5) In the programs resulting from any of the above four problems, add more than one \n next to each other in the `printf()` statement to see its effect on the output.

6) Remove the `#include<stdio.h>` directive from any of the programs in the above five problems to see the effect this has.

7) Remove the `#include<stdlib.h>` directive from any of the programs in the above five problems to see the effect this has.

Variables, Memory, and Operators

2

Now that we are past the nearly trivial first chapter, we're going to crank up the level of "interesting-ness" a bit more. In this chapter, we will work on defining and declaring variables and performing some simple operations on them. In the process, you will gain some additional experience with the output function `printf()`.

1   Variables – A Brief Introduction

In its most basic terms, a computer program instructs the computer in which it resides to acquire, manipulate and output data in some form or another. Therefore, data manipulation can be said to be an essential part of computing. Computers cannot sing or dance, but they can manipulate data to display a singer or a dancer, and even control a dancing robot. To do that, data must be placed somewhere while they are being manipulated and then stored somewhere after they have been processed. *Variables* are the most basic element with which to do this in a computer program. They are designed to store and retrieve data easily.

The concept of a *variable* in algebra is that a mathematical term (a symbol) holds a computable value that can be changed, hence its name variable. The symbol that represents the variable is itself non-computable. For example, one cannot add the characters a and b, as such an operation in mathematics is in and of itself meaningless. However, if the a and b symbols (variables) were to somehow stand for numerical values, the operation could replace the symbols a and b by their numerical values, which would be added, and carry out the operation successfully. In algebra, a variable can be *assigned* a specific value, or it can be left *unbound* (i.e., it holds no value ... yet).

In computer programming, however, variables are not the highly abstract concepts that they are in algebra. Instead, they are actual locations in the computer's memory where a value can be stored, retrieved and then later re-stored after being processed (if that is what the program calls for). This could happen many times during the course of a program's execution.

Memory in a computer is a veeeeeeeeeery looooooooong string of binary elements called *bits*, each of which can hold either a 0 or a 1. Fortunately, a computer's memory is equipped with an indexing system (beyond the scope of this book) that allows any location in this long string to be found rather efficiently. Thus, locations in memory have *addresses* where a particular segment of memory can be found, just like a street address (house number, street name, city, state and zip code) can uniquely pinpoint the location of a small house in a big country. Unfortunately, addresses in computer memory

© Springer Nature Switzerland AG 2020
A. J. Gonzalez, *Computer Programming in C for Beginners*,
https://doi.org/10.1007/978-3-030-50750-3_2

are quite cryptic, making it difficult for a programmer to keep track of what address in memory holds a particular value of interest. Fortunately, high-level programming languages such as C make it easy on the programmers by providing the ability to assign a name to a memory location where the value of a variable is to be kept. Such names can be selected by the programmer and are much easier to remember and keep track of without needing to know their actual locations in memory (i.e., their addresses). A variable in computer programming, therefore, is a symbol that serves as a <u>label</u> for a particular location in memory where a specific value is being stored.

The name of a variable is selected by the programmer, but it is subject to some restrictions:

1) Only letters, numbers, and the underscore character (_) are allowed in the name.
2) The variable name is case-sensitive – upper and lower case letters are different.
3) The first character must be either a letter or an underscore.
4) The name must not be one of the 37 reserved keywords in C.

Keywords are words that mean something special in the C language. So, they cannot be used as variable names, lest the compiler becomes very confused. The 37 reserved keywords are:

```
auto, double, int, struct, break, else, long, switch, case, enum,
register, typedef, char, extern, return, union, const, float,
short, unsigned, continue, for, main, signed, void, default, goto,
sizeof, volatile, do, if, while, static, _Boolinline, _Complex,
restrict, _Imaginary
```

We will use most of these keywords (but not all) in one form or another in this book.

So, now launch your Code::Blocks or other IDE and let's start working with variables. We will cover how to *define* variables, how to assign values to them and how to retrieve values from them. Note that all the code described below is to be placed within the body of the main () function, and nowhere else.

---

2   Some Operations on Simple Variables

Before we continue with variables, we first need to explain what an *operator* is, as we cannot show you much here without doing some sort of operation on the data, even if only a simple operation. An operator is an instruction that performs some kind of manipulation on data. The data can be retrieved from a variable, or be stated explicitly in the instruction. Most operators in C are pre-defined and available for use by the programmer through the standard C libraries. However, it is important that the programmer understands exactly what a specific operator does and the type of data it can work on. Operators that carry out arithmetic operations such as add (+), subtract (−), multiply (*) and divide (/) are the simplest of operators, but for this discussion, not the most important.

The most important operator in the context of this discussion is the *assignment operator*. It is used to assign a value to a variable that has already been defined. In effect, it tells the processor to store a particular value in the memory space already allocated to a specific variable name (its label). The assignment operator plays an essential role in data manipulation, as without it, values could not be assigned to variables. The symbol used for this operator is the equal sign (=). For the simplest of examples, the statement

```
var = 10;
```

Sets the value of variable var to 10.

It is important to understand the difference between the assignment operator (=) and the *equality operator* (==). Rather than assign a value to a variable, the equality operator (==) is a test to determine whether the value found on its left side is equal to that found on its right side. If so, it will respond with **true**; otherwise, with **false**. Actually C does not use the labels **true** and **false** per se. Instead, it will respond with 1 if true and with 0 if false.

So, now we will jump ahead and use the assignment operator in this section.

Set up your program in Code::Blocks and name the program that we are about to build Chap-2.

The source code file will be named main.c by the system. You can leave the name of the source file as is, or you can change it later if you want.

Start the program source code with two comment lines. The first one should indicate the name of the program as shown below. In the second line, type out a very brief one-line description of this program, in your own words. For example,

```
// Chapter 2 - Variables and operators - <your last name>
// In this exercise, we will work with variables and operators
```

Next, include the two .h files we discussed in Chap. 1 (stdlib.h and stdio.h). As discussed in Chap. 1, this should <u>always</u> be done, but future chapters will not remind you of this any longer.

Next, of course, is the main() function with its opening and closing curly brackets. So, your source code should now look like this: (Notice that blank lines are allowed in the source code and have no effect on the program.)

```
// Lab 2 - Variables and operators - <your last name>
// In this exercise, we will work with variables and operators

#include<stdio.h>
#include<stdlib.h>

int main()
{



        return 0;
}
```

All the code that we will add in the exercises of this chapter will be placed inside the curly brackets of main() and <u>above</u> the return 0; statement. We saw this return statement in the Hello World! program of Chap. 1. It simply means that the function main() is to exit and *return* the number 0. The return statement is the last statement executed in a function and causes the function to exit. The fact that the term int is found in front of the main() function definition indicates that main() is expected to return an integer number, which, of course 0 is. It should be noted that in this particular case, returning something is not necessary, as any value returned by main() is not processed any further because the program ends upon exiting main(). Nevertheless, many programmers prefer to do this by convention (as do we).

2.1   Data Typing in Variables

There are many different types of data that can be stored in a variable. These different types of data can take up different amounts of space in the memory. Therefore, C requires that the variable have enough space allocated to it in memory to be able to hold the type of data it will be assigned. You will now need to know that a *byte* is a string of 8 consecutive bits in memory, and it is the smallest unit of memory that is addressable. The most common types of data are:

- **Integer values**. These are natural numbers and are indicated by the keyword int. Most computers set aside 4 bytes (32 bits) for integer variables, although some can allocate 8 bytes (64 bits). Older computers allocated 2 bytes (16 bits) for integers, which limited the size of the integer number to be stored to 65,535 (1111111111111111 in binary).
- **Floating point values**. These are real numbers with a decimal point and are indicated by the keyword float. Most compilers will allocate 4 bytes (32 bits) for variables of this type.
- **Double precision floating point values**. Same as the float data type above, except with more precision. Given the abundance of memory in modern computers, this is the standard type used for any floating point operations. It is indicated by the keyword double. Compilers will normally allocate 8 bytes (64 bits) for this type of variable.
- **Character values**. These represent a single non-computable character and are indicated by the keyword char. Compilers will allocate 1 byte (8 bits) for this type of variable. (For full disclosure, char values are in fact integers that are mapped to characters in the so-called *ASCII Table*. So, they could, in fact, be made computable. However, by default they are not computable. We leave this discussion for another day.)

Of course, there are many other data types, but for now we will only use the four above. These other data types will require different sizes of memory blocks. Let's now proceed to defining variables.

2.2   Defining and Initializing Variables

All variables in C must be explicitly defined before they can be used. Definition of a variable tells the compiler that the programmer wishes to set aside a block of memory to store some specific piece of data that is to be used in the program. This is done through a C statement located somewhere above (i.e., before) where the variable is first used, that *declares* the existence of this variable, its name, and importantly for C, the *type* of data it will hold. Optionally, an initial value can also be assigned during declaration, but it is not required.

We should note that strictly speaking, defining and declaring a variable are not the same thing. Defining a variable means that a variable name is created and a memory block is allocated and associated with it. A variable declaration simply means that a variable that is already defined elsewhere is declared to be valid in a file. This becomes important when we discuss multi-file programs in Chap. 10. Unfortunately, the two terms have become conflated, and we often say that we declare a variable when we actually mean that we define a variable.

Indicating the type of data that a variable is to hold is one of the features that sets C apart from most other languages, and is why C is often called a *heavily typed* language. This feature imparts great efficiency in memory use, as the location in memory that holds a variable is allocated at just the right size for the type of data to be stored. This goes back to a time when memory was a limited resource, which is generally no longer the case today, although that can still be true for embedded computing applications, such as for small instruments. Unfortunately, it is also the source of many headaches for beginner programmers who sometimes mismatch the data to be stored in a variable with the type expected by the variable. More about this later in this course. Now let's see how to define and initialize variables.

Defining a variable requires that the programmer provide the: 1) type of data to be stored in the variable being defined; 2) The name of the variable being defined; and 3) Optionally, its initial value. The general format is as follows:

```
<data type> <variable name> = <initial value - optional>
```

We'll use integer variables for our exercises, as they are the most common. Integer variables are typically (although not only) used for counting things. By convention, they are named `n, i, j` or `k,` but this is not a requirement – so, you can name an integer variable `supercalifragilis-ticexpialidocious` if you want. But to keep things as easy as possible, let's stick to simple variable names that are meaningful to the programmer. Go ahead and type in the following statement inside the `main()` function in your program.

```
int n;
```

You have defined a variable called `n` of type integer; however, it has been left *unbound* (i.e., it has no specific value). We now write some statements to display the value that is held in `n` (i.e., retrieve its value), so add the following line to the source code, just under the definition of `n`. This line is to display the value assigned to `n` (in this case, none specifically):

```
printf("n = %d \n", n);
```

Compile the code. You will note that the compiler will issue a warning saying that `n` is uninitialized. We know that, so let's continue anyway. As we discussed in Chap. 1, warnings do not prohibit compilation of the program (as do errors), and an executable file is built in spite of the warnings. Go ahead and run the program now. You will see that it will display some meaningless number in the black output window. Our computer printed the following:

```
n = 2147307520
```

There are two things to note here. One is that we used `printf()` to accomplish more than simply print literal text as we did in Chap. 1. In this case, we used it to retrieve the value of a variable and print it out. We did that by using the `%d` symbol as a placeholder in the printed line for where the value of a variable is to be printed. This is called a *type specifier* for the `printf()` function. The name of the variable whose value is to be printed in that placeholder (i.e., `n`) immediately follows the closing quotation mark and is separated from the quoted field by a comma.

Second, it turns out that because we failed to initialize `n`, the `printf()` displayed the value held in the memory location allocated by the compiler to our variable `n` when it was defined. This value is simply the decimal equivalent value of whatever 0's and 1's had been left over in those bits from some prior operation. This is what the `printf()` function retrieved when asked to print out the contents of this memory location. If you were to compile the program again and re-run it, a different number might or might not be printed out. This argues for the good practice of <u>always</u> initializing <u>all</u> variables when they are defined. Many logic errors occur because of uninitialized variables.

So, let's initialize `n` to 0 and run the program again.

```
int n = 0;
printf("n = %d \n", n);
```

Now there are no warnings, and as expected, the output says

```
n = 0.
```

Several variables of the same type can be declared and initialized in the same statement. For example, if we want to declare three int variables named a, b and c and initialize them to zero, we can do so in one line as follows:

```
int a=0, b=0, c=0;
```

2.3   Setting and Reading the Values of Variables

Now we will see a bit more about how to assign values to variables, as well as reading and printing these values. We'll start with integer variables.

2.3.1   Integer Variables

Let's take n, which has been initialized to 0, and set it to 21. So, add the following statement:

```
n = 21;
```

Your main() function code should now look like this:

```
int n = 0;
printf("n = %d \n", n);
n = 21;
```

Go ahead and compile and run the program. The output will still say n = 0. Why? Well, because at the time printf() retrieved the content of n, it was indeed still 0. The statement that assigned a value of 21 to it did not execute until afterward. This tells you that when printf() encounters a variable whose content is to retrieved for display, it will retrieve its contents at that instant of time, not later. If we now change the location of the n = 21; statement to before the printf(), then the desired value will be displayed (n = 21). Try it. Thus, the location of statements can matter. This might seem to be a bit trite, but many errors result from reading the value of the right variable but at the wrong time.

Continuing with the thought of minding the location of a statement in the sequence of statements in a program, what do you think would happen if we set the value of n to 21 before we declare the n variable? Go ahead and compile the following code:

```
n = 21;
int n = 0;
printf("n = %d \n", n);
```

Yep! You guessed it - compilation error. The compiler had not yet allocated memory to variable n before we asked it to set it to 21. In fact, it didn't even know what variable n was. So, you see, compilers do not (for the most part) read ahead.

2.3.2 Floating Point Variables

We can define and initialize floating point variables just as easily. The memory allocated to this type of variable is at least 4 bytes (32 bits). Unlike integer variables, float variables can use the scientific notation to represent large numbers, so there is practically no limit to the size of the number it can hold. Go ahead and declare max, a floating point variable.

```
float max = 10.0;
```

Let's slightly modify the printf() function to be able to *read* (another word for retrieve) the value of max and display it. So, our program will look like this:

```
float max = 10.0;
printf("max = %f \n", max);
```

You will see that it will compile just fine and will display the following result:

```
max = 10.000000
```

We will learn to control the flood of zeroes displayed after the decimal point in a later chapter, so for now, just ignore this annoying number of zeroes. Also note that the placeholder field (type specifier) for a floating point number is %f, rather than the %d used for integers. This further suggests that the type of variable to be read must agree with its type specifier – a recurring theme in C.

2.3.3 Double Precision Floating Point Variables

Double precision floating point data are almost identical to floating point. Their difference is in how many significant digits can be represented for greater precision in the computations. This is important for some applications where small errors can accumulate after many operations. However, we will not deal with such applications in this book. Like float variables, double type variables can also represent its contents in scientific notation, but have more digits to represent the real number, thus providing the capability for greater precision.

In any case, for the sake of completeness, see the code below. Note that the type specification for the placeholder for a double-precision floating point value is %lf. These variables can be defined with the keyword double.

```
double max = 10.0;
printf("max = %lf \n", max);
```

The output will be the same as for float:

```
max = 10.000000
```

2.3.4   Character Variables

Furthering the completeness of this section, we do need to do character variables, as they are some-what different than the three types discussed above. We'll keep it simple for now, so type in the following lines of code:

```
char letter = 'x';
printf("letter = %c \n", letter);
```

The output correctly displays letter = x as expected.

Note two things about character variables: 1) the character x to be assigned to the variable letter had to be placed between single quotes. This is required for character *literals*. 2) The format specification used was %c, reinforcing the need to make sure that there is a match between the type of variable and the placeholder type.

2.4   Mixing up Data Types

As we discussed earlier, C is very heavily typed. It depends on correctly matching the data types and their specifications; else it has conniptions – sometimes, but not always – and that's the problem. Let's see some of these.

If instead of assigning max a floating point value (with a decimal point), we assign it what would be considered an integer (without a decimal point). Try the code below.

```
float max = 10;
printf("max = %f \n", max);
```

It turns out that max is undaunted. It assumes that we meant to put a decimal point at the end, and still prints out.

```
max = 10.000000
```

This is good. However, if for some reason we really (and mistakenly!) believe max to be an integer variable, even though we mistakenly defined it as a floating point variable, and as a result, we specify it as an integer in printf() with a type specification of %d instead of %f:

```
float max = 10;
printf("max = %d \n", max);
```

Well, now the conniptions begin. It compiles, but with a stern warning that should never be ignored (i.e., that it expects int rather than float). If we go ahead and execute the program, it prints the value of max as a 0 (max = 0) – clearly an incorrect output! A programmer who chooses to ignore the warning will find that she has a working program that provides an incorrect answer. This can be considered a logic error.

Let's now do the converse for integer variables, starting with assigning n a floating point value (with a decimal point). Try the following:

```
int n = 10.0;
printf("n = %d \n", n);
```

As with the floating point example above, the C compiler second-guessed us correctly and ignores the decimal point. It correctly displays:

```
n = 10
```

However, when we specify the wrong type specifier in the output for variable n (see code below), it behaves similarly as the example earlier for an integer: Gives a stern warning but compiles anyway. However, the output obtained was n = 0.000000, a clearly incorrect value. Try it.

```
int n = 10.0;
printf("n = %f \n", n);
```

The main lesson to be learned from this section is that C makes some guesses as to what we really mean when we unwittingly introduce a data type mismatch. In some cases, it guesses right, but in others not so. This seeming unpredictability in C (to most programmers) suggests strongly that the programmer should always be sure that all data types and specifications match, and all warnings are to be always heeded.

Next, we will deal with operators that are more interesting than the simple assignment operator with which we have worked so far.

3   Working with Variables and Operators

It is important to understand the assignment operator, but it is easy to understand, and there is not much more to it once you know how it works. Let's now work with (slightly) more interesting computations. The really interesting stuff will come later in the course.

The first operators to discuss are the basic arithmetic operators: addition, subtraction, multiplication, and division. The first three are rather straight-forward, and we will deal with them rather quickly. We will save our attention for division, which is slightly more interesting.

3.1   Addition, Subtraction, and Multiplication

These are simple operators. Just remember to set the result of the operation to a variable of the appropriate type. Otherwise, the result will be lost. Let's begin with the addition operator, indicated by the plus sign (+). So, type in the following lines (yes, as we saw earlier, more than one variable can be defined and initialized in the same line as long as they are of the same type).

```
int a=1, b=2, c=3, d=4, total=0;
total = a+b+c+d;
printf("total = %d \n", total);
```

The (correct) result displayed, of course, will be

```
total = 10
```

We can do the same thing with subtraction, which uses the minus sign (−) as the operator: (Note that spaces between terms in an equation are ignored by the compiler, so they can be used to facilitate readability (by humans).)

```
int a=1, b=2, c=3, d=4, total=0;
total = a - b - c - d;
printf("total = %d \n", total);
```

The correct result of `total = -8` is displayed. Note that the negative sign was properly indicated. This is because `int` is for a *signed* integer, so it encompasses negative numbers. If instead we were to have specified `total` as `unsigned int` and we use the unsigned integer output type specification (`%u`) as below, ….

```
int a=1, b=2, c=3, d=4;
unsigned int total=0;
total = a - b - c - d;
printf("total = %u \n", total);
```

Well, not so good. The program compiles <u>without giving warnings</u> and runs just fine, but the output now is some nonsensical number. Try it. This reinforces the fact that data types must match in C, even in the absence of warnings, to avoid problems later on.

The symbol for the multiplication operator is the asterisk ⋆. Using the code above, simply replace the + or − sign by an * and observe the results. Try it. We do not show it here, as it is rather trivial after the discussions above.

3.2   Division

Division is a different story. Floating point division and double-precision floating point division work as one would expect from our old math courses in grade school. The symbol used to represent these types of division is the forward slash /. For example,

```
float a=11.0, b=4.0, total = 0.0;
total = a/b;
printf("total = %f \n", total);
```

The result would be.

```
total = 2.750000
```

Easy enough, right? Integer division, however, is much more interesting.

3.2.1   Integer Division

There are two different types of integer division (*Euclidian division* is the formal name) when the dividend and the divisor are both integers. The first operation, which uses the / symbol, returns the quotient of the operation. This is an integer number that indicates how many times the divisor fully "fits into" the dividend. In effect, it *truncates* the results of a floating point division, and only returns the left side of the decimal point (without the decimal point). For example, if we divide the integers 11 / 4, we can see that 4 only fits completely into 11 twice. If we look at the real number division of 11.0 by 4.0, we would get 2.750000 as indicated above. The left side of the number is 2. Let's give it a quick try:

```
int a=11, b=4, total=0;
total = a/b;
printf("total = %d \n", total);
```

The output displayed will be total = 2 because 4 fully fits into 11 only twice.

The second type of integer division, *division with remainder* (aka, *modulus*) on the other hand, uses the percent sign (%) as the operator symbol, and returns the <u>remainder</u> of the division. It represents the leftover fraction. Now let's try it:

```
int a=11, b=4, total=0;
total = a%b;
printf("total = %d \n", total);
```

This program output displays total = 3, which is what is left over.

Easy enough, right? Now what happens when we mix up integers and floating point variables? Hmmm, this gets much more interesting…

3.2.2   Mixing up Integer and Floating Point Division
First, let's divide an integer by a floating point and set the value to a floating point.

```
int a=11;
float b=4.0, total;
total = a/b;
printf("total = %f \n", total);
```

The result is a floating point value

```
total = 2.750000
```

This is correct if a floating point value is indeed what we wanted. It turns out that the compiler by itself converted integer a to floating point and proceeded as if it were a floating point operation, displaying the result obtained. If we ignore the extraneous zeroes (for now), then all is good. The same thing happens if we have a floating point numerator and an integer denominator. Try it.

Now, what happens if we set the result to an integer variable?

```
int a=11, total;
float b=4.0;
total = a/b;
printf("total = %d \n", total);
```

The result displayed is total = 2, which reflects integer division.

Last, what if we mix up the mod division, which is only defined for integers? Let's quickly try that.

```
float a=11.0, b=4.0;
float total;
total = a%b;
printf("total = %f \n", total);
```

It didn't like it at all (appropriately so), did it? That's correct because % is not defined for floating point. It results in a compilation error. What if we now set the result (total) to an integer variable? Well, it makes no difference: it is still a compilation error. The mod operator % requires both operands (numerator and denominator) to be integer values. Period.

3.3   Increment/Decrement Operators

Increment and *decrement operators* are shortcut ways for incrementing or decrementing an integer value by 1. In effect, they shortcut the operations:

```
n = n + 1; // increments
n = n - 1; // decrements
```

The symbols for these operators are ++ and −−. They are examples of what is called *unary* operators in that they only operate on a single operand. They can replace the expressions above simply and succinctly with n++; and n−−; . This conciseness can be a big advantage and these operators become very useful when we get to repetition structures (loops) later in this book.

However, where these operator symbols are placed in relation to the variable they are to increment or decrement is important. There are two variations – the *pre-* and the *post-* operators - and they are subtly different. Thus, we need to fully understand how they work.

The *post-increment* and the *post-decrement* operators increment/decrement the value of its integer variable by 1, but only <u>after</u> the value of the variable has been retrieved. Let's see this in action by executing the following code:

```
int n=5;
printf("%d ", n);
printf("%d ", n++);
printf("%d ", n);
```

The output of the code above is 5 5 6. (Note that we didn't use the \n newline operator in the printf()'s, so the three outputs are printed out on the same line.) The post-increment operator used in the third line above increments the value in the variable (in this case n) <u>after</u> the value has been retrieved by the second printf(). Only thereafter does it assign the newly-incremented value to n. This is why the second printf() displays 5 rather than 6. It takes the third printf() to read and print the newly-incremented value of n. It is important to note that the increment operator also performs an implicit assignment operation in that it assigns the incremented value to the variable on which it operates.

The same is true for the *post-decrement* operator (n−−) if used in the second printf() above in lieu of n++, resulting in an output of 5 5 4.

As the name suggests, a *pre-increment/decrement* operator increments/decrements the value and assigns it to the variable <u>before</u> its value is retrieved. A second short program shows a *pre-increment* operator.

```
int n=5;
printf("%d ", n);
printf("%d ", ++n);
printf("%d ", n);
```

The result is now 5 6 6 because the pre-increment operator incremented the value of n <u>before</u> it was retrieved by the second printf() above for printing. Try replacing the ++n by --n. You will get 5 4 4.

These examples also provide further evidence of the relevance of exactly when an instruction is executed. In other words, when programming a computer, one must be aware of what value a variable is expected to hold when its value is read. This is normally a common source of errors for beginners as well as for experienced programmers alike.

3.4   Boolean Operators

The nineteenth Century English mathematician George Boole conceived the mathematical representation of logic concepts. These later became one of the foundations of computing hardware. He formalized the concepts of *and*, *or* and *not* (among many other things that are irrelevant to this discussion). His formalizations use the *truth value* of a statement as being either *true* or *false*. In C, some expressions can be evaluated to return a value of 0 if they are **false**, or 1 if judged to be **true**. For example, the expression 2 == 2; will evaluate to **true**, while 2 == 3; will return **false** (0). Please enter the following code in your editor:

```
int main()
{
    printf("The answer is %d\n", 2==2);

    return 0;
}
```

The program will output

```
The answer is 1
```

Likewise, if we change the last part of the printf() statement to 2==3; the program will output:

```
The answer is 0
```

Boolean operators, as they are called, permit a programmer to determine the truth value of *compound expressions* – an expression consisting of two or more *component expressions*. The symbols for the logical AND in C is && and it is placed between the expressions to be "and'ed" together; for the logical OR, it is ||, similarly placed between expressions to be "or'ed" together; Lastly, the symbol for the logical NOT is "!", placed before and adjoined to the expression whose truth value is to be reversed. To illustrate this, let's say we have two expressions, abstractly referred here as A and B – let's call them the *component expressions*. Each can have a truth value of either **true** or **false** (in C, 1 or 0 respectively).

Table 1 below shows the truth value of a compound expression (A and B), expressed as (A && B) in the C language. Note that the compound expression is only **true** when all its component expressions evaluate to **true**. If at least one of the component expressions evaluates to **false**, then the compound expression will evaluate to **false**.

Table 1   The AND Boolean Operator

A	B	A&&B
True	True	True
True	False	False
False	True	False
False	False	False

Table 2   The OR Boolean operator

A	B	A||B
True	True	True
True	False	True
False	True	True
False	False	False

Table 3   The OR Boolean operator

A	!A
True	False
False	True

Conversely, for the OR Boolean operator, as long as at least one of the component expressions evaluates to **true**, the compound expression will do likewise. Therefore, the only way the compound expression will evaluate to **false** is when all of its component expressions evaluate to **false**. See Table 2.

Lastly, the NOT Boolean operator will merely flip the truth value of its argument expression to the opposite value. See Table 3.

Boolean operators will become important in the next two chapters when we will need to test the truth values of certain expressions.

An interesting thing happens with logical expressions linked by Boolean operators, called the *short-circuit evaluation*. This states that the processor will evaluate a component expression within a compound logical expression only if it has to do so. An example will make this clear.

Let's say some sort of test is composed of several component expressions linked by the AND operator &&. The component expressions will be evaluated one by one, in sequence, starting with the left-most one first. This overall compound expression will evaluate to **false** as soon as one component expression evaluates to **false,** as it only takes one false expression to make the entire AND'ed compound expression **false**. The succeeding component expressions will <u>not</u> be evaluated because it would not be necessary to do so, as no result would change the overall evaluation of **false** for the compound expression. For example,

```
int a = 10, b = -10;
(a != 10) && (b < 0);
```

The processor will never evaluate the second expression (b < 0) in the compound expression because the first one (a != 10) turns out to be **false**, immediately making the compound expression **false.** Therefore, it will continue to evaluate the component expressions, one by one, as long as they keep evaluating to **true**.

Likewise, if the component expressions are linked by the OR operator | |, the overall compound expression will be evaluated as **true** as soon as one of the component expressions evaluates to **true**, without bothering to evaluate any succeeding expressions. For example:

```
int a = 10, b = -10;
(a == 10) || (b > 0);
```

In the program snippet above, the processor will never evaluate the (b > 0) expression because (a==10) turns out to be **true**, already making the compound expression **true,** regardless of the value of the second expression (which turns out to be **false**).

3.5 Embedded Operations in C

In the spirit of just-in-time learning, there is one interesting thing to discuss in the code above. Recall how the code above actually contained an expression for the incrementing and decrementing operators inside the `printf()` statement that was executed just before its computed value was printed. The same thing happened for the evaluation of the Boolean operators inside the `printf()` statement (e.g., 2 == 3). This indicates that we can embed operations within other operations. Without digressing too far, we need to expand on this a bit here. Whenever an operation (or a function, for that matter) is called in C, it executes on the spot, and the value *returned* is what is used further in the larger operation.

Using this concept can often save having to define variables that are in some sense, useless, and therefore, save memory (if that were to be an issue). For example, the code we used in the floating point division example, which we reprint below exactly as in Sect. 3.2 above:

```
float a=11.0, b=4.0, total = 0.0;
total = a/b;
printf("total = %f \n", total);
```

We could, instead, avoid having the variable `total` altogether and write the program more succinctly as:

```
float a=11.0, b=4.0;
printf("total = %f \n", a/b);
```

In this case, rather than it being simply a matter of retrieving the value of a variable (i.e., `total`), the values of variables a and b are retrieved (i.e., read), and the operation a/b is executed on the spot. The value returned from this operation then is what gets printed by `printf()`.

Of course, we may want to keep the value computed for further processing, rather than merely printing it out and losing it thereafter. In this case, having the variable `total` would be advantageous. Nonetheless, the point is that the ability to embed operations/functions within other operations/functions is a simple, yet useful concept in all computer programming languages.

4   Input/Output Functions

C has several standard, pre-defined functions to do input and output, whose prototypes reside in either `stdio.h` or `stdlib.h`. We have already seen and worked with the primary output function `printf()`, so we won't go over that one here. There is a chapter later in this book (Chap. 9) that discusses input/output at much greater depth. In it we cover other features of the `printf()` function that allow for formatting the printed output.

Of particular interest here is an input function for introducing data from the keyboard. Thus, the input function of interest here is `scanf()`. On the surface, `scanf()` is somewhat similar to `printf()`, but its function is radically different, as it not only accepts input from the keyboard but also saves that input to a designated variable in the same step.

The format of the `scanf()` is:

```
scanf("%type_specifier", &variable);
```

Let's see how to use it. Say you are writing a simple program that can convert temperature in degrees Centigrade to degrees Fahrenheit. First, the program asks the user for the ambient temperature in °C through a `printf()` statement. `scanf()` will then provide her/him with an opportunity to enter it. Let's write the code as follows:

```
int main()
{
    float tempC = 0.0, tempF = 0.0; // always initialize!!
    printf("What is the temperature in °C? \n");
    scanf("%f", &tempC);
    tempF = 32.0 + (9.0*tempC)/5.0;
    printf("The temperature in °F is %f \n", tempF);

    return 0;
}
```

The program will ask for the temperature and wait for the user to enter the information and hit return (it will just sit there quietly and wait until he/she does). Once entered, the value is saved to the variable `tempC` and the Fahrenheit equivalent is computed. The result is then printed out in the `printf()` that follows it. The output looks like this:

```
What is the temperature in °C?
```

35 return (entered by the user)

```
The temperature in °F is 95.000000
```

So, you might wonder, why the `&` in front of `tempC` in the `scanf()` but not on `tempF` in the `printf()`? It is too early in the discussion to be able to explain it properly, but let's just say that it is one of the many maddening oddities of the C language.

Let's remove the `&` in front of `tempC` in the `scanf()` statement above for a moment and see what happens. Re-compile it. You'll find that it does compile, although it gives a warning (and we did say never to ignore warnings). Interestingly, the warning misdirects the unsuspecting programmer, as the description has seemingly little to do with the real problem.

In spite of this, go ahead and execute the compiled code. You will see that it fails to terminate – it crashes! You have now experienced your first **run-time error**. The first `printf()` will work as intended, asking the user for the temperature in °C. If one enters a value (such as 35), the `scanf()` statement tries to save the value to the variable `tempC` but cannot find it because it has been incorrectly specified (without the `&`). It grinds its wheels for a few seconds and then crashes.

OK, so we know that for some strange reason, in `scanf()` we need to use the `&` in front of the name of the variable that is to hold the value entered. This will be properly explained when we get to *pointers*, but for the time being, let's agree to always use the `&` in `scanf()` as required, and continue with our discussion.

The next question is can we enter more than one input on the same line? Of course, yes. Let's say that we want to calculate the relative humidity in a room. For that, we will need to enter two temperatures: the *wet bulb* and the *dry bulb* temperatures. Unfortunately, we would need a Mollier Diagram to compute the relative humidity -- a complex chart that is beyond the scope of our work here. So, we will simply compute the difference between the two temperatures (which would be an input to the Mollier Diagram). So,

```
int main()
{
     float tempWet = 0.0, tempDry = 0.0, tempDiff = 0.0;
     printf("What are the wet & dry bulb temperatures in Deg C? \n");
     scanf("%f %f", &tempWet, &tempDry);
     tempDiff = tempDry - tempWet;
     printf("The difference in temperatures is %f Deg C\n", tempDiff);

     return 0;
}
```

Let's compile and run it and input the values 35 for the dry bulb temperature and 32 for the wet bulb.

```
What are the wet & dry bulb temperatures in Deg C
35,32 return (entered by the user)
The difference in temperatures is 35 Deg C
```

The answer is obviously wrong. So, what happened? The program compiled flawlessly but computed the answer incorrectly. The error here was in the comma entered by the user in his input. In this situation, the comma does not work as a delineator. One must use a space as the delineator in the input line. Execute the program again and enter 35 32 return. You will see that it will work properly now.

```
What are the wet & dry bulb temperatures in Deg C
35 32 return (entered by the user)
The difference in temperatures is 3 Deg C
```

Inputs of different types can be entered in the same input line as long as the variable types are properly specified and there are no mismatches in data types along the way.

You will need to use the `scanf()` function many times in this course, so this is just the beginning.

5   Constants

In some cases, one may wish to make a value constant throughout the entire program. Of course, one way to do this is to define a variable (pi for example), assign it the desired constant value (e.g., 3.14159) and then make sure it is never changed. The last requirement, however, can be burdensome, as someone else may use your source code and not understand that it is never to be changed. The C language provides a way to make sure the value of a "constant variable" never changes. The keyword const (one of the 37 reserved keywords) placed in front of a variable when it is defined and initialized makes sure of this. For example,

```
const int VAR = 10;
```

Note that the variable to be made constant must be initialized in the same line in which it is defined. This value cannot be changed from this point on in the program code.

By convention (not required by C), the name of a constant is in all caps as indicated by VAR above. This "locking up" of a value in a variable can be important in large programs where a programmer would share her program with other programmers, but would not want anyone changing the value of a constant.

While this works well, there is another way – at least for simple constant values. The #define preprocessor directive gives us a computationally cheap and easy way to define constants. Let's say we want to make computations with π, and want to set it to 3.14. We can define PI through a preprocessor directive as follows:

```
// blah
// blah blah

#include<stdlib.h>
#include<stdio.h>

#define PI 3.14

int main()
{
   float area = 0.0, radius = 26.5;
   area = PI * radius * radius;
   printf("The area of a circle of radius %f is %f \n", radius, area);

   return (0);
}
```

The number 3.14 will replace every instance of PI in the source code prior to compilation. This has the effect of not requiring any memory for a variable and incurs no overhead when retrieving a value that never changes. Plus, it cannot be changed because it is not a variable per se. But there is more. Let's say that the programmer now wants to increase the precision of the computation and would like to use 3.14159 for PI instead of the earlier number. All she would have to do is simply go to one statement in the source code and change the value of PI in the #define directive that is typically at the top of the source code. Try it.

6 Summary

In this chapter, we have introduced the important concept of variables – the most basic way to manage data. We discussed how to define variables, how to assign a value to them, and how to retrieve that value. Furthermore, we discussed the different types of variables and how sensitive the C language is to mismatched data types. Some mismatches are recognized and corrected by the compiler, but others are not. Such unrecognized mismatches lead to errors, often insidious errors. We also discussed the good practice of always initializing variables to avoid potential errors later on. This will become more important when we get into more complex types of data structures later in the book.

This chapter also discussed simple mathematical operators and basic input/output functions. The concepts learned in this chapter, while basic and relatively simple compared to what we will see later, provide a foundation in programming with C.

Equally importantly, the exercises provided the dutiful learner with increased experience in writing, compiling and executing these simple programs. This has hopefully built up confidence in the learner's ability to write such simple programs. Next, we provide an increasingly more challenging set of problems for the learner to practice by him/herself to build up that confidence.

7 Problems

1) You are planning a road trip around the western USA. Unfortunately, for some reason, the map you have gives you the distances between cities in Kilometers (Km) rather than miles. You would prefer to plan your trip on the basis of miles. Write a program that will convert a distance from Km to miles when a number is entered from the keyboard. Look up the conversion factor from the internet. Test it by entering 15 Km as `15 return`. It should give you approximately `9.32 miles`. Clearly, you should be using floating point variable types, right? What if you were to use integers? Use the `const` feature to "lock-up" the conversion rate, as this value will never change.

2) You are planning a series of long flights but hate to fly. So, you want to know how long a flight would be in hours from wheels up to touchdown (yes, there are websites that can tell us this, but let's program it anyway). Therefore, knowing the distance between two airports, you would like to estimate the duration of a flight. The distance between two airports (cities) can be found in the Internet (e.g., NY to LA is 2451 miles). Assume that the typical cruising ground speed of a modern jetliner is 550 MPH. Additionally, knowing that airplanes have to slow down as they approach their destination and must also take time to align the aircraft with the runway, add 25 min to the total time computed. Your program should ask the user for the distance in miles and prints out a statement that indicates the duration of the flight in minutes as well as in hours. Use the `const` feature to "lock up" the variable holding the speed constant, as the speed of a jetliner is not likely to change (much).

3) Write a program that converts the Euro into US Dollars. Do not use the const to define a constant but instead use the `#define` pre-processor directive, because the exchange rate changes frequently (daily). You can find the conversion rates in the Internet. A user will enter the number of units of Euros, and your program will calculate and print out the equivalent US Dollars (USD). Because this value is likely to change daily, use the `#define` p[re-processor directive rather than the constant variable used in the previous two problems.

4) Slightly more complex. With respect to the same problem #3 above, make your program able to convert the currency in both directions - that is, convert from Euros into USD as well as from USD to Euros.

5) Even more complex. You'd like to keep track of how many calories you are consuming. You are hoping that keeping track of this information will nudge you into making better food choices. Unfortunately, the labels on the foods you eat do not display the number of calories. Luckily, they are labeled with the number of grams of protein, carbohydrates and fat that they contain.

Write a program that asks the user to enter these three values (grams of protein, carbohydrates and fat) consumed, and prints out the total number of calories in that food. The formula is to multiply the number of protein/carbs/fat, times the constants below respectively, and add them up. Please use the following constants in your program:

CALS_PER_GR_PROTEIN = 4
CALS_PER_GR_CARB = 4
CALS_PER_GR_FAT = 9

Sample Run (User Input in Bold and Italics)

```
How many grams of protein did you eat?
50
How many grams of carbohydrates did you eat?
75
How many grams of fat did you eat?
15
You ate 635 calories of food.
```

Selection Structures

3

Up to this point, we have been working strictly with *sequential structures* in our simple C programs. A sequential structure is simply a fancy name for a series of C statements that are executed in sequential order. While it may be overkill to even refer to these as *structures* – after all, a sequence of statements is the most basic way to build programs – it is nevertheless the precursor to more complex structures of code. In this and the next chapter, we will see two other types of structures that are not only more complex than the sequential structure but are also very important in computer programming. These are the *Selection Structure* and the *Repetition Structure*. Both deviate from the idea of sequentially executing statements, one after the other in the order set forth by the programmer. In this chapter we cover the Selection Structure.

In short, a selection structure, also called a *conditional structure*, or more commonly, an *if-then structure*, allows the processor to selectively execute alternatives blocks of code depending on the value of some expression (either computed, entered from outside the program, or referenced from memory). In this chapter, you will learn about and work with the four main selection structures: *single selection, double selection, multiple selection,* and the *switch*. So, once again, we crank up the level of interestingness a bit more. We will learn how to use these structures and how not to misuse them.

1   Selection Structures – A Short Introduction

Selection structures permit re-directing the execution of statements, from merely the next statement in the sequence to an alternative statement or block of statements. These structures allow the programmer to decide what statement or block of statements should be executed by the processor, depending on one (or possibly more) test(s) performed on specific data. The decision as to whether to re-direct the execution and where to re-direct it is based on evaluating a *test condition* (or conditions), whose results will be used to make this determination.

For example, we have often faced situations when our decisions depend on some information. For example, if it is raining, then I'll take my umbrella. Whether to take the umbrella or not depends on some information about a process that we may not control, such as whether it is raining. The test here is whether it is raining at this moment or not. The re-direction of the execution is to either bring the umbrella or leave it in the apartment. Such decision-making is very common, indeed essential, in

© Springer Nature Switzerland AG 2020
A. J. Gonzalez, *Computer Programming in C for Beginners*,
https://doi.org/10.1007/978-3-030-50750-3_3

computer programming, and the selection structures assist the programmer in easily implementing such logic in his program. For example, in a highly abstract representation of our "umbrella code":

```
If (it is raining) then execute <bring umbrella>
     Otherwise, execute <leave umbrella at home>
```

The above is an abstract example of a code *construct* that allows a programmer to implement such a decision-making mechanism. This construct is often called a *conditional statement.* Furthermore, noting that such decisions almost always begin with an "if" and follow with a (possibly implicit) "then", we most often simply call them *if-then statements* (although not all of the conditional constructs contain these words).

We begin with the simplest of these structures – the *single selection structure.*

2   Single-Selection Structures

Single selection structures ask a question through some *test.* If the test evaluates to **true** (i.e., 1), then a designated statement or block of statements is executed. Otherwise, that statement (or block) is skipped and the processing continues with the first statement <u>after</u> that designated statement (or block of statements). It is as if we tell the processor: If <test> is **true**, then do this. Otherwise, don't do it and move on.

The format and syntax for the single selection construct is as follows:

```
if ( <test> )
     {
             <designated statements>
     }
<next statement>
```

The if is a reserved keyword in C. When the processor encounters an if, it proceeds to evaluate the associated test condition within the parentheses. If this test condition evaluates to **true** (1), it will execute the designated statements. If, on the other hand, it evaluates to **false** (0), then it will execute the first statement <u>after</u> the designated code. Note that there is no semicolon after the if (<test>) line. It is followed by the designated code block. Let's code something now.

```
int main()
 {
    char rain = 'y';
    if(rain == 'y')
      {
              printf("I will take my umbrella! \n");
        )
    return 0;
 }
```

In this simplest of programs, the output will be:

```
I will take my umbrella!
```

Now let's go to the same program source code and change the value of the variable `rain` to 'n' (or actually, any character except 'y') .

```
int main()
{
    char rain = 'n';
    if(rain == 'y')
      {
            printf("I will take my umbrella! \n");
      }
    return 0;
}
```

You will see that now nothing will happen. That is because the statement that follows the designated code is simply the `return 0;` statement that causes the `main()` function to exit. The program does not ask the processor to do anything else.

Now let's complicate the test question. The only way we can take an umbrella is if it is raining AND we own an umbrella. If we don't own an umbrella, then we can't take one, even if it is raining. So, recalling the Boolean operator `&&` from Chap. 2, let's make a compound conditional statement:

```
int main()
  {
    char rain = 'y', own = 'y';
    if(rain == 'y' && own == 'y')
        {
              printf("I will take my umbrella! \n");
        }
    return 0;
  }
```

In this case, the two tests with `rain` and `own` evaluate to **true** (both hold the values 'y'), so the output of the program is:

```
I will take my umbrella!
```

Alternatively, if one of them holds a value other than 'y', the compound expression will evaluate to **false** (will fail) and nothing will print. Try changing the value of `own` to 'n' and you will see that nothing happens. This is because just like in the case of the simple test that only needed to know whether it was raining, the next statement following the conditional structure is the `return 0` statement, which causes the program to end.

2.1   Exactly What Is Defined as the "Designated Code"?

Now is a good time to make an important point about what constitutes the so-called "designated statements" in a selection structure. In our examples above, we enclosed the designated statements within curly brackets { } (also called *braces*) as a block of code, even when the block contains only one statement. This works fine, as the compiler assumes that the designated statements block follows the test definition. However, if the designated statements number only one statement, as is the case in our examples above, we can dispense with the curly brackets and merely place the designated statement after the test condition definition. So, the code below:

```
        .
          .
          .
if(rain == 'y' && own == 'y')
      printf("I will take my umbrella! \n");
return 0;
```

would work equally well. In fact, while it is customary to indent the designated code (or block of code) from the test definition to make it more obvious to the human, it is not necessary to do so. Thus, the code

```
.
.
.
.
if(rain == 'y' && own == 'y')
printf("I should take my umbrella!\n");
return 0;
```

would also work, as the compiler interprets the `printf()` statement **as** the designated statement and the `return 0` as the next statement after the construct. However, this can be confusing to the human, so the use of curly brackets, or at the very least the indentation, is always encouraged, even when the block contains only one statement.

2.2   How Does One Handle the "Otherwise" Case?

To answer the question posed in the title of this sub-section: <u>you cannot</u> with the single selection structure. The reason is that the processor will always execute the statement <u>after</u> the end of the structure, regardless of whether it executes the designated code or not. For example, see the following code:

```
int main()
  {
    char rain = 'y';
    if(rain == 'y')
      {
          printf("I will take my umbrella! \n");
      }
    printf("I think I'll leave my umbrella at home \n");

    return 0;
  }
```

This processor will execute the designated code (the first `printf()`) because the test succeeded, but it will <u>also</u> execute the second `printf()` anyway and print out:

```
I will take my umbrella
I think I'll leave my umbrella at home
```

This is, of course, contradictory as well as incorrect (not to mention rather idiotic). This is a good lesson to learn that programs must be tested extensively to find all bugs, as logic errors such as this can creep in easily.

So, the single selection structure should never be used when there is an "otherwise" case – that is, when we want to execute an alternative statement or block of statements if the test condition fails. For that, C offers the *double selection structure*.

3 Double-Selection Structures

Double selection structures give the programmer the ability to define two alternative statements (or blocks of statements). One is executed if the conditional test succeeds and the other is executed if it fails (the "otherwise" case). This gives the programmer much more flexibility in defining conditionals. This selection structure uses what we commonly say when defining an alternative block of statements – the *else* statement. In effect, we tell the computer "If the test is true, then do this; else, do that". The format for the double selection is as follows:

```
if (test)
        {
                < designated code>
        }
else
        {
                <alternative code>
        }
<next statement>
```

As you might expect, `else` is a reserved keyword in C.

Now for some examples. Say we have a program to determine whether a user is allowed to legally drink alcohol. The program asks for the user's age. If 21 or greater, it will say yes. If not, then it will say no.

```
int main()
{
    int age = 0;
    printf("How old are you? \n");
    scanf("%d", &age);

    if(age >= 21) // the >= symbol stands for "greater than or equal to"
        printf("You are permitted to drink alcohol. \n");
    else
        printf("You are not permitted to drink alcohol. \n");

    return 0;
}
```

Try it. Run it once and enter 18; then run it again and enter 25. This is something one could <u>not</u> do with a single selection structure. Note that we did not use curly brackets to enclose the designated and alternative statements because there is only one statement for each of the blocks (just to keep the code succinct). Had it been more than one statement, we would have had to use the { } to enclose the statements as a block of code.

4   Multiple-Selection Structures

While the double selection structure allows us to do more than the single selection structure, it allows us to have only one conditional test. In the example used above for the double conditional, the only test was the age test. Yes, the double selection structure allows us to have compound tests using the AND or the OR Boolean operators, but these are not really separate tests, just a combination of various tests. This single test can only have two results – **true** or **false**.

What if we have a situation where we need to ask different questions, or one question with several possible answers, each of which will cause a different alternative code to be executed? The multiple selection structure allows a programmer to define completely different tests for each set of alternative code. The format of the multiple selection structure is as follows:

```
if ( <test1> )
     {
          <alternative statement 1>
     }
else if ( <test2> )
     {
          <alternative statement 2>
     }
else if ( <test3> )
     {
          <alternative statement 3>
     }
else
     {
          <alternative statement 4>
     }
<next statement>
```

Note that the last statement uses an else, rather than an else if, as do the first three cases. As in the double selection structure, the else defines the "otherwise" case (i.e., if <u>all</u> the prior tests fail, then execute these statements). Note also that the else case is optional and, if there is to be one, always goes last. So if there isn't an else set of statements, the execution will continue on to the first statement after the multiple selection construct – in this case, <next statement>.

Let's look at an example. Say we have to determine a letter grade for a student based on the numerical grade received on a test. Our program will map a numerical score to a letter grade. We'll use the conventional grading scale of 90 to 100 = A; 80 to 89 = B; etc.

```
int grade;
printf("What grade did you get? \n");
scanf("%d", &grade);
if (grade >= 90)
     printf("You have an A \n");
else if (grade >= 80)
     printf("You have a B \n");
else if (grade >= 70)
     printf("You have a C \n");
else if (grade >= 60)
     printf("You have a D \n");
else
     printf("You have failed the test \n");
```

Write the program above in your editor, compile and execute it. You will see that you will obtain the correct answer as long as the input is an integer value between 0 and 100.

One curious thing to note in the code above is that the second, third and fourth test conditions (the `else if`'s) were not defined as being between 80 and 90 for a B, between 70 and 80 for a C, or between 60 and 70 for a D. Rather, these tests merely ask whether the entered number is >=80, >=70 or >=60 respectively. This appears to be incorrect until we come to learn that in a multiple selection structure, the tests are executed in the sequence presented, but that as soon as a test succeeds, the corresponding alternative code is executed and the processor <u>exits</u> the double selection structure. The subsequent tests <u>are not evaluated</u>, and neither is the `else` case, so those blocks of alternative statements are not even considered for execution. This is why we obtained the correct answers above. This reminds one of the short cut evaluations of compound Boolean expressions that we saw in Chap. 2.

There are three other things one should note about the code above:

1) No curly brackets were needed for the alternative statements because there was only one statement in each group (one `printf()`). Had there been more than one statement, then `{ }` would have been necessary to enclose the statements as a block of code. You should already know this, but this is a reminder.
2) We did not use a semicolon at the end of the lines that contained the `if`, the `else` or the `else if`. You should also already know this, but more reminders can't hurt.
3) The example above actually asks the same question for all four cases. The value entered for the variable `grade` is what makes a difference in the output. Nevertheless, we could have had a different question for each test (in some other application) and it would also have worked.

One last note: good programming practice would have included another test to make sure that the number entered was an integer between 0 and 100. If not, then the user would be told that the entry was invalid and be provided another opportunity to enter a valid number. At this point in the course, however, the only thing we know enough to be able to do would be to exit the program without providing an answer. After Chap. 4, we will learn how to give him/her a second chance to enter a valid number (… and if necessary, a third, and a fourth and …). A test like this would look as follows:

```
if ((grade < 0 || grade > 100))
   {
     printf("The value you have entered is invalid.  Good bye! \n ");
     return 0;
   )
```

This would then be followed by the multiple selection structure that we showed above.

Alternatively, one could make this condition the first test in the multiple selection structure. For example:

```
int grade;
printf("What grade did you get? \n");
scanf("%d", &grade);
if ((grade < 0 || grade > 100))
   {
     printf("The value you entered is invalid. Good bye! \n");
     return 0;
   }
else if (grade >= 90)
     printf("You have an A \n");
else if (grade >= 80)
     printf("You have a B \n");
else if (grade >= 70)
     printf("You have a C \n");
else if (grade >= 60)
     printf("You have a D \n");
else
     printf("You have failed \n");
```

The fact that the first test succeeds when an invalid number is entered would by itself get the processor out of the selection structure. However, in this case, the `return 0;` statement executed as part of the designated block of code ends the program altogether.

---

5   The `break;` and the `return;` Statements

Before continuing, we need to learn about a statement in C that causes execution to immediately exit the structure in which it currently is, and continue to the first statement after said structure. This is the `break;` statement and it is a single statement by itself. `break` is a reserved keyword in C. Its works for selection as well as *repetition structures* (discussed in Chap. 4). This statement is used extensively by our last selection structure (the `switch`), introduced in Sect. 6 below.

As you should already know from our earlier use of it in our `main()` function, the `return` statement is similar to the `break`, except the `return` takes the execution out of the entire function altogether, not just the structure. If in `main()`, it also ends the program. Thus, the `return` is a more global version of `break`, so to speak. Furthermore, the `return` statement permits the programmer to specify what he wants to have the function leave in its place once the execution exits the function. We will discuss the `return` statement more extensively when we introduce user-defined functions in Chap. 5.

6   The switch Structure

The switch structure is the last selection structure to be discussed in this chapter. It does the same thing as the multiple selection structure, except it does it a bit more elegantly, although it can be somewhat harder to understand and has a more intricate format. The format is as follows:

```
switch(controlling expression)
    {
        case label_1:
                <statement 1>;
                break;
        case label_2:
                <statement 2>;
                break;
        case label_3:
                <statement 3>;
                break;

                .
                .
                .

        case label_n:
                <statement n>;
                break;
        default:
                <statement x>;
    }
```

The controlling expression is a test expression that will return a value when evaluated (It could just be the value of a variable.) This is similar to the tests of the single, double and multiple selection structures. However, it is different in two subtle ways: 1) while the former ones can only evaluate to **true** or **false**, the controlling expression in a switch structure can return any value. The case identifies a value to be expected from the controlling expression (or variable). If this value matches the output of the controlling expression, then the test succeeds and the statements below case are executed. Otherwise, the execution moves on to the next case. 2) While the multiple selection structure can ask a different question in every else if, the controlling expression in switch can only ask one question, albeit with multiple possible answers.

The break; statement, as mentioned above, breaks the execution out of the switch structure whenever it is executed. Note that in the multiple selection structure, the function of breaking out of the structure is implicit. Not so for the switch – it needs to have the break; statement explicitly stated. The default: is the same as the else in the multiple selection structure – it will execute this alternative code only when all tests above it have failed. It is also optional.

Let's now work with a more complex example that involves an arithmetic operation selector program. Say we have two numbers embedded in the source code (of course, we could easily ask the user for them). For simplicity, let's say both are floating point numbers. We may want to add them together ('a'), or subtract the second from the first ('s'), or multiply them ('m') or divide the first by the second number ('d'). The user gets to say which operation she wants. To do this, we implement the following code, which you should enter in your IDE editor.

```
int main()
{
    float num1 = 75.3, num2 = 101.6, total = 0.0;
    char op;

    printf("What operation would like to perform? \n ");
    scanf("%c", &op);

    switch(op)
    {
        case 'a':
                total = num1 + num2;
                break;
        case 's':
                total = num1 - num2;
                break;
        case 'm':
                total = num1 * num2;
                break;
        case 'd':
                total = num1/num2;
                break;
        default:
                printf("You have entered an invalid input. Good bye! \n");
                return 0;
    }

    printf("Total = %f \n", total);


    return 0;
}
```

Compile and execute the code, entering valid (a, s, m or d) as well as invalid entries. There are several things to note in this code:

1) The block of code under each case <u>did not</u> have to be placed between curly brackets { }, even though there are more than one statement. Once again, these are the inconsistencies of C. You will get tired of hearing about these inconsistencies.

2) If either a, s, m or d are entered, the statement break; breaks the execution out of the switch structure after executing the corresponding arithmetical operation. If the break; statement is mistakenly left out, the processor will continue executing the statements below it. Try taking out one of the break; statements and enter the character that will make this alternative code execute. See what happens.

3) There are two return 0; statements in the code – one in the default: block and another at the end of the main() function body. That is OK because the processor would never encounter both of them, as return 0; is a terminal statement. The return 0; embedded within the default: case serves to avoid having the last printf() execute, as the computations are

irrelevant if the value entered by the user is anything other than a, s, m or d. This was discussed earlier under good programming practices.

4) The controlling expression in the code is just retrieving the value of a variable. However, it can be more than this. It could include a more complex expression. The value returned by this expression is what is compared to the value expected in the case label.

5) Notice further in the code above that we have two sets of curly brackets – one for the main() function and another for the entire switch structure – one inside the other. The brackets for main() enclose the entire switch structure as well as other statements before and after it, so they are considered to be the outer pair of brackets. The "inner" set is to be placed in a manner indented from the "outer" pairs. Programming convention dictates that the pair of corresponding { } curly brackets be lined up with each other. While the C compiler doesn't care about this, it is much easier for us humans to see which opening bracket/brace/parenthesis lines up with which closing bracket/brace/parenthesis.

7   Summary

In this chapter, we introduced the first of two major structures that are so important to computer programming, regardless of the programming language used. The selection structure allows a programmer to provide alternate code to be executed depending on the results of a test. This is indeed an essential feature in computer programming. We discussed four such structures, from the simplest single selection structure, to the most complex multiple selection structure and the switch structure. In the process, we introduced the break; statement and the learner acquired more practice with coding in C.

8   Problems

1) Write a program that asks a user to enter an integer value and returns an indication of whether the number entered is even or odd. (Hint: Use the mod division % to determine this.)
   (a) Use a double selection structure.
   (b) Use a switch structure.

2) Write a program that when a user enters a water temperature in degrees Fahrenheit (as real numbers between 110 and –10), converts it into degrees Centigrade and determines whether the water is about to boil (>100 °C), about to freeze (<= 0 deg. C) or in a liquid (somewhere in between). Reject any entries from the user that are outside of the range indicated.

3) The water in a swimming pool should be kept at a neutral pH level. A common test for pool water pH is to put in a few drops of a solution in a small sample of pool water and observe its color. If purplish, this indicates a high pH (alkalinity). Alternatively, an overly orange shade will indicate low pH (acidity). If the shade is reddish/mildly orange, this indicates a neutral pH. Write a program that indicates the pH of the water if the color of the sample is entered as "p" for purple, "o" for orange or "r" for reddish.
   (a) Use a multiple selection structure
   (b) Use a switch structure

4) Write a program that accepts an integer value from 0 to 10 and prints out the number entered in words (e.g., 2 → two). Reject any entries other than integers from 0 to 10. Use a switch structure.

5) You've decided that it's critical for you to take advantage of the "Buy One Get One" (BOGO) free offers at the nearby grocery store. Write a program that determines the total cost of buying orange juice under the BOGO offer. Note that if you want to buy an odd number of cartons (as in not even), you pay full price for the last one.

Your program should ask the user to enter the number of cartons being purchased and the regular price of one carton of juice. Assume no sales tax or any such other added cost to the total sum.

Sample Run (User Input in Bold and Italics)

```
What is the cost of one container of OJ in dollars?
3.79
How many containers are you buying?
4
The total cost is $7.58.
```

Sample Run (User Input in Bold and Italics)

```
What is the cost of one container of OJ in dollars?
4.50
How many containers are you buying?
5
The total cost is $13.50
```

Repetition Structures

4

Selection structures are not the only structures that shift the execution to an alternative statement or block of statements. There are times when we might want to execute <u>the same</u> statement or block of statements over and over again. A *repetition structure* (also called a *loop structure* or just simply a *loop*) can do this. As you will see later in this book, there are many cases where such repetition becomes necessary. It is virtually impossible to do anything useful in computing without multiple selection and/or repetition structures in the program. In this chapter, you will work with the three main repetition structures: the *for loop,* the *while loop,* and the *do-while loop.* We will learn how to use these structures and how not to misuse them. So, once again, we crank up the level of interestingness still a bit more.

1   Repetition Structures – A Short Introduction

Repetition structures cause the same statement or block of statements to be executed again ... and again ... and again in a loop, until something happens to stop the looping. Normally, when the looping ends, the processor goes on to execute the first statement after the loop structure; that is, outside and after the loop.

The programmer must decide how to end the repetition. The decision of whether to continue looping or to stop is based on evaluating a test condition (or conditions) – this is called the loop *exit criteria*. There are two types of criteria that can be used to decide whether to re-execute a block of code or exit the loop and continue on to the next statement after the loop construct. One criterion is the number of times the loop is to be executed. These are called *counter-controlled loops*. In these types of loops, the statements in the loop are executed a pre-set number of times. A *counter variable* is used to keep track of the number of times the block was executed. After the count limit has been reached, execution then continues on to the first statement after the end of the loop structure. In the great majority of applications, each *iteration* (as one pass through the loop code is commonly called) executes something slightly different within the loop code. Setting the end criteria (i.e., the number of loops to execute) can be done internally within the specification format of one of the loop constructs. However, it can also be done through a selection structure within the *loop body* (i.e., the block of code to be repeatedly executed); this can provide added flexibility, as we will see later. Examples of applications where count control is relevant include data collection, such as logging a temperature reading of something every hour of every day for a month (720 iterations).

© Springer Nature Switzerland AG 2020
A. J. Gonzalez, *Computer Programming in C for Beginners,*
https://doi.org/10.1007/978-3-030-50750-3_4

Alternatively, there are other applications where we don't know how many times the loop body should be executed (and it may not be important). Instead, stopping the loop depends on the value of one or more variables. The looping ends when this (these) variable(s) reaches a pre-determined value. We refer to these loops as *sentinel controlled loops*. The *sentinel* is the variable or variables whose value(s) are to be continually monitored during each iteration until it/they attain (or exceed) a certain benchmark value, at which point execution of the loop statements ends and the processor moves on to execute the statements after the end of the loop. One example of a sentinel controlled loop would be when pre-heating an oven, a program would monitor the temperature inside the oven every second until the pre-set value of the desired temperature is reached, at which time the loop would end and an alarm would sound to alert the user.

There is one other issue in loops about which we will need to become familiar: where is the decision about loop continuation/stoppage being made? It can be done at the beginning of the loop body or at the end of the loop body. The former is called an *entry condition loop* while the latter is known as *exit condition loop*. An exit condition loop guarantees that at least one run through the loop body code will be made, as it doesn't check the exit criteria until the end of the loop. No such guarantee exists for an entry condition loop because the decision of whether to execute the loop body or not is done before the processor "enters" the loop body. Before you ask, no loop structure exists in C that intrinsically makes this decision anywhere except at the beginning or at the end of the loop code block. Nevertheless, if a programmer were to have an untypical situation where that would make sense to do, a well-placed selection structure with a `break;` statement, placed at the appropriate location within the loop body code, could serve that purpose. We'll see examples of this later in this chapter as well as in Chap. 12.

So, we can categorise loops as 1) counter-controlled/entry condition loop (the most common); 2) sentinel-controlled/entry condition loop (the next most common), and; 3) sentinel-controlled/exit condition loop. There are no counter-controlled/exit condition loops, at least not in C.

One last thing to consider: what exactly does the programmer need to define in order to unambiguously specify the operation of the loop? There are four things:

Exit control variable: It is essential to clearly and unambiguously specify a variable whose value can be cause for the lopping to end. Otherwise, *infinite loops* can occur, where the looping goes on infinitely until the program crashes or execution is aborted by the user. As we discussed above, all loops require exit criteria to be defined (somehow) and these criteria must be attainable. An exit control variable can hold a value equal to the number of iterations that have been executed at any point in time, or more generally, the value of the sentinel criterion whose value at some point will cause the loop to exit.

Initial value of exit control variable: The initial value of the exit control variable must be unequivocally and unambiguously specified. It should be a value that does NOT cause cessation of the looping process; otherwise, the loop won't execute at all if it is an entry condition loop or only once if it is an exit condition loop.

Final value of exit control variable: Declaring the exit control variable per se is not enough. The programmer still needs to define what specific value of this exit control variable will cause the looping to end, or more accurately, will cause the looping to continue.

Update of exit control variable: How does the exit control variable change throughout an iteration of the loop? If it is a counter controlled variable, then it typically increments or decrements (depending on the loop design) by 1 after each iteration. If it is a sentinel control variable, then how does this value change? It is important that this updating procedure "move" the value of this variable towards the exit criterion. If the exit criterion value is skipped over or not otherwise ever satisfied, the looping will continue forever (or crash).

We discuss all the above issues in this chapter and provide some practice with these loop structures.

2   for Loops

We begin with the for loop – a counter-controlled/entry condition loop structure. The for loop is the most commonly-used loop structure in C.

The for loop construct is very strictly specified. That is, it requires explicit specification, right in the loop definition, of several parameters that control the looping process. These parameters are all specified within a parenthetical expression that immediately follows the reserved keyword for. The format for a for loop is as follows:

```
for(<init>; <continuation condition>; <increment>)
    {
        <loop body statements>;
    }
```

init sets the initial value of the counter control variable; continuation condition specifies the condition <u>for continuing looping</u> (not for exiting); and increment defines how the counter control variable is to be incremented or decremented in each iteration. We reiterate that the continuation condition indicated above is a criterion for <u>continuing</u> the looping process, not for ending it. Therefore, it is not an exit criterion per se, but rather a *continuation criterion*, even though we will continue to call it an "exit" control variable herein. So, when the continuation condition is evaluated to **true**, the looping continues. It only stops when the continuation condition evaluates to **false**.

It is important to state here the importance of defining the counter control variable prior to entering the for loop structure. Some C compilers permit the *in situ* definition of the counter control variable, right inside the parenthetical expression, just ahead of its initialization. This makes sense to do; it also limits the *scope* (the extent of the code where a variable's definition is recognized) of the variable to the confines of the repetition structure only. We will further discuss the scope of a variable later in this course when you will actually need to consider it. In the meantime, let's assume that our compiler does <u>not</u> allow *in situ* definition of counter control variables, and let's instead define them outside and before entering the for loop (we come back to discuss *in situ* definition of counter variables later in this chapter.) Furthermore, it is customary (but <u>not</u> required by the C compilers) that n, i, j, or k be the names of choice for the counter control variables. No special reason, it's just convention.

Let's see how this for loop works. Write the following program in your IDE editor:

```
int main()
{
    int n, k=0; // The counter control variable n is defined here
    for(n=0; n<25; n++)
        k++;
    printf("The value of n is %d \n", n);
    printf("The number of iterations was %d \n", k);
    return 0;
}
```

Compile it and execute it. The output of this program should be:

```
The value of n is 25
The number of iterations was 25
```

At the end of the 25th iteration, the value of n was increased from 24 to 25 by the for loop's internal mechanism that executes the n++ operation. As the loop tried to enter the loop body on the 26th iteration, the continuation criterion (n < 25) evaluates to **false**, thereby causing the processor to exit the loop. Therefore, the value of n is 25 when it is printed by the printf() statement after the end of the loop structure. Note that we set the initial value of n as 0, and not 1. That is because in C (like most computer programming languages), counting starts from 0, and not from 1.

The counter control variable is just a variable for determining when to stop the looping. It does not always count the actual number of iterations of the loop -- that depends on its initial value as well as how it is incremented. In this simple example, we use the variable k as the true iteration counter. The program will execute the k++; statement over and over as long as n is less than 25. When n reaches 25, it will then stop looping and go on to the first printf() to print the final value of the counter variable n. The variable k counts the number of times the loop body was executed. The second printf() states the number of times the loop body was actually executed. Its correct printout should say:

```
The number of iterations was 25.
```

However, if we were to change the initial value of n to, say 3. See the code below.

```
 int main()
 {
     int n, k=0; // The counter control variable n is defined here
     for(n=3; n<25; n++)
            k++;
     printf("The value of n is %d \n", n);
     printf("The number of iterations was %d \n", k);
     return 0;
 }
```

The output would still say that n is 25 just the same, as that is still the exit condition. However, the number of iterations that it took the processor to get there is now 22 rather than 25. So n, in this case, does not really count the number of iterations – that is done by k. The variable n just serves as the exit criterion. However, the counter variable (n in this case) can serve as the actual iteration counter if it is initialized to 0, and it is incremented by one in each iteration.

Now is a good time to introduce the continue; statement and the role it plays in loops. Let's first show by example by saying that we will use n to count the number of iterations (i.e., we no longer need to know the actual number of iterations) in the above code. So, we no longer need the variable k nor the k++; statement. However, because we presumably need to have at least one statement to execute in the loop body, we replace the k++; statement with a continue; statement in the loop body. See the code below.

```
int main()
{
    int n; // The counter control variable n is defined here
    for(n=0; n<25; n++)
        continue;
    printf("The number of iterations was %d \n", n);
    return 0;
}
```

So, then, what does this `continue;` statement do and why do we need it?

The `continue;` statement tells the processor to go back to the beginning of the loop body and skip any statements underneath it (within the loop body). In effect, it aborts the current iteration and tells the processor to begin the next iteration from the top of the loop body. It can be used inside a selection structure to skip the execution of statements in the loop body under certain conditions, but not to exit the loop, as the `break;` statement would do. Much more commonly, however, `continue;` is used by many programmers as the last statement in a loop body, just to indicate that the loop body ends here. Of course, the processor already knows this, making the `continue;` statement superfluous in such cases. Nevertheless, it can be helpful for a human to unequivocally see where a loop body ends.

Let's see how it works. Compile and run the program. It should print out:

```
The number of iterations was 25
```

Which is correct.

As we saw, there has to be at least one statement in the loop body that is to be executed. In this case, it is the `continue;` statement. As discussed above, it does nothing useful in this particular case, but it is the one statement to be executed in the loop body. Nevertheless, what would happen if we took out the `continue;` statement altogether from the code above? See below.

```
int main()
{
    int n; // Note how the exit control variable is declared here
    for(n=0; n<25; n++)
    printf("The number of iterations was %d \n", n);
    return 0;
}
```

Note that we are leaving the `for(n = 0; n < 25; n++)` statement without a semicolon at its end! This seems like a sure compilation error. Nevertheless, please compile and run it. Surprisingly, it compiles just fine and it executes without errors.

But hmmm! The output is now:

```
The number of iterations was 0
The number of iterations was 1
The number of iterations was 2
            .

            .

The number of iterations was 24
```

However, this is not what we wanted. So, what happened here? After thinking about it, we see that it should <u>not</u> have been surprising that the program compiled just fine and ran. The `printf()` now became the statement immediately after the loop definition, so the compiler interpreted it to be the loop body, and executed it 25 times, resulting in the 25 printed lines.

OK, fine, but we notice that the last printout says the loop counted 24 times and not 25, as we had discussed above. Why? Well, this is because the `printf()` is now inside the loop, rather than after it. Therefore, it printed the value of n while <u>inside</u> the loop body, albeit at its end. The value of n gets updated by the `for` loop's "internal mechanism" only <u>after</u> the iteration ends and <u>before</u> the start of the next iteration. But the process never enters the loop body again after n becomes 25, as it fails the continuation criterion precisely because the value of n is 25. Since the `printf()` is in the loop body, it never gets the chance to execute when n is 25. In the original program, the value of n to be printed was its value <u>after</u> the loop exited, thereby causing the continuation criterion to fail; but the value of n had been already set to 25.

While the above discussion may seem trite and possibly hard to follow, many errors are made by inexperienced programmers when determining the number of iterations to execute in a loop because they do not understand exactly how the `for` loop works and when it updates the counter variable. This discussion hopefully helps the learner understand some of the intricacies of `for` loops in the hope of avoiding such errors.

As for the `continue;` statement, alternatively, one could simply put a semicolon; right after the `for(....);` statement. Let's try it:

```
int main()
{
    int n; // Note how the exit control variable is declared here
    for(n=0; n<25; n++);
    printf("The number of iterations was %d \n", n);
    return 0;
}
```

Interestingly, the output is now:

```
The number of iterations was 25
```

This is correct! But why? Well, it is because the compiler interprets the; as the end of another statement that does nothing. This do-nothing statement <u>is</u> the loop body – the same role played by the `continue;` statement. This now places the `printf()` statement outside the loop body and immediately after the end of the for loop structure, making it execute just once, when the value of n is indeed 25.

However, this is can be misleading to the human eye because the `for(...)` statement does not syntactically have a; following it. Of course, one could place the; in the following line, and this will work also, but it is rather awkward and can also be visually misleading. This is why the `continue;` statement is typically used in such cases – it does nothing, but makes it obvious to the human code reader. Try this both ways so you can see for yourself.

Another thing to notice is that we did not use the curly brackets to enclose the statements in the loop body. The same ideas that we discussed for the selection structures (except, of course, for the `switch`!) apply here. If there is only one statement in the loop body (immediately following the loop specification line `for (...)`), then curly brackets are optional. However, they become necessary when the loop body consists of more than one statement.

Let's now change the values of this `for` loop construct a bit more to illustrate some other aspects of `for` loops.

Going back to the question of *in situ* definition of variables, first take out the statement defining the variable n and re-compile the program. Of course, it will fail to compile, as every variable has to be defined before it is used. But we knew that already, right?

Second, with the statement that defines n still out, let's now try an *in situ* declaration of n. The loop specification line should now look like this (all else remains the same):

```
    .
    .
    .
for (int n=0; n<25; n++)
    .
    .
```

The compilation will fail. The resulting error says something to the effect that this is only allowed in C99 mode. So, some compilers will allow it; others won't. This one won't.

Next let's see what an infinite loop looks like. In the code above, we introduce a mistake (on purpose, of course) and set the value of the update to n-- instead of n++. This means that the counter variable n will decrement from its initial value of 0, never being able to reach 25. Consequently, it will loop forever if the computer were to let it do so. See the full code below.

```
int main()
{
    int n;

    for(n=0; n<25; n--)
          continue;

    printf("The number of iterations was %d \n", n);

    return 0;
}
```

Compile this code. You will notice that the compiler does NOT detect this error! It compiles just fine. Now execute the program. In our computer, it ran for a few seconds and then returned.

```
The number of iterations was 2147483647
```

This loop actually did end, so it technically was not infinite. However, it only ended because the counter control variable n reached the limit for the value it can store, which is exactly the number above. We have not discussed this yet, but it is the largest number that a 32-bit long signed integer variable can hold. Lucky that it ended; in most cases, the loop will run forever until the computer runs out of memory (if memory is employed in the loop body) or the user aborts the execution. In either case, the outcome is most definitely undesirable.

One more thing to discuss about the `for` loop here. The increment/decrement operator is by far the most common one used in `for` loops. However, it does not matter whether it is pre- or post-; it can be either one, although post- is used most of the time by habit.

Lastly, the operation that changes the control variable does not have to strictly increment/decrement it by 1. Say we want to set the value of n to increase by 2, using the shorthand notation of n+=2. Type in, compile and execute the following code:

```
int main()
{
    int n=0, sum = 0;
    for(n=0;n<100;n+=2)
        {
            printf("n = %d \n", n);
            sum = sum + n;
        }
    printf("The number of iterations was %d \n", n);
    printf("The total value of sum is %d \n", sum);

    return 0;
}
```

The execution stops at 98 instead of 99 because the loop is now incrementing by 2, and the next value is 100, which is not <u>less than</u> 100, as required for continuation. Note that the first printf() outside the loop:

```
printf("The number of iterations was %d \n", n);
```

causes the output to (erroneously) state:

```
The number of iterations was 100 times .
```

Of course, it didn't. It only counted 50 times. This is because, as we discussed earlier, n is not an iteration counter per se in this case. It merely serves here as a counter control variable. How can we fix this so that it prints out the number of iterations executed? Note how the value of n increases by 2 in each iteration of the loop. The final value of n is 100, but it gets there faster than if it was n++. We could solve this by introducing a true iteration counter in the loop body, such as what we did in an earlier example with k++.

Next, note that the two statements printf("n = %d \n", n); and sum = sum + n; now have to be enclosed in { }, because there are now more than one statement to be executed in the loop body.

Finally, could we have used n + 2 as the update operation? As in

```
        .
        .
        .
for (n=0; n<25; n+2)
        .
        .
```

The answer is no because n+2 does not perform an implicit assignment as do n++ and n+=2. So the counter variable n would not be updated. This is not good. Let's see what happens. Make this simple change in your code and compile it. We note that it compiles, but puts out a warning, saying that the relevant statement has no effect. This is true, of course – it will have no effect, as n will never update, and will be 0 every time. But it is only a warning, right? So, let's run the program anyway. The result is that we will get a true infinite loop.

```
n = 0
n = 0
n = 0
n = 0
   .
   .
   .
```

It will print this out forever, as the value of the variable n will always be 0 and thus, never reach its maximum value. Unlike our previous example of an infinite loop that turned out not to be truly infinite after all, this one is indeed infinite. Hit CTRL C to exit the program. This also serves to tell us that the update operator needs to include an assignment function in order to work properly. The increment/decrement operator and the += operator do it implicitly.

Another way to fix it is to include an explicit assignment in the expression. So, instead of n+2 we can specify it as n=n+2. Try it. It works fine although it is a bit more cumbersome to use than n+=2.

While specifically designed to be counter controlled, for loops could also be used as sentinel-controlled loops by placing a single selection structure in the loop body, where the sentinel control variable is evaluated at every iteration. If the test condition (i.e., the exit criterion) is satisfied, then the alternative statement is a break; statement that causes the processor to exit the loop and continue on to the first statement after the end of the loop. Of course, this assumes that this happens before the maximum number of iterations is reached. Nevertheless, it is awkward to use for loops in this manner and this is not normally recommended. C provides other constructs much better suited for sentinel control than for loops. But it can be done if necessary.

Next, let's take a look at what happens when we use a sentinel value rather than a counter to end the looping.

3   The while Loop

The while loop is a sentinel-controlled/entry condition repetition structure. It does not require quite as strong a specification as the for loop, but instead leaves it to the programmer to put the initialization and the update conditions as part of the loop body code. The while loop has the following format:

```
<variable_type> sentinel_var = <initial val>;
while (loop continuation test on sentinel_var)
      {
            <statement1>;
            <statement 2>;
            <statement 3>;
            <update sentinel_var somehow>;
      }
```

The keyword `while` is also a reserved keyword in C. Like the `for` loop, the loop continuation test represents the conditions that permit the loop to <u>continue</u> (rather than to stop). Therefore, it is only when the loop continuation test returns **false** that the loop ends. The name of the `while` construct suggests this – "while the following condition is true, execute the following statements".

Note that the definition and the initialization of the sentinel variable take place outside and above the loop. The update operation for the sentinel variable is defined in the loop body as a statement, typically (but not necessarily) at the very end of the loop body. Let's complete our first example now:

```
int product = 2;
while (product <= 1000)
        {
            product = 2*product;
            printf("The value of product is %d \n", product);
        }
```

The loop will print out the value of `product` at every iteration of the loop as long as the value of `product` is less than or equal to `1000`. This means that the loop will end only when the value of `product` exceeds `1000`. Note that in our case, after nine iterations, the value of `product` will reach `1024`, but only after the loop has been entered for the ninth time. So, the value of `product` is `512` when the decision is made to continue looping at the top of the structure just prior to the ninth iteration. However, it will become `1024` during this ninth iteration and will keep that value when it gets to the `printf()` statement. In the next iteration (the soon-to-be-aborted tenth iteration), however, the processor will realize that the value is now `1024`, and thus greater than `1000` at the point of entry, and will thus end the looping.

The output will be:

```
The value of product is 4
The value of product is 8
The value of product is 16
The value of product is 32
The value of product is 64
The value of product is 128
The value of product is 256
The value of product is 512
The value of product is 1024
```

Next, let's examine what happens when we flip the order of the two statements in the loop body. The code will now look like this:

```
int product = 2;
while (product <= 1000)
        {
            printf("The value of product is %d \n", product);
            product = 2*product;
        }
```

Compile and run it. The result will be that there are still nine iterations, but because the value of product is printed prior to it being updated, the initial value will be 2 (rather than 4) and the final value will be 512 (rather than 1024). We should point out that the actual value of product at the end of the iteration is 1024, just like in the previous version of the program. However, its value when the printf() statement is encountered has not yet been updated. This tells us that in an entry condition loop structure like a while loop, the sentinel variable is updated somewhere in the loop body, while the processor is executing the loop body. However, exactly where the update operation is placed within the loop body can affect what the statements in the loop body do. Again, this may seem like a trite point to make, but understanding this can prevent errors later on.

Lastly, to again see what an infinite loop looks like, set the initial value of the sentinel variable product to 0 as follows.

```
int product = 0;
while (product <= 1000)
        {
          product = 2*product;
          printf("The value of product is %d \n", product);
        }
```

You will see that the program will indeed compile correctly and execute, but will keep printing out.

```
The value of the product is 0
```

over and over .... until you close the window (CTRL C). This is the classic infinite loop! The reason it is infinite, of course, is that anything multiplied by 0 is always 0, so the value of product will never change. As we discussed earlier, infinite loops can be a real problem for all programmers, but especially for inexperienced ones, and one should try to avoid them by being careful in how the loop is defined.

For our last repetition structure, we next examine a version of the while loop that is exit controlled.

4   The do-while Loop

The do-while loop is a sentinel controlled/exit condition loop. That means that it will execute the loop once, regardless of whether the value of the control variable has reached the exit condition (actually, whether the continuation condition fails). If the control variable has reached the exit condition, it will be detected only <u>after</u> it has executed the loop statements. The format is as follows:

```
<variable_type> sentinel_var = <initial val>;
do      {
              <statement 1>;
              <statement 2>;
              <statement 3>;
              <update sentinel_var>
      } while (loop continuation test on sentinel_var);
```

Note the required ; at the end of the continuation condition specification after the while().

Using the same code we used for the `while` loop example but adapting it to the `do-while` loop construct, we have the following:

```
int product = 2;
do {
      product = 2*product;
      printf("The value of product is %d \n", product);
   } while (product <= 1000);
```

In this case, the answer is the same, 1024. This is because whether the value is checked at the end of one iteration or the beginning of the next, the value of `product` will be the same. So, from this standpoint, the two loop structures are equivalent.

Nevertheless, what if we set the initial value of `product` to 1001? One would think that given that the value of `product` is already equal to 1001 to begin with, which meets the stopping (i.e., non-continuation) condition, this would cause the loop to not even execute. However, because it is an <u>exit condition</u> test, it will run once, setting the value of `product` to 2002. Then the continuation test is performed. Try the following code:

```
int product = 1001;
do {
      product = 2*product;
      printf("The value of product is %d \n", product);
} while (product <= 1000);
```

You will see that the resulting printout will say:

```
The value of product is 2002
```

This is because it multiplied the initial value of 1001 times 2 once and then stopped when the continuation test was done at the end of the (first and only) iteration. The important thing to note here is that the loop executed once even though the initial value of the sentinel variable already exceeded the stopping (non-continuation) criterion.

Next, we will see how the three loop structures can be manipulated to do things that they were not specifically designed to do. However, before we do that, being true to our just-in-time learning philosophy, we need to introduce the concept of random number generation. We do this next.

5   Generating Random Numbers in C

Generating random numbers in a computer program can be very important for some applications. Consequently, most programming languages, C included, have means to generate such random numbers. We should mention here that the random number generator used in C does not generate true random numbers in purely mathematical terms. This is because computers are deterministic in nature. That is, the random numbers are not truly random. Nevertheless, they are considered close enough to being random that it doesn't matter for the great majority of applications that require random numbers. Any further discussion of this subject would be beyond the scope of this book, so we will leave it at that and move on.

The statement (actually, a function, but we have not yet discussed functions formally) that returns a random number is:

```
rand();
```

This function returns an integer value between 0 and RAND_MAX – a number equal to the largest size stored in an integer variable. In 16-bit integer variables, RAND_MAX would be 32,767. In a more modern 32-bit integer variable size, RAND_MAX would be 2,147,483,647. The problem is that if the program is run more than once, rand() would return the same sequence of random numbers each time it is run. Let's see. Write the following program in your IDE editor.

```
int n;
for (n=0; n<10; n++)
      printf("The random value generated is %d \n", rand());
return 0;
```

In our computer at the particular time we ran this program, it printed out the following (your output is almost certain to be different):

```
The random value generated is 41
The random value generated is 18467
The random value generated is 6334
The random value generated is 26500
The random value generated is 19169
The random value generated is 15724
The random value generated is 11478
The random value generated is 29358
The random value generated is 26962
The random value generated is 24464
```

It seems random enough, right? Well, perhaps, with the caveat discussed above about not being truly mathematically random. But there is more. Close the output window and run the same program again without recompiling. The same exact sequence! Not very random, right? This is because the function was not *seeded*. Seeding means that you can tell the rand() function (more or less) where to start its computation, One popular way to seed the rand() function is to use the current time of the computer's clock. To seed the random function, use a second function:

```
srand(time(NULL));
```

This function is only used once, at the start of the program code. The time() function will return the time since 00:00:00 UTC, January 1, 1970, measured in seconds. Of course, this value will change every second, thus making the seed different every time the program is executed. Time() is a standard C library function whose prototype is found in the time.h file. This means that we will have to include time.h as a pre-processor directive.

```
#include <time.h>
```

So, armed with this new knowledge, put these statements in the code above. It should now look like this:

```
#include <stdio.h>
#include <stdlib.h>
#include <time.h>

int main()
  {
     int n;
     srand(time(NULL));
     for (n=0; n<10; n++)
          printf("The random value generated is %d \n", rand());
     return 0;
  }
```

Compile and run this program. Note the output (not shown here). Now close the program output window and run the program again without recompiling. You should get a different sequence of numbers than the first time you ran it. Now it looks more random.

Another issue is that our application may need a random number between 0 and 20, rather than between 0 and RAND_MAX, which can be a very big number. How can we do that? The mod division is the answer. Given that the rand() function returns an integer value, we can mod divide the value returned by rand() by the maximum number of the range; for example 20. Let's do this with the code above, placed inside main(). We leave out the pre-processor directives and the main() function here for the sake of brevity in display (although, of course, they need to be included in the actual code).

```
int n;
srand(time(NULL));
for (n=0; n<10; n++)
    printf("The random value generated is %d \n", rand()%20);
return 0;
```

Compile and run it. You will see that the numbers will be between 0 and 19. Try it with other dividends.

6   Alternative Ways to Work with the Repetition Constructs

Sections 2, 3 and 4 describe and discuss how the three repetition structures in C should be used. However, creative and devious as programmers can be, there are ways to get around the built-in mechanisms of these loop constructs. For example, as we mentioned earlier, the for loop can be easily converted into a sentinel controlled structure, and a while loop can likewise be converted into a counter-controlled loop.

For example, say we want to write a program that will generate random numbers between 1 and 10, and add them up. We will now impose on the loop more than one stopping criterion: 1) stop when the maximum number of iterations exceeds 100; 2) exit the loop if the random value generated is 0. After exiting the loop, print the value accumulated and the number of iterations it took to get this number. So, this loop will be a combination of counter controlled and sentinel controlled.

We start with the program we used in the previous section, except that we'll have to make several changes. Write the following code in your IDE editor inside main() and be sure to include the appropriate pre-processor directives:

```
int n, sum = 0, rand_value = 0;
srand(time(NULL));

for (n=0; n<100; n++)
  {
      rand_value = rand()%11;
      sum = rand_value + sum;
      if (rand_value == 0)
        break;
  }

printf("The sum of the random numbers is %d \n", sum);
printf("The number of iterations to obtain a 0 were %d \n", n);

return 0;
```

Compile and run the program and you see that it will work. To make sure, insert the following statement in the loop body, just above the if construct.

```
printf("The random value in this iteration is %d \n", rand_value);
```

This will allow you to see that the program is working properly as it executes. Count the number of iterations it took rand() to produce a 0 and you will see that it is one more than the number displayed by the last printf(). Why? Well, as we discussed a few sections above, the value of n is not incremented until after each for loop iteration ends naturally; that is, through the normal internal mechanism of the for loop structure. This happens in every iteration except the last one, when rand() produces a 0. In this iteration, the processing breaks out of the loop unnaturally through the break; statement. Therefore, the counter variable is never updated in this last iteration, and is therefore not counted. Once again, by understanding these types of things, one can avoid errors, or at least be able to fix them easily.

Likewise, we can also use a while loop as a counter-controlled loop. The key here is to set the value of the condition check operation within the parenthetical expression to 1, which will always evaluate to **true**, thereby continuing the looping process indefinitely. Additionally, we must define the counter control variable and initialize it to 0. Moreover, we have to increment this variable by 1 within the loop body. Finally, use a selection structure with a break; statement to get out of the loop. Let's use a variation of the program above, where the loop now stops when it gets to 10 iterations.

```
int n=0, sum = 0, rand_value = 0;
srand(time(NULL));

while (1)
    {
        rand_value = rand()%11;
        sum = rand_value + sum;
        printf("The random value in this iteration is %d \n", rand_value);
        if (n == 10)
            break;
        n++;
    }

printf("The sum of the random numbers is %d \n", sum);
printf("The number of iterations were %d \n", n);

return 0;
```

We not only succeeded in turning the `while` loop into a counter-controlled construct, but also an exit-controlled one. Inspect the output by counting the number of times the loop executed, up to and including the `printf()` inside the loop. You will see that it is 11, which is correct. But why does the last printout line say it is 10? You will need to figure this one out yourself.

7   Nested Loops

Loops can be nested within other loops. This is a powerful feature that will allow manipulation of multi-dimensional data. We will see more interesting applications of embedded loops when we get to arrays in Chap. 7, but for now, we will stick to simpler problems. While there is no maximum level of nesting in C, for practical purposes within the scope of this course we will only discuss nested loops to a depth of two. That is, we will learn how to embed one loop inside another one. Let's also keep our discussion to `for` loops, although the concept works just as well for `while` and `do-while` loops.

A nested pair of loops can be defined as follows:

```
for (i=0; i<10; i++)
    for (j=0; j<5; j++)
        continue;
```

The upper `for` loop is called the *outer loop*, while the lower one called the *inner loop* and is usually indicated by being indented. This indentation means nothing to the compiler – it is just for ease of human readability. For each of the 10 iterations of the outer loop, the inner loop will execute 5 times. So, there will be a total of 50 iterations. Note that the counter control variables used in each of the loops should be different (i.e., `i` and `j` in our program). Applications of nested loops without the use of *arrays* (Chap. 7) are difficult to conceive, so let's write a simple program that prints out the number of the inner and outer loop iteration to see how the process works.

```
int main()
{
   int i, j;

   for (i=0; i<10; i++)
     {
        printf("This is iteration no. %d of the outer loop \n", i);
        for (j=0; j<5; j++)
           printf("   This is iteration no. %d of the inner loop \n", j);
     }
        return 0;
}
```

The output of the second `printf()` was purposely indented with three blank spaces for ease of visualization. Enter this code in your IDE editor, compile it and run it. You can see that the inner loop executes five times for each iteration of the outer loop. This is a simple example, but it will do for now until we get to other chapters later in this course.

8   Summary

In this chapter, we have learned about the all-important repetition structure. Like the selection struc-ture before it, there are very few problems that can be solved in computing without the benefit of a repetition structure. We discussed the three repetition structures in C: the `for` loop, the `while` loop, and the `do-while` loop. Each is designed for somewhat different tasks. The `for` loop is counter-controlled and entry-controlled; the `while` loop is sentinel-controlled and entry controlled; the `do-while` loop is sentinel-controlled but exit-controlled. The `for` loop needs to be very tightly specified while the other two somewhat less so. However, in the last section, we saw how they can be used in almost any way by obviating the built-in mechanisms.

We also had a quick look at building nested loops. Lastly, we also learned how to generate random numbers in C.

9   Problems

1) Write a program that generates random numbers between 0 and 100. Do this for 100 iterations. Print out how many of these random numbers were even and how many were odd.
2) Same as problem #1 immediately above, except the range now is now for random numbers between 50 and 100.
3) Same as problem #2 above, except now the program is to calculate the average value of the random numbers generated in 100 iterations. Be sure to get the number of iterations correct.
4) Write a program that generates random numbers between 0 and 100. Do this until the random number generated is 0. Compute and print out the average of these random numbers. Be sure to get the number of iterations correct.

5) Write a program that determines how many calls to a random number generator it takes to match a number between 0 and 99 that is entered by a user. The program should request a number between 0 and 99 from a user. Then the program will repeatedly generate a random number and compare it to the number entered by the user. Count the number of iterations it takes for a match to take place. Be sure to use integer numbers and not floating point numbers. The output should be:

```
It took <number> random numbers generated to match the number <number>
entered by you.
```

6) Embed the above program within a second loop that makes this computation 50 times and prints out the average number of times that the program took to find a match for the one number entered by the user. The output should now be:

```
It took an average of <number> numbers generated to match the number
<number> entered by you.
```

Defining and Calling Functions

5

Now that we know how to write simple programs using (only) the `main()` function, we need to take the next step in our evolving programming education: how to write larger and more complex programs. This involves learning how to define our functions and invoke them properly. The concepts explained herein are important in order to continue your learning about more complex issues that will come up later in this course. Please read this chapter and execute it carefully and in sequence to understand all the nuances about building your own functions in C.

1   Defining and Calling Functions – A Short Introduction

As programs get larger and more complex, it becomes more and more inefficient to put an entire program in `main()`. Sure, it can be done, but it is not good programming practice because a) `main()` can grow to be very large – too large for easy management; but more importantly, b) all the code would be placed at the same level of *abstraction,* which is not good because it makes structuring a complex program cumbersome. It is better to have different levels of abstraction to make the program easier to write and maintain. But what do we mean by *abstraction*?

Abstraction means that when we think about some object, we only consider the higher level ideas and general aspects associated with it while ignoring the details that compose the object. For example, abstraction of the concept of car means that some people think of a car as a mechanical vehicle that gets us from one place to another very fast. Others of us think of a car as a source of pride or a source of fun (e.g., going very, very fast), while others see it as a necessary black hole for our hard-earned cash. The car is also composed of details, however, such as the gasoline combustion engine, the gears in the transmission, the electrical generator, the battery and voltage regulator, the cooling system, etc.

Abstraction also applies to complex tasks. We use abstraction very frequently in our daily lives. When we were young children and our parents asked us (or more likely told us!) to brush our teeth, they didn't go into a detailed explanation of how to brush our teeth every time. That would have meant them giving us the following instructions <u>every single time</u> we had to brush our teeth:

1) Go to the bathroom.
2) Stand in front of the sink
3) Reach for your toothbrush.
4) Grab the toothpaste tube

© Springer Nature Switzerland AG 2020
A. J. Gonzalez, *Computer Programming in C for Beginners,*
https://doi.org/10.1007/978-3-030-50750-3_5

5) Open the cap
6) Squeeze the tube onto the toothbrush
7) Move your toothbrush back and forth over your teeth
8) ......
9) .... well, we get the drift!

Giving us these detailed steps every time would have been wasteful of effort and rather awkward. It would be better to explain the low-level details once at the beginning, and then simply refer to the process as "brush your teeth", which the child would understand and proceed to execute all the low-level steps associated with brushing her teeth. This is what we mean by abstraction: we abstract the procedure of brushing one's teeth into a label that the child understands (*"Brush_your_teeth"*) as representing a series of low-level steps. There are clearly two levels here: the low level that includes the detailed instructions, and the higher, abstract level represented by the label *Brush_your_teeth*.

Computers are like children, except not nearly as smart, in spite of recent progress in Artificial Intelligence (AI). They must be given low-level instructions in order for them to do what the programmer wants them to do. Defining functions in C (or in any other language) serves a similar purpose – they allow the programmer to abstract a process and simply refer to it by a label, which carries with it a whole set of lower-level instructions to be performed by the computer. We define and put these lower-level instructions into a *function* that when *called*, executes the instructions it contains on some provided data. The program simply *invokes* or *calls* the function and accepts whatever it outputs (i.e., *returns*), possibly using it for further processing. We have already seen the concept of returning values by operators, but we will see more of it as it applies to functions.

A function (other than `main()`) is said to be *invoked* (or *called*) when it is told to execute. This can be done through an instruction (a C statement) that contains the name of the function to be executed, along with any inputs it might need to do its intended task. Such function calling statements are normally placed in functions other than the one being executed (recursive functions being one big exception) – including possibly, but not necessarily `main()`. Of course, the `main()` function is automatically invoked immediately upon initial program execution, but other functions are called when the instruction that does so is executed by the processor. When this happens, the machine language form of the called function is placed at the top of the *runtime stack* (a holding space that holds and "sends" the instructions to the processor, one by one in the proper sequence), and the function is executed. Upon completion, it is said that a function *terminates* (or *finishes)*, and then *exits*. The runtime stack then continues from where it left off before the called function was loaded at its top. When a completed function exits, it has the option (determined by the programmer) of just exiting, or exiting and leaving some value behind (perhaps the result of its computations) to the instruction that called it. The latter permits further processing of the results of the called function by the instruction that called it. This process of "leaving a value behind" is called *returning a value*. It is a way to provide the output of the function for further processing, even though outputs can be made available in various other ways in the execution of the function itself (before finishing and exiting).

On the input side, data can be *passed* to a function when it is invoked. Data play an important (virtually essential) role in computing, so input data must be able to be passed to a function when it is called. For example, if you were to write a function that added two numbers, you would want to pass to it the two numbers you would like to have added. Passing input data to a function is optional – some functions may not require that data be explicitly passed to them. Following is a brief conceptual example of passing inputs to a function and returning a value by that function. Say we have a function named `add` that sums two numbers passed to it and returns the result. Of course, this is silly because the + operator already does this, but let's play along. Moreover, say that we wish to embed this addition within a larger mathematical expression. So:

```
var = 3 * (add 2 2)
```

In the above expression, we want to multiply 3 times the result of a function that adds 2 and 2. The function add is passed the two inputs 2 and 2, and is asked to execute by virtue of having its name in the statement. It loads onto the runtime stack, executes, adds $2 + 2$, its resulting value (4) is left behind (returned) and placed in the physical location where add was called in the calling function for further processing (multiplying it by 3).

```
var = 3 * 4
```

The entire expression returns 12 and assigns that value to the variable var.

For a more realistic example, say we have an application that requires computation of the average values of several different sets of numerical data. If we were to do this strictly in main(), we would have to explicitly direct the computer to add the values and divide them by the number of values every time we wanted to compute an average. With the ability to write functions, we could write a function that, given a set of data, can return its average value. The programmer has just abstracted that process into a function that he chooses to name average(). Whenever the program needs an average value computed, all he needs to do is write a statement that calls the average() function, and provide it with the correct data whose average it is to compute. This is what we are going to learn in this chapter.

2   Defining Functions

Calling a function is easy – simply refer to it by its appropriate name (e.g., average), provide it with the inputs it requires (if any), and then let it go to work. However, before a function in C can be called (invoked), it must first be defined. But defining a function properly is not so easy. This requires that the programmer understands what he is doing when calling the function. Functions in computer programs are composed of three things:

1) The body of the function – the lower-level instructions that do what the function is meant to do. This is required, otherwise, why bother to define the function?
2) The inputs (also called pre-conditions) that are given (*passed*) to the function to operate on. Inputs are optional, i.e., there may be none.
3) The outputs (also called post-conditions) to be *returned* by the function. Returning something is not required; for example, the objective of a function may simply be to print something. Moreover, outputs can be extracted in other ways as we will see in later chapters.

Actually, we have been calling functions every time we have called printf(), which is a pre-defined C standard library function. The pre-conditions are what is included inside its parentheses – the literals within quotation marks, the variable names, etc. The output is the display of the desired output on the screen. Same with scanf(). These functions require that we provide them with the inputs, in the format that they were designed to expect. These inputs are called the *arguments* of a function call. If the arguments are not stated correctly with respect to the expectations in the function definition, then a compilation or run-time error will result.

It is important that you understand that when a function is called, its *definition* must already exist somewhere. printf() and scanf() have already been defined and their definitions are found in the standard C library. However, if a function is not pre-defined, the programmer must define it before it can be called. Makes sense, no? So, let's learn how to define functions and then we can discuss how to call them.

User-defined functions, as these are called (*programmer-defined functions* would be a more appropriate but more cumbersome name), are typically defined after the `main()` function has been defined in the source file. They can also be placed at the beginning of the source file, above where `main()` is defined. The compiler doesn't care. However, functions <u>cannot</u> be defined inside other function definitions (e.g., inside of `main()`). Each definition must be placed at the highest hierarchical level of the program – at the same level as `main()`.

In reality, you already know how to define functions in C because when you write the `main()` function, you are in fact defining it. After all, `main()` is a user-defined function! It is just that it can't be called explicitly because no other function calls `main()`. `main()` is called automatically when the program is executed.

The information one must include in the definition of a function in C are the following:

- The *name* of the function – the label through which we will *invoke* (i.e., *call*) it. The name must be unique, not a reserved keyword in C (see Chap. 2 for the list) and follow the other restrictions for naming variables, namely that the function name can be composed of numbers and characters as well as the underscore, but the name cannot begin with numbers or with symbols (<u>including</u> the underscore). Upper case characters can be used, but they are considered different from lower case, so the name is case-sensitive. Generally, function names are, by convention, relatively short and meaningful. Some programmers like to use the so called *camelBack notation*, but this is not required.
- The *type* of value *returned* (if any).
- The *types* and the *names* of the variables that will hold the values of any *arguments* passed to it (if any).
- A *definition* of other local (also called *automatic*) variables (if any are necessary).
- The *body* of the function – the statements that the processor will execute when the function is called. This is the heart of the function definition and it is essential.

A function definition format contains a *header* and a *body*. The header template is as follows:

```
<return_type>  <function_name>(<parameter list>)
```

The header declares the name of the function being defined (`function_name`); the type of value (`return_type`) it will return (i.e., send back) to the function that calls it (the *returned* value); and the inputs (arguments) that are to be passed to the function when it is called (`parameter list`). In the context of defining a function, the arguments of a function are called the *parameters* of the function. Each parameter in the `parameter list` is actually a set of comma-delineated pairs composed of a `parameter_name` that indicates the name of the variable that will "take on" the value passed to the function which represents that argument. The `parameter_name` is preceded by the `parameter_type` that indicates the type of data to be "received" by the function as that particular parameter. These parameters are in fact the definitions of variables to be used in that function's body, except they are also designated to receive and hold the values passed to the function when it is called. Parameters/variables can be and are used as regular variables inside the function body without having to be defined again. We'll see examples of this later in this chapter.

The parameters are defined in the `parameter list` within parentheses as comma-delineated pairs as follows:

```
(<parameter1_type>  <parameter1_name>, <parameter2_type> <parameter2_name>,
            <parameter3_type>  <parameter3_name>, ......)
```

There is no limit for the number of arguments (parameter pairs) to be passed to a function. However, common sense dictates that it should not be a very long list, lest the programmer become confused by the numerous pairs. If a function is to have no arguments passed to it, the space between the parentheses can be left empty (as `main()` typically is) or the reserved keyword `void` can be inserted within the parentheses where the parameter list would go such as:

```
<function_name>(void)
```

The body of the function is a sequence of C statements that represent the instructions for the function to execute, thereby accomplishing what the programmer wants it to do. These statements must <u>always</u> be enclosed within curly brackets { }, just like we do in `main()`. Note that no semi-colon follows the closing curly bracket, just as there isn't a semi-colon after the closing bracket when we define `main()`.

OK, let us define our first, very simple user-defined function. Say we want to write a function that squares a double precision floating point number passed to it, and returns the answer as a double precision floating point value. We will call this function `square`.

```
double square(double x)
    {
            double y = 0.0;
            y = x * x;
            return y;
    }
```

We created a function named `square` that frees us from having to multiply a number by itself every time we want to compute its square. So, all we have to do is call it, give it the number we want to have squared and it will do it for us. (Full disclosure: there already exists a standard C library function called `pow()` that can do this, but it requires two arguments – the base value and the power to which the base value is to be raised.)

The first `double` before the name indicates that the function will return a double precision floating point value. The name of the function (`square`) follows, and the parameter list states that it will accept one argument of double precision floating point type and save it to a variable named x. Note how x is used as a variable in the function body without being formally defined within the body. As we mentioned before, the parameter definition serves as its definition as a double precision floating point type here. Go ahead and type it into your IDE editor as is above, after (but <u>not</u> inside!) `main()`. Don't write anything in `main()` yet. Don't compile or run anything yet either.

Returning a value is not required of a function. One can place the keyword `void` where the `return_type` should go, and this lets the compiler know that this function does not return anything. In such cases, no `return` statement can be present in the function body, as that would confuse the compiler.

We now define a more complex function named `dist` that calculates the distance between two points in a Cartesian plane. In this example we make use of a pre-defined standard library function in C called `sqrt()` which calculates and returns the square root of its only argument (of type `double`). The header for `sqrt()` is included in `math.h`, so let's add the following line of code to our pre-processor directives:

```
#include <math.h>
```

Also, let's make sure its arguments are double precision floating point numbers (`double`). The code for this function definition is as follows for points (x_1, y_1) and (x_2, y_2):

```
double dist(double x1, double y1, double x2, double y2)
    {
        double answer = 0.0;
        answer = sqrt(((x1 - x2)*(x1 - x2)) + ((y1 - y2)*(y1 - y2)) );
        return answer;
    }
```

Go ahead and type it into your program code after the end of the `main()` function. But don't do anything yet with `main()`. We are building up to something here.

While not a particularly difficult function to define, it does require that several parameters be passed to it, rather than just one as we saw with the definition for `square()`.

So, we have learned how to define simple user-defined functions (`square()` and `dist()`) and included them in our program. However, as we mentioned earlier, this is only half the story, as we need to know how to use these newly-defined functions. This comes next.

3   Calling Functions

Now let's see how to call the two functions defined in the previous section – that is, how to actually make use of them. For that we need to see how we can call from `main()` those functions we just defined. This will also serve to further discuss the idea of returning values.

Before we start working on `main()`, we need to define some more terminology. We must now distinguish between the function that is <u>called</u> (or invoked) and the function that <u>calls</u> (or invokes) it. These are referred to respectively as the *called function* and the *calling function*. In the exercise coming up, the called functions will be `square()` and/or `dist()`, and the calling function – the function from where a called function is called, will be `main()`. Let's start with an easy exercise.

In the `main()` function let's add the following code. The function `main()` is to be located above the definitions of `square()` and `dist()`.

```
int main()
{
        double distance = 0.0;
        distance = dist(5.37, 9.6, 11.16, 21.78);
        printf("The distance between the points is %lf \n", distance);
}
```

Go ahead and compile it and execute it.

It gave you a bunch of errors and warnings, right? Something about conflicting types and implicit declarations of the `dist()` function you just defined. Why is that, you may wonder? This is because we didn't do something very important when defining C functions – included a *prototype* of the function. A function prototype is an indication to the compiler that a function with the information specified in the prototype is being defined somewhere in this program. So, when the compiler sees the user-defined function called in `main()` (or anywhere else, for that matter) before it gets to its definition, it would know it is OK, as long as the data types match. These prototypes serve as a kind of declaration (but not a definition!) of a function before it is called. The prototypes are what is contained in the header (`.h`) files for standard C library functions that we discussed in Chap. 1. They are required in C for most modern compilers.

So, what information does a prototype contain and where do we put it? Easy! It is a single statement that looks very much like the function header in the function definition, except that the names of the parameters in the parameter list can be omitted (but do not have to be). So, for the two functions that we have defined, the following prototype statements should be added:

```
double square(double);
double dist(double, double, double, double);
```

Where do we put them? Right at the top of the source code file, above main() and just below the pre-processor directives. So, here is how our code looks now:

```
#include <stdio.h>
#include <stdlib.h>
#include <math.h>

double dist(double, double, double, double);
double square(double);

int main()
{
    double distance = 0.0;
    distance = dist(5.37, 9.6, 11.16, 21.78);
    printf("The distance between the points is %lf \n", distance);
    return 0;
}

double dist(double x1, double y1, double x2, double y2)
{
    double answer = 0.0;
    answer = sqrt(((x1-x2)*(x1-x2)) + ((y1-y2)*(y1-y2)));
    return answer;
}

double square(double x)
{
    double y = 0.0;
    y = x * x;
    return y;
}
```

One detail to note. We won't be using the square() function just yet, even though it is already defined and prototyped in our program – we don't need it to make our next point. Depending on the compiler used, that may produce a rather silly warning that we have the function defined and prototyped but do not use it. Just ignore it if it comes up.

Now go ahead and compile and run it. You will see that it will work, giving an answer of 13.486160, which is correct.

In this example, main() is the calling function because it is within it that the function dist() is called. dist(), of course, is the called function. But main() need not always be the calling function. Other user-defined functions can also serve as calling functions. So, let's continue along that thought.

Look at the statement in dist () that includes (x1-x2) * (x1-x2) and (y1-y2) * (y1-y2). Why do we need to multiply the value (x1-x2) by itself twice? (Also the value (y1-y2).) Sure, mathematically it is just fine, but it is cumbersome and certainly not elegant. We can use the square () function to make this easier, right? So, let's now change the code to make use of the square () function:

```
#include <stdio.h>
#include <stdlib.h>
#include <math.h>

double dist(double, double, double, double);
double square(double);

int main()
{
    double distance = 0.0;
    distance = dist(5.37, 9.6, 11.16, 21.78);
    printf("The distance between the two points is %lf \n", distance);
    return 0;
}

double dist(double x1, double y1, double x2, double y2)
{
    double answer = 0.0;
    answer = sqrt(square(x1-x2) + square(y1-y2));
    return answer;
}
double square(double x)
    {
        double y = 0.0;
        y = x * x;
        return y;
    }
```

Compile and run it and you will see that you will get the same correct answer. In this case, square() is called by dist(), and not main(). The dist() function acts as both, a called function (by main()) and a calling function (of square()). In this example, we managed to abstract the distance formula between two points, as well as the squaring a number.

Now let's inject some errors on purpose. As they say, failure is the best teacher. For our first failure, let's include a mismatch in the number of arguments passed to a function. So, the statement below passes only three values to dist (), which is expecting four.

```
        .
        .
        .
distance = dist(5.37, 9.6, 11.16);
        .
        .
        .
```

The only thing we changed in `main()` was that we left out the last argument (y_2) when we called the `dist()` function. Everything else in `main()` and in the other function definitions are unchanged, so we do not re-display those here to save trees. Now compile the program. You will see that the compiler caught it right away and the compilation failed. So, lesson #1 here is to always ensure that the number of arguments passed match what the function expects in its parameter list.

For our second error, let's mismatch the data types (a recurring headache for inexperienced programmers). We fixed the call to `dist()` to include y_2, but changed the definition of the variable `distance` to be an integer. Everything else remains unchanged.

```
        .
        .
int distance = 0.0;
distance = dist(5.37, 9.6, 11.16, 21.78);
        .
        .
        .
```

Now we only get a warning about the mismatch, but not an error. So, let's go ahead and run the program. It executes fine (i.e., no run-time error), but prints out `0.000000` as the answer. Lesson #2 here: data mismatches can and will generally cause problems. Lesson #3: pay attention to warnings!

We could have saved ourselves the need to define the variable `distance` by simply calling `dist()` within the `printf()` function. However, `dist()` requires a relatively long list of arguments, so for (human) clarity, it is better to use the `distance` variable as an intermediate.

4 Returning Values

The code above allows us to learn a bit more about returning values. We have used this term before and briefly defined it, but will discuss it in greater detail here. An analogy in real life would be getting a tennis racket re-strung. Say your beloved tennis racket breaks a string and it is no longer usable. Because you don't know how to re-string a racket, you take it to the pro shop and you give them the racket to re-string, with a specification for the proper tension to put on the new strings. When the job is done, they will return to you your same racket except with new strings that are properly tensioned. If the pro shop was a computer, the equivalent would be that you called a function named `string_ my_racket()` that took two arguments as inputs: my racket of type carbon composite, and an integer string tension value of 35 psi. The returned value would be my racket with the new strings at the correct tension.

More realistically, in C code, the value returned by a called function after it finishes its work takes the physical place in the instruction where the function was called. We saw this above. The variable `dis- tance` in `main()` took on the value returned by `dist()` after the latter did its thing. This was the way that `dist()` provided its output – by returning its output to the function that called it. The returned value can then be further processed. Same for the `square()` function that returned the square of its arguments within `dist()`, which were then further processed by the `dist()` function.

As we stated earlier, what the processor actually does when it sees a function call is that it immediately stops what it is doing, loads the definition of that function onto the *runtime stack* with the appropriate arguments, executes the called function and places the returned value in the same location where the function was called. Then it resumes what it was doing before the function call; except now it uses the returned value in place of the function call in subsequent computations.

Likewise, in the `dist()` function definition, the first call to the `square()` function returned its value, which was added to the value returned by a second call to it, and the resulting sum was "square-rooted" to compute the final answer, which was then returned by `dist()` to its calling function `main()` so that the `distance` variable could be assigned this value.

As we saw earlier, a function need not return anything. It can also return something and the calling function can ignore what it returns. Let's make some changes to our code above to eliminate values returned, yet leaving the computations as they are.

In the definition for `square()`, we will re-define this function to have it not return anything. We do that easily by placing the keyword `void` in the first position in its header as well as in the prototype (they have to match!). We also need to comment out the `return y;` statement in the body of the definition. See below.

```
    ...
void square(double) ;
    ...
    ...
    ...
void square(double x)
    {
        double y = 0.0;
        y = x * x;
        // return y;
    }
```

We leave everything else alone. Go ahead and compile the code. It will naturally give you a compilation error, as the computation involving `square()` on the `dist()` function will be left with nothing meaningful, given that it now returns nothing. The error says.

```
Error: void value not ignored as it ought to be
```

The error points to the line in the `dist()` definition that contains the following statement.

```
answer = sqrt(square(x1-x2) + square(y1-y2));
```

Note that there is nothing wrong with the way we defined `square()`. The problem is with how we use it in the calling function `dist()`, which assumes that a value is returned and placed in its place for subsequent computations. The same error can be generated if we set `dist()` to not return anything by placing `void` in the header and in the prototype. The assignment operation that sets the value returned by `dist()` to the variable `distance` in `main()` would then not work.

Lastly, we should note that there are other ways to output the results of a user-defined function that do not involve returning a value. For example, maybe we just want the function to print something out. In that case, the output could be implemented with one or more `printf()` statements. Another example would be to have the function change the value of a *global variable* directly from its body. We will discuss global variables later.

5   Passing Values of Variables to Functions

You noticed that when we called dist() on main(), we inserted actual numbers as arguments for dist(). Of course, there is nothing wrong with that – it worked fine. However, it would be very limiting if we could only put actual values (numbers, character literals, etc.) as arguments in function calls. So, C and other programming languages allow the programmer to place variables as arguments in the function call. The variable is read (the better word to use is *referenced*) and the value retrieved is put in place of the variable name. That's what referencing a variable does. It is the same basic process as returning a value, except in a different context. Now let's modify our code a bit and define some new variables in main() whose values we are going to *pass to* dist(), rather than pass the actual numbers as we did before. The pre-processor directives, the prototypes and the definitions for square() and dist() are not changed from their original correct versions (i.e., they return something), but we left them out of the code below to not unnecessarily repeat them. However, you know that you will need to include them in your code.

```
int main()
{
    double x_one = 5.37, y_one = 9.6, x_two = 11.16, y_two = 21.78;
    double distance = 0.0;
    distance = dist(x_one, y_one, x_two, y_two);
    printf("The distance between the two points is %lf \n", distance);

    return 0;
}
```

You will see that this compiles and executes correctly. So, we managed to pass the value of variables to a called function as part of its arguments. The important thing to note here is that only the underlined values of the variables are being passed to the called function (dist() in our case), and not the variables themselves. Therefore, the variable(s) are evaluated before loading the function definition into the runtime stack, and only the values returned by this evaluation are passed to the function for execution. This is called *Passing by value*. Most modern programming languages work as pass-by-value when calling functions.

The significant implication of pass-by-value is that the called function (in this case, dist()) cannot change the value of a variable that is defined in the calling function (in this case, in main()), even when the variable is seemingly passed to it. Remember that a variable is simply a block of memory of a specific size, big enough to hold a specific type of value, with an address. A called function that only receives the value of a variable has no idea where that variable is located in memory (i.e., it doesn't know its address), so it is not able to change it.

We can and will look into pass-by-value further. But before we do that, we need to discuss the *scope of variables*, and this now becomes necessary to better understand pass-by-value.

6   Scope of Variables

We know that variables are locations in memory where a value associated with a specific name is stored. Now that we know about the existence of user-defined functions, the question that comes up is whether variables declared in one function are recognized as the same variable (i.e., the same location in memory) in other functions in the same program. To answer this, it is now appropriate (even essential) that we discuss the *scope* of a variable.

The scope of a variable defines exactly how far and wide it is recognized as the same variable (same memory location). The easiest to understand is the *global* variable, whose scope extends to all functions in the program, so we will start with them.

6.1   Global Variables

Global variables are the easiest to understand because they are easy to relate to. That is, a global variable is recognized by its name across all functions in the program (as long as the entire program is in one file; we'll discuss that when we get to multi-file programs). When compiling and linking the source code, the compiler will assign a memory address to that variable name, and then when building an executable in machine language, will replace the name of the variable with its address. Thus, the name of the variable becomes irrelevant once the executable is built. In the case of a global variable, this address is fixed and constant throughout the entire program. Its value, therefore, can be changed from any function in the program.

Global variables are also easy to use. To make a variable global in scope, it must be declared outside of any function definition, including `main()`. However, while they can be useful in some applications, their use is generally discouraged. This is because their unlimited accessibility can be dangerous, especially when user-defined functions are shared among several programmers in a group. If one of these programmers makes a change to a shared user-defined function that changes the value of a global variable, then all hell breaks loose with the other programmers whose code does not expect this. Nevertheless, we will work with global variables a bit later in this course. For illustration, let's use the distance formula code that we used above, except that we will make `distance` a global variable. So,

```
double distance = 0.0; // defined outside of any function
int main()
{
    double x_one = 5.37, y_one = 9.6, x_two = 11.16, y_two = 21.78;
    dist(x_one, y_one, x_two, y_two);
    // dist() doesn't return anything, so it is not assigned to any
    // variable. It sets the value of the global distance directly
    printf("The distance between the two points is %lf \n", distance);

    return 0;
}


void dist(double x1, double y1, double x2, double y2)
{
    distance = sqrt(square(x1-x2) + square(y1-y2));
    // variable distance is not defined here b/c it is global
}
double square(double x)
    {
        double y = 0.0;
        y = x * x;
        return y;
    }
```

This code does some things differently: 1) it declares the variable `distance` as global by placing its definition outside of any function. 2) The variable `distance` is used in `dist()`, but it is not defined within it. This is OK because `distance` is global and therefore recognized in `dist()`. 3) The function `dist()` assigns a value to `distance` directly, which it can do because the latter is global. Write this code in your IDE's editor, compile and execute it. You will notice that it will work correctly.

We thus managed to affect the value of a global variable from a called function, and read its correct value from a different function without having to rely on returning anything.

Let's continue with an introduction of the simplest and most common type of variable vis-à-vis its scope (as opposed to its data type): the *local* variable.

6.2 Local Variables

As the name implies, local variables are those whose scopes only extend to the function where they are declared and used. This is what we had been doing up until the exercise just above. Local variables are formally called *automatic* variables in C. They are preferred because of their ability to compartmentalize. That is, the exact same name for two different local variables defined in different functions will have different addresses, and therefore be completely different variables. How addresses are assigned to local variables is a bit more complex because when a function (other than `main()`) exits and is called again, the same variable may have a different address. Thus local variables are given what is called a *stack address*, which changes every time the function is called. However, this discussion is clearly beyond the scope of this book.

To prove that the values of local variables to one function cannot be changed by another function even if they have the same name, let's slightly modify the code used in the previous section. Note that the variable `distance` is no longer global, but goes back to being local, as in earlier versions of this program. The changes are shown in underlined and bold font for your ease of identification.

```
int main()
{
    double x_one = 5.37, y_one = 9.6, x_two = 11.16, y_two = 21.78;
    double distance = 0.0;
    distance = dist(x_one, y_one, x_two, y_two);
    printf("The distance between the two points is %lf \n", distance);

    return 0;
}

double dist(double x1, double y1, double x2, double y2)
{
    double distance = 0.0;
    distance = sqrt(square(x1-x2) + square(y1-y2));

    return distance;
}

double square(double x)
    {
        double y = 0.0;
        y = x * x;
        return y;
    }
```

We merely changed the name of the old variable answer in dist() to distance, in order to coincide with the name of the variable distance in main(). Try it – it works! This is because nothing has really changed – the two variables named distance are in fact two different local variables with different memory addresses, with no relationship to one another. The function dist() still returns a value that is assigned to distance in main(). There is no attempt here to modify the value of distance in main() directly by assigning the value to distance in dist().

Now we take this one step further. Given that it has the same variable name (distance), if it were the same variable in dist() as the one in main(), we would only need to call dist() from main(), right? This is what we did when distance was global – and it worked – except that distance is now local to each function. It worked when distance was global. Will it work now that they are two local variables?

To pursue this line of thought, we now define dist(), as not returning anything (void), and just reference distance in main() to see if its value set in dist() carries over to that in main(). This is how the code would look now. Any new code added is shown as bold faced and underlined for ease of illustration. Don't forget to change the prototype for dist() to void for its return value!

```
void dist(double, double, double, double);
int main()
{
    double x_one = 5.37, y_one = 9.6, x_two = 11.16, y_two = 21.78;
    double distance = 0.0;
    dist(x_one, y_one, x_two, y_two);
    printf("The distance between the two points is %lf \n", distance);

    return 0;
}


void dist(double x1, double y1, double x2, double y2)
{
    double distance = 0.0;
    distance = sqrt(square(x1-x2) + square(y1-y2));
}

double square(double x)
    {
        double y = 0.0;
        y = x * x;
        return y;
    }
```

Interestingly enough, it compiles just fine, as there is nothing in this revised code that is illegal. However, when executed, it says that the value of distance is 0.000000, which is to what we initialized the distance variable in main(). So, all it did after all that work was to print out the initial value of distance as assigned in main()! Obviously, calling and executing dist() did not affect the value of the variable distance in main(). That is an illustration of the compartmentalization of local variables.

We should add that in order to give a called function (e.g., $\texttt{dist ()}$ in our example) the ability to affect a local variable in the calling function, we would have had to pass to it the <u>address</u> where this variable lives. This can be done, and the process is called *pass-by-reference*, (also *call-by-reference*); however, we can only explain it after we get to *pointers* later in this course.

6.3   Static Variables

Static variables are the third major type of variable (with regards to scope). It is neither local nor global but has elements of both. Static variables are seldom used, but they fill a very specific need. There are two basic uses of static variables. In otherwise local variables declared in functions that will be called repeatedly, but need to "remember" the value of a variable from call to call, a static variable will fill that need. Otherwise, local variables would be lost when a function exits – not just their value, but also their essence (they no longer exist).

In otherwise global variables, static designation means that a global variable will not be recognized as such in some selected files, such as those to be shared with other programmers. Thus, the static designation will limit the "globality" of a global variable as desired by the programmer.

Static variables are identified by placing the keyword $\texttt{static}$ before the type of the variable when first declared. We will further discuss static variables when we get to multi-file programs later in this book.

7   Summary and Conclusion

This is an important chapter to understand. Well, they all are, but especially this one, as writing user-defined functions becomes essential when building larger and more complex programs. In this chapter we discussed how to define and call user-defined functions. We also described and showed examples of passing values to functions and what it means for them to return something to the calling function. Importantly, the scope of variables was introduced and some examples and exercises were shown with this concept to illustrate how the visibility of a variable depended on its scope.

The concept of call-by-value was introduced, and its alternative, call-by-reference was mentioned and will be discussed in depth in Chap. 6. This is a very important concept in C.

8   Problems

The problems are now becoming more complex. You will have to use what you have learned in previous chapters to be able to solve the problems below.

1) Write a program that includes a user-defined function called $\texttt{hi\_lo ()}$ that when called, generates 50 random numbers one at a time, between 0 and 100, and selects the highest and lowest of the numbers generated. It then prints out the resulting high and low numbers. The output of the function should be:

```
The highest number generated = <x>;
The lowest number = <y>.
```

2) Modify the program in problem #1 above so that the user enters the range of the random numbers to be generated by `hi_lo()`, starting from 0 (e.g., 0 to 500) and prints out the highest and lowest numbers generated in the range specified by the user. The range of the random numbers should be requested in `main()` and passed as an argument to `hi_lo()`. The same output as that of problem 1) should be used.

```
The highest number generated = <x>;
The lowest number = <y>.
```

3) Write a program that compares the average of ten numbers to the average of another ten numbers, and computes the difference between the two averages. To do this, write a user-defined function called `average()` that generates three random numbers between 1 and 10, computes their average and <u>returns</u> the result to the calling function. The `average()` function is called a second time to do the same thing (but generates different numbers), and the two averages returned are compared as specified above. (Don't forget to seed the random function, else you will get the same average for both function calls.) The output should look as follows:

```
The first average = <some value>;
The second average = <some value>;
Their difference is <some value>.
```

4) Write a program that calculates the area of one of various simple shapes, such as a rectangle, (r)) square (s), circle (c) and equilateral triangle (t). The program should ask the user for what type of shape should the area be computed (enter the character representing the shape as indicated above), and depending on the answer, request the correct data. The program must use at least one user-defined function that requests the correct inputs from the user depending on the shape entered, calculates the area and <u>returns</u> the computed area to the calling function (`main()`) where the output is printed. The output should be:

```
The area of the <shape entered> is <y>.
```

5) Write a program where a user-entered integer between 1 and 26 is passed to a function called `alphabet()`, that returns the character in the English alphabet that corresponds to that integer (e.g., 1 = a, 2 = b, 3 = c, 4 = d, etc.). The function `alphabet()` will return the resulting character to the calling function `main()`, from where it will be printed out to screen. The output should be: (hint: use a `switch` structure.)

```
The alphabet character corresponding to number <number> is <character>.
```

6) Write a program that when given the length of two sides of a right triangle, will calculate the hypotenuse. Do this as a user-defined function that returns the hypotenuse to the calling function (`main()`). Look up in https://en.wikipedia.org/wiki/Pythagorean_theorem how to compute the hypotenuse of a right triangle. This requires that the user enter two values from the keyboard – the two perpendicular sides of the right triangle. Test it by entering 3 4 return. Should give you as the answer:

```
The length of the hypotenuse is 5
```

7) Now for something a little more complex. You have laid out the western US in a Cartesian coordinate grid. In this grid, each destination has a set of coordinate points as x and y, placed in the format (x, y). For the sake of simplicity, let's assume that the grid is centered at the origin (0, 0) and only positive displacements from that point are possible (i.e., all values are positive). Assume you are situated at an x and y location to be entered by the user. Write a user-defined function to calculate the distance between your current location and a location whose x- and y-coordinates are also entered by the user from the keyboard in `main()`. The function returns the distance to be printed out from `main()`. Look up the distance formula in a Cartesian plane for the math required. The output should be:

```
Your desired destination is <number> miles away
```

Pointer Variables

6

At this point, the easy part of the course is over. Now we enter the most difficult stretch. This stage begins with the introduction of and discussion about *pointer variables*. *Pointers*, as these pointer variables are commonly called, are very important in C (and in C++). They provide a window into the computer that allows a learner to better see and understand some of the internal workings of a computer. Few other programming languages offer such a window. This is why we believe that C is the best language for teaching computer programming, although certainly not the easiest. As usual, please read this chapter carefully and do the exercises in sequence in order to understand all the nuances of pointers.

1   Pointers – A Short Introduction

Pointers have been a painful subject for all new C programmers. Inexperienced programmers hate them; experienced programmers quickly grow to love them. So, what exactly are pointers? Well, they are nothing more than variables, just like all the other variables we have studied so far in this book (we'll refer to those as "normal" variables here to easily distinguish them from pointers – but that is not an official name!) Pointers have to be defined and their type has to be specified in their definition, just like "normal" variables do. Values can be assigned to them and these values can be changed, just like normal variables. However, there is one very important difference. Rather than holding "normal" values (e.g., of type int, or float, or char, or ... of whatever other pre-defined type), as the normal variables do, pointer variables actually hold the addresses of other variables as their values. Therefore, they really do figuratively *point* to other variables. These other variables pointed at are generally normal variables, but they can also be other pointers, files, user-defined data types or even user-defined functions! So, a pointer variable must hold an address as its value.

Pointers provide a second way to reference variables. The first one, of course, is *directly* through a variable's name, as we have learned to do in the preceding chapters by simply stating the variable's name. Pointers allow a backdoor, so to speak, into the variables to which they point. This backdoor permits us to make changes to the values of the pointed-at variables without actually referencing them directly. This gives us many advantages, as we will see here later. So, one can read and change the value of a variable indirectly through a pointer that has that variable's address. This is called *indirect referencing*, or more commonly, *indirection*.

© Springer Nature Switzerland AG 2020
A. J. Gonzalez, *Computer Programming in C for Beginners*,
https://doi.org/10.1007/978-3-030-50750-3_6

Pointer variable   `int` variable

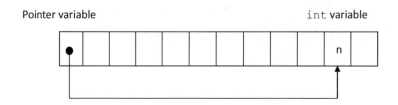

Let's begin our exercise by learning how to define and set values to pointers.

2   Declaring and Initializing Pointers

As mentioned earlier, pointers have to be defined just like normal variables. When defining pointers, it is important to know not the type of variable the pointer itself is (i.e., it will just hold an address!), but rather the type of variable at which the pointer will be pointing. Because a pointer can be used to indirectly read and write to a variable (which is explained later), the compiler needs to know what type of value the pointed-at variable contains. Otherwise, it couldn't do this in the context of C, which is so heavily typed. So how does one define a pointer?

An asterisk * is used to indicate the "*pointerhood*", so to speak, of a variable. If the name of the variable being declared is preceded by an asterisk, then the compiler knows that a pointer variable is being defined. Other than that, it looks very much like defining a normal variable.

For example, let's say we want to define a pointer named `ptr` that points to an integer variable. (Put this inside `main()` or some other user-defined function.)

```
int * ptr;
```

The space between the asterisk and the name of the variable is not necessary. The following will also work (although we prefer to leave a space for more clarity):

```
int *ptr;
```

We have now defined a pointer variable called, appropriately enough, `ptr`. It doesn't yet have a value (an address as its value) because it is not "pointing" to anything at the moment. In order to do this, we have to assign an address to it. However, holding meaningless addresses is not what pointers are about. They need to hold addresses of meaningful elements of the program, such as other variables. But as we said above, they can also point to other pointers, to user-defined functions, to files and to other things that we haven't seen yet. So pointers must point to something meaningful. Another consideration is that addresses only identify the location of one byte in memory. Yet most variables take up more than one byte of space (except for the `char` type, which takes up exactly one byte). The pointer holds the address of the first byte of the variable to which it points, but by knowing the type of variable to which it is pointing, it can know the size of its memory block. This is important when indirectly reading or writing to that variable.

Therefore, to set the value of a pointer to something meaningful, we need to learn about the *address-of operator*. This operator is a unary operator (like the increment (++) and decrement (−−) operators that we saw earlier) and it is represented by the *ampersand (&)*. It is placed right next to and before the name of the variable whose address we want to discern; the value returned is the address where that variable is located in memory. So, we are now able to set the value of ptr as follows:

```
int var = 0;
int * ptr = &var;
```

What the above statement says, in effect, is "define a variable called ptr that holds the address of integer variable var". Sure, we could print out the contents of ptr using the printf() function and see the actual address of var, but it doesn't really matter that we know. The processor will know, and that's all that is important. We just care that its address is now known by ptr so that it can reference it to read it and change it indirectly. Let' see now how to make changes to the variable var indirectly.

Just like we have done up to this point, we could change the value of var directly through the assignment operator and the name var as follows:

```
var = 76;
```

We can also access the value of var indirectly through the pointer ptr, because the latter knows where the former "lives". However, before showing you how to do that, we need to learn about another pointer-specific operator – the *indirection operator (*)*. Unfortunately, C uses the asterisk as the symbol to represent this operator, thereby causing potential confusion for inexperienced programmers with the multiplication and with the pointer definition operators; but you will grow used to it as your experience grows. Indirection is also a unary operator, so the asterisk is placed adjacent to and in front of the pointer name. This is why we prefer that a space be left between the asterisk and the pointer name when defining a pointer – to avoid confusion with the indirection operator (actually, both the definition of a pointer and the indirection operator permit a blank space between the asterisk and the variable, but it is not done by convention in the indirection operation.) Therefore, in our developing snippet of code above, we can set (change, in this case) the value of var to 97 indirectly by doing the following:

```
*ptr = 97;
```

Just as if we had written var = 97; . We are in effect telling the processor, "change the value of the variable pointed at by ptr to 97". ptr doesn't know that it is pointing to var. It just knows its address and can change the integer value located in that address.

We can also use this approach in more complex operations. For example, write the following simple program:

```
int main()
{
     int var1 = 20, var2 = 30, total = 0;
     total = var1 + var2;
     printf("The value of total = %d \n", total);

     return 0;
}
```

Naturally, the answer will be `The value of total = 50`. Easy, right? Now let's do the same thing indirectly:

```
int main()
{
    int var1 = 20, var2 = 30, total = 0;
    int * ptr1 = &var1, * ptr2 = &var2;
    total = *ptr1 + *ptr2;
    printf("The value of total = %d \n", total);

    return 0;
}
```

You got the same (correct) answer, right? The equation `total = *ptr1 + *ptr2;` makes no direct mention of `var1` or `var2`, yet is able to do the same thing via indirection. Now let's take this a bit further and declare another pointer, `ptr3` that points to `total`, and let's see whether that works. (We'll just show the changes to the code above.)

```
int var1 = 20, var2 = 30, total = 0;
int * ptr1 = &var1, * ptr2 = &var2, * ptr3 = &total;
*ptr3 = *ptr1 + *ptr2;
printf("The value of total =  %d \n", total);
```

The answer will still be the same. This shows the power of indirection by pointers.

Here we come upon a teachable moment about how C initializes variables upon their definition. Instead of defining the normal variables (`var1, var2` and `total`) and the pointer variables (`ptr1, ptr2` and `ptr3`) in two separate statements, let's do it in one that looks as follows:

```
int var1 = 20, var2 = 30, total = 0, * ptr1 = &var1, * ptr2 = &var2, *
ptr3 = &total; // in the same line as above
```

Surprisingly, this will work in GCC despite the fact that the definitions of the pointers depend on the definition of the normal `int` variables, which are in the same statement. This is called *parallel assignments*. The variables `var1, var2` and `total` were created and assigned a location in memory before the statement completed execution. This way, `&var1, &var2` and `&total` already knew their addresses. Such parallel assignments don't always work in all compilers, so be careful in how you use them.

There are many more interesting things we can do with pointers besides the seemingly pointless task of setting the value of a variable indirectly (which we can already do directly anyway). We will get to those in due time. Before we do that, lets' discuss how to do input and output with pointers.

3   Input/Output with Pointers

As with normal variables, the contents of a pointer can be printed out. We hinted at this earlier in this chapter. There would normally not be much need for that, but it can be done. Likewise, pointer values can be input through `scanf()` although there would be even less reason to do so, at least for most applications. So, at this time, we'll just stick to printing out the values of pointers.

The printing type specifier for pointers is %p. We now specifically want to print out the content of a pointer variable – its address. Let's print out the contents of our pointers in the above code snippet. Please add the following statements:

```
printf("The value of pointer ptr1 is %p \n", ptr1);
printf("The value of pointer ptr2 is %p \n", ptr2);
printf("The value of pointer ptr3 is %p \n", ptr3);
```

You will see that it will output something like this (in our computer):

```
The value of pointer ptr1 is 0022FF10
The value of pointer ptr2 is 0022FF0C
The value of pointer ptr3 is 0022FF08
```

The addresses, of course, are in hexadecimal numbers. These addresses are selected by the compiler, so there is no telling what these will be when you run your program on your computer. The above is just what our program outputted when we ran the code in our computer. You will most likely (almost certainly) get something different when you run your code. Go ahead and do it.

A couple of more things to cover in this section. Initializing pointers is as important as initializing normal variables. However, we should use NULL to initialize pointers. This is a primitive in C that corresponds to an address of 00000000. You can also initialize to 0, but C does not consider that to be an address per se. It is better to use NULL . NULL is a reserved keyword and will become very important later when we learn to do linked lists.

User-defined functions can also return addresses. We know how to define what user-defined functions return, so we build on that to see how to return addresses as pointers. Three things the programmer must do:

1). Reflect in the prototype that the function will return a pointer. This is easy – we do this by simply inserting an asterisk after the return type and before the function name.

```
int * simple_function(int); // this is the prototype
```

2) Have the function header in the definition reflect that it returns an address:

```
int * simple_function(int x)
{
        int y = abs(x);
        int * xptr = &y;
        return xptr;
}
```

3) Make sure that the function does return a pointer! That is, make certain that the argument to the return statement is indeed a pointer (e.g., return xptr; in the above code).

This simple_function returns a pointer that holds the address of a variable (i.e., y) that is assigned the absolute value of the integer passed to the function (i.e., x). Remember that the return statement returns the evaluation of its argument (a variable or an expression). In this case, this is the content of a pointer, which is an address.

We should mention that while this actually works, keep in mind that the variable y will cease to exist after simple-function() exits, so the address returned to the calling function will turn out to be generally meaningless. However, the value held in its address will persist and can be retrieved through the pointer. Let's work with this a bit more. See the following code:

```c
#include <stdio.h>
#include <stdlib.h>

int * test(int);   // the prototype

int main()
{
    int var = -20;
    int * ptr = NULL;
    ptr = test(var);

    printf("This is what we got back in main(): %d \n", *ptr);
    return 0;
}

int * test(int k)
{
    int y = abs(k);
    int * ptr1 = &y;
    printf("The value of y in test() directly is %d \n", y);
    printf("The value of y in test() indirectly is %d \n", *ptr1);
    return ptr1;
}
```

The output is:

```
The value of y in test() directly is 20
The value of y in test() indirectly is 20
This is what we got back in main(): 20
```

So, it did indeed work. The value of 20 remained in the memory location of variable y even though the latter no longer existed. There would be little reason to do this, as we could just have returned the value of y directly. However, it allows you to see how to return pointers.

---

4   Calling Functions by Reference with Pointers

In the previous chapter we discussed the concept of *call-by-value* and (very briefly) *call-by-reference*. To refresh our memory, C is naturally a call-by-value language. That means that when passing variables as arguments to a called function, the only thing passed is the value of the variable(s) passed. In Chap. 5 we did some brief exercises with calling-by-value and found that a called function cannot change the value of a local variable in the calling function that is passed as an argument. This is because the variable itself is not passed -- only its value at the time it is referenced. So, the called function does not know its address, because such information is not passed in a call-by-value scheme (such as in C).

However, now that we know about pointers, we can implement a call-by-reference scheme where the called function does not pass the value of a variable, but rather its address -- a pointer to the variable! Now the called function knows exactly where that variable "lives" in memory and can affect its value through indirection. Sneaky, right? It is another way of "returning" the output of a function to its calling function without actually formally returning it. Let's see how to do this. We'll use an example that involves defining a function called cube_it() that cubes the only argument passed to it. It doesn't return anything, but rather, places the value computed into a variable defined in the calling function (main() in this case). To make it easy, we'll say that the argument must be an integer.

```
void cube_it(int); // this is the prototype
int main()
{
      int number = 5;
      printf("Original value = %d\n", number);
      cube_it(number);
      printf("New value = %d\n", number);
      return 0;
}


void cube_it(int number)
{
      number = number * number * number;
}
```

The output of this will be:

```
Original value = 5
New value = 5
```

Of course, because C is pass-by-value, the value of the variable "passed" to cube_it() (number) remained as 5. So, nothing changed. The variable number declared in main() and the variable number declared in cube_it() are actually two different local variables with no knowledge of each other, even though they have the same name.

Now we will call cube_it() by reference and see how it can change the value of number in the calling function (main()). However, we must change the function cube_it() to look as follows:

```
void cube_it(int *); // this is the prototype
int main()
{
      int number = 5;
      printf("Original value = %d\n", number);
      cube_it(&number);
      printf("New value = %d\n", number);

      return 0;
}
```

```
void cube_it(int * nptr)
     {
           *nptr = (*nptr) * (*nptr) * (*nptr);
     }
```

Now the output is:

```
Original value = 5
New value = 125
```

We were able to change the value of the local variable number in main() right from the called function cube_it() even though number is a local variable in main(). We did this by indirectly modifying the variable number, without needing to return anything or using global variables. In fact, we just did call-by-reference. Let's look closely at what we did:

Rather than passing the variable's name (i.e., number), we passed its address by including &number in the argument of the function cube_it() when it was called from main(). To accomplish this, we had to change some things in the original code. First, note that the prototype for cube_it() has in its argument list (int *). This indicates that it is expecting the address of an integer variable as an argument. Likewise, the parameter list in the header of the definition of cube_it() includes (int * nptr). This declares a new pointer variable in cube_it() named nptr. This pointer variable "picks up" (formally said, "is assigned") the address of number that is passed to cube_it() as an argument when it is called. So, using indirection on this pointer allows the new version of the cube_it() function to modify the value located in the address passed to it, which, again, happens to be where the variable number lives.

So, the only thing the programmer had to do was to pass &number rather than number, and, much more importantly, set up the definition of cube_it() to accept an address, assign a pointer variable to this address (nptr) and use this address to indirectly change the value of number.

Call-by-reference is commonly used in C programs. This will become useful in understanding arrays and how to pass them to other functions (covered in the next chapter). Plus, the fact that you know how call-by-reference works gives you an insight into pointers and indirection. Please make sure you understand this well.

5   Pointer Math

If you thought you hated pointers already, here is further fuel for your hatred. Now we will do *pointer math*, also called *pointer arithmetic*. Yes, one can do a limited amount of math on pointer variables – or, better put, on the addresses contained in the pointers. Fortunately, pointer math is very limited in its scope and only limited to the contexts in which these operations are valid. Why one would even bother to do pointer math will become clear when we introduce arrays in Chap. 7. For now, let's look at what can be done.

Addresses are valid operands in (some) mathematical operations, assignment expressions, and comparison operations. However, not all operators are valid with pointers, and those operators that are valid <u>do not</u> work the same way as they do in normal arithmetic.

Addresses can be incremented (++) and decremented (--). They can be added and subtracted to/from other addresses as well as to/from integers (but not from floating point numbers, as decimal points make no sense in addresses). Multiplication may be valid under some circumstances, but <u>only</u> indirectly. Addresses cannot be divided nor operated upon by any other mathematical function -- it wouldn't make any sense. So, we only need to worry about addition and subtraction, and maybe a bit of multiplication. However, these operations don't work exactly as we know them to be. How so? Well, let us see.

When adding integers to pointers, the value of the integer added is the number of <u>memory blocks</u> to be added, and <u>not</u> the integer value itself! A memory block is the block of memory sized to hold the value of a particular variable. For example, as memory block could be 32 bits, if that is the size of an integer variable in one's computer. This implies that the addition of pointers is closely tied to the type of the variables to which they point. Therefore, the actual answer depends on the size of the memory element being pointed to by the pointer. Assuming that in our particular computer, an integer variable `int` is 4 bytes (32 bits), and that our pointer points to an integer variable, see the following snippet of code:

```
int * yptr = 3000;
yptr += 2;
printf("The value of the pointer yptr now is %p \n", yptr);
```

Notice that when initializing `yptr` upon its declaration, we did not use the address-of operator (`&`) to assign it the address of some existing variable, as we had done previously in this chapter. Instead, we directly assigned it an address. In reality, memory addresses are normally expressed in hexadecimal numbers, so the address of 3000 is only a representative number used to illustrate our point here and is not a realistic one.

Please compile and run the program above in `main()`. One may be surprised to see that the output will say: The value of the pointer yptr now is 3008 rather than what one would expect: 3002. This is because we are adding two integer-size memory blocks to it. So, 2 * 4 (bytes per `int` memory element) = 8 bytes. In other words, the pointer moved two integer data blocks away from its original address. Since an integer data block is 4 bytes it moved 8 bytes.

The ++ and -- operators work the same way. They add the size of one data block to the address (say, 4 bytes).

```
int *ptr = 3000;
ptr++;
```

Output:

```
ptr = 3004
```

Of course, this assumes that an integer variable takes 4 bytes (32 bits) in the computer where this code is run.

Since `char` variables are 1 byte in size, the arithmetic will be normal for pointers that point to character variables. Let's do some brief examples. Because we can't predict what addresses will be assigned, or even know whether one's computer uses a 16-, 32- or 64-bit integer, the results will only be relevant to the computer you are using, as well to when you are using it; running the same program at a different time, after the computer has been used for other things, may yield different addresses on the same computer.

```
int main()
{
  int * ptr1 = NULL, * ptr2 = NULL;
  int var;

  ptr1 = &var;
  ptr2 = ptr1 + 5;

  printf("The value of pointer ptr1 is %p \n", ptr1);
  printf("The value of pointer ptr2 is %p \n", ptr2);

  return 0;
}
```

The results will be:

```
The value of pointer ptr1 is 0022FF14
The value of pointer ptr2 is 0022FF28
```

Converted to decimal for easier understanding, the hexadecimal number 0022FF14 = 2,293,524 in decimal. Likewise, 0022FF28 = 2,293,544. The difference between them is 20 bytes, which just happens to be 4 bytes for each integer space, multiplied by 5, which is how many memory spaces the program is adding to ptr1. Thus, it is not the number that one adds to an address, but rather, the number times the size of the variable type being pointed to. This is where multiplication comes in, albeit implicitly.

Let's do the same thing except with double precision floating point variables. Now the size of the memory block to be added is that of a double precision variable (8 bytes). Note that all we changed was the declaration of the variables ptr1, ptr2 and var, which are now double. Nothing else changed.

```
int main()
{
  double * ptr1 = NULL, * ptr2 = NULL;
  double var;

  ptr1 = &var;
  ptr2 = ptr1 + 5;

  printf("The value of pointer ptr1 is %p \n", ptr1);
  printf("The value of pointer ptr2 is %p \n", ptr2);

  return 0;
}
```

The results are:

```
The value of pointer ptr1 is 0022FF10
The value of pointer ptr2 is 0022FF38
```

These values correspond, respectively, to 2,293,520 and 2,293,560. The difference is 40 bytes, which corresponds with the size of a double precision floating point variable being 8 bytes (8 × 5 = 40). Do this for other values added as well as for other variables types such as `char` to gain practice.

6   Double Pointers

As we said earlier in this chapter, pointers can also point to other pointers. After all, pointers are also variables, right? When a pointer points to another pointer (which in turn points to a normal variable), the pointer is called a *double pointer* (for obvious reasons). As long as you understand that a double pointer points to another pointer, there is really no reason to become confused.

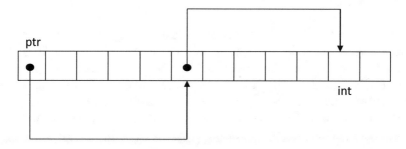

The double pointer contains the address of a pointer variable. If we indirectly reference the pointer pointed at by the double pointer (we'll call it the *intermediate pointer* here to avoid confusion, but it is not an official term), what will it read? An address, of course! However, that address is where a third variable is located (we'll call this the *ultimate variable*), so one can indirectly affect the value of the ultimate variable through this intermediate pointer. We just have to do some things twice. For example, when we declare a double pointer, we do it with two asterisks:

```
int * * dbl_ptr;
```

or

```
int **dbl_ptr;
```

This tells the compiler that the pointer `dbl_ptr` points to a pointer (our so-called "intermediate pointer") that in turn, points to an integer variable (the "ultimate variable").

The address-of operator (`&`) works in the same way. When used with a pointer variable, it returns the address of that pointer variable. Not the address it holds as a value, mind you, but rather the address where the pointer variable itself lives.

What about the indirection operator? Well, it depends on what one wants. If it is the <u>address</u> of the ultimate variable, then `*dbl_ptr` will return that address. This is because that is what the intermediate pointer holds as its value, and the * operator returns the value held by the variable pointed at by a pointer.

On the other hand, if we want to access the <u>value</u> of the ultimate variable, then we need to apply the indirection operator twice.

```
*(*dbl_ptr)
```

or just

```
**dbl_ptr.
```

Let's work with this next.

```
int main()
{
    int * * dbl_ptr = NULL, * i_ptr = NULL;
    int ult_var = 100;

    i_ptr = &ult_var;
    dbl_ptr = &i_ptr;

    printf("The value of the ultimate variable ult_var is %d \n", ult_var);
    printf("The address of ultimate variable ult_var is %p \n", &ult_var);
    printf("The value of the intermediate pointer i_ptr is %p \n", i_ptr);
    printf("The address of ultimate variable ult_var is %p \n", *dbl_ptr);
    printf("The address of intermediate pointer i_ptr is %p \n", &i_ptr);
    printf("The address of intermediate pointer i_ptr is %p \n", dbl_ptr);
    printf("The value of the ultimate variable ult_var is %d \n",
           **dbl_ptr);

    return 0;
}
```

The output of the program, when it ran in my computer, was:

```
The value of the ultimate variable ult_var is 100
The address of ultimate variable ult_var is 0022FF14
The value of the intermediate pointer i_ptr is 0022FF14
The address of ultimate variable ult_var is 0022FF14
The address of intermediate pointer i_ptr is 0022FF18
The address of intermediate pointer i_ptr is 0022FF18
The value of the ultimate variable ult_var is 100
```

Admittedly this is a bit confusing, so let's break down each line.

In the first `printf()` statement, the value of the variable `ult_var` referenced directly is clearly 100, so that is correct.

The second, third and fourth `printf()` statements display the same answer, an address of 0022FF14. Let's see whether that is correct: From the code, we can see that the second `printf()` statement contains the address of `ult_var`. This is expressed through the address-of operator acting upon `ult_var` itself, so we must assume that the address is correct as allocated by the compiler. Check √. The third `printf()` statement outputs the contents of the intermediate pointer i_ptr. Also from the code, we can see that pointer i_ptr points to `ult_var`, and therefore should contain the address of `ult_var` as its value. Therefore, it should be the same as the output of the second line, which it is. Check √. The fourth `printf()` statement accesses the address of `ult_var` but this time indirectly, by using the indirection operator on `dbl_ptr`, which points to the intermediate pointer `i_ptr`. Given that the indirection operator (*) can access the contents of the memory location pointed at by a pointer, and given that in the case of `dbl_ptr`, it is another pointer (`i_ptr`), then it should give the value held by `i_ptr`, which is the address of the variable pointed at by `ptr`. This is indeed the address of `ult_var`, which it is. So, check √ again. These three `printf()` statements all deal with where `ult_var` lives. We can conclude that the results for `printf()` statements 2, 3 and 4 are correct, if not a bit confusing.

The fifth and sixth `printf()` statements output the location in memory of the intermediate pointer `i_ptr`, each in a different way. These addresses, of course, should be different than the address of `ult_var` that was the output of the previous three `printf()` statements. Additionally, this would be the value held by `dbl_ptr`, so it should be something different than what is displayed in `printf()` statements 2, 3 and 4, all of which pertain to the address of `ult_var`. So, one would expect an address, and it should be different from those of `printf()` statements 2, 3 and 4, which it is. So, check √ once again.

That leaves the seventh and last `printf()` statement, which simply accesses the value of `ult_var` through double indirection. It outputs `100`, which is of course, correct. Check √ one last time.

The question remains about where one would apply double pointers. There are only a few applications for them, at least at a beginner's level, but one common one is when the programmer wants to pass a pointer variable by reference to a called function. Because to pass by reference we must pass a pointer to the variable being passed, in the case of passing a pointer by reference, one would have to point to a pointer, or … a double pointer!

7   Summary and Conclusion

In this chapter, we introduced and discussed the concept of pointer variables. Pointers are probably the most difficult part of learning C by novice programmers, and sometimes even by intermediate programmers. The one thing to keep in mind that will help you think through what you are trying to accomplish with pointers is: Pointers are just variables that hold addresses.

We have learned how to define and assign values to pointers. We have also seen operators that are used for manipulating pointers, such as the indirection and address-of operators.

In a more advanced context, we learned about call-by-reference and how we can pass the addresses of local variables to called functions and allow the (local) variables to be modified directly from the called function.

Likewise, in a yet slightly more advanced context, we learned about double pointers and how to manipulate them to obtain values through other pointers.

Pointers are very important in understanding arrays, which is covered in the next chapter.

8   Problems

1) Write a program that compares the average of three numbers to the average of three other numbers, and prints out the difference between the two averages. This is similar to Problem 3 in Chap. 5. To do this, write a user-defined function called `average()` that generates three random numbers between 1 and 10, computes their average and, through call by reference, sets the value of a variable within the calling function to the value of the resulting average. The `average()` function is then called a second time to do the same thing with three other numbers and a different variable

in the calling function. Then the two averages are compared in the calling function by computing and printing out their difference. The output should be:

```
The first average = <x1>;
The second average = <x2>;
Their difference is <y>.
```

2) Write a program where two variables (can be integers) are defined and are assigned values in main(). Then write a function called switch1() that will switch the values of the variables in main() without returning anything to main(). That is, it should be done via call-by-reference.
3) This is a challenging problem that requires the learner to understand the concept of pointers very well. It also requires understanding of passing by reference. Write a program that contains a user-defined function called move_address() that when passed an integer-type pointer by reference (hint: use double pointers), will add two integer blocks to the address passed to it, and modifies the value of the pointer variable in the calling function (main()). The output should be:

```
Original address = <address>
New address = <address>
```

Arrays

7

Up to this point, we have been limited to using simple variables to store data. That is, variables that can hold only one piece of data. While that may have been sufficient for the kinds of problems we have addressed so far, they are far from adequate for the more complex problems that we will be seeing as we progress in this book. For example, if we want to hold 20 pieces of similar data (real numbers, as in ambient temperatures over a 20-h period), we would have to declare 20 individual float-type variables, each with a unique name. To read the 20 numbers, we would have to reference each variable specifically by its unique name. Thus, to do it in a loop of some sort would be virtually impossible, even though it is the same process over and over, 20 times. OK, we might be able to bite the proverbial bullet and do it for 20 temperature values, but what if it was for 500? 10,000? Impossible! This is where *arrays* can help.

Arrays are a very important part of every programming language; without them, manipulating large volumes of data becomes very cumbersome – practically impossible. Arrays are an arbitrarily long collection of variables <u>of the same type</u> that have the same name. What distinguishes each of them from the other is an index, placed inside square brackets, that indicates the "place in line", so to speak, that each of the variables occupies. This allows them to be uniquely identified from the others, even though they have the same name. Now that we know about pointers, we can more easily understand arrays, as they are intimately intertwined. So let's begin:

1   Arrays – A Short Introduction

One of the biggest advantages of computers is that they can easily work with large volumes of data that would take humans much time and effort to collect and manipulate. For example, a nuclear power station is an incredibly complex system that must operate within rather narrow operational constraints. Otherwise, safety risks can arise. Therefore, it is critical to monitor thousands of inputs throughout the reactor and its auxiliary systems to be sure they are working within this narrow range of values. These include temperatures, pressures, flows, voltages, currents, (mega) watts, as well as many other variables from many sensors. The sensors that produce these data must be interrogated several times per minute – some several times per second – and the data must be analyzed to see whether they are within the normal limits.

Now imagine if we had to declare and manipulate a uniquely-named variable for every individual reading as we have done up to now. That would make it practically impossible to collect such large

© Springer Nature Switzerland AG 2020
A. J. Gonzalez, *Computer Programming in C for Beginners*,
https://doi.org/10.1007/978-3-030-50750-3_7

volumes of data. Therefore, ways to group data are available in C (and all other languages) that make it practical to store and retrieve such large volumes of data. The general name for these powerful variables is *data structures*. In particular, we now discuss one of these data structures: *arrays*. When combined with loops, the contents of arrays can be easily stored, read and manipulated.

So, arrays are groupings of indexed variables under the same variable name. The types of data held in an array must all be the same. One <u>cannot</u> mix different types of data in the same array. C provides us with another data structure to do that, which we will see in Chap. 8.

This indexing feature of arrays allows us to define each variable in an array as an indexed version of the array name. One can think of an array as in the figure below:

Array **a**:

a[0]	a[1]	a[2]	a[3]	a[4]	a[5]	a[6]	a[7]	a[8]	a[9]	a[10]	a[11]

Each "*cell*" in this 12-cell array a, shown pictorially above, has the name of the array (a), plus an index number between straight brackets [ ]. The index begins at 0 and increments by one, going from the first cell to the last. The index number is represented by an integer value. Of course, it can also be represented by an int variable, such as a[n], where n can be incremented or decremented as desired. This enables their use within loops, as the processor can go from one cell to the next by incrementing or decrementing the index variable (n in our example) by one. More significantly, the processor can jump between cells that are not adjacent to each other (e.g., a[3] to a[11]) in one step. This is called *random access* (although the access is not random per se), and it is an important feature of arrays, as we will see later.

One more notable feature of an array, as suggested in the drawing above, is that the cells are physically next to each other in computer memory. That is, they are in *contiguous memory*. This makes it very easy and efficient to access each cell and enables the "random access" mentioned above. The disadvantage is that the compiler must find one block of <u>contiguous</u> memory large enough to hold the entire array. For very large arrays, that may not be so easy. Even if the computer has plenty of memory but it is not in a single contiguous block long enough to store this array, it will not otherwise have enough memory to store this large array.

Why would we use an array? One example that we briefly discussed above would be if we want to collect the temperatures from a temperature sensor that measures a particularly important part of our nuclear power plant (e.g., reactor outlet steam). We want to collect that temperature value once every second for an entire day (86,400 times), then calculate the average temperature, the maximum and minimum temperatures, plus maybe some other more exotic calculations (e.g., rate of rise). Where do we put all that data? Well, we can do it by declaring an array of a specific type of data (i.e., double for this application). Remember, all cells have to be of the same variable type. The array would be of size 86,400 from 0 to 86,399. The temperature value captured every second would be progressively placed in the array, where the temperature logged at 00:00:01 (AM) would be placed in a[0], the temperature captured at 00:00:02 would be placed in a[1] and so on until the temperature for one second before midnight (23,59,59) would be placed in a[86399]. Of course, this would be done inside a loop, but we will discuss that below.

One disadvantage of arrays is that their size has to be specified by the programmer during code development, and before compilation; it cannot be changed during run time. This places the burden on the programmer to predict how large the array will have to be. Too small and data may be lost; too large and memory will be wasted. Other data structures in C can grow and shrink during run time as it becomes necessary – we will see some of these later, but the array size must be fixed during development. For now, let us just look at the mechanics of defining and initializing arrays.

2 Defining and Initializing Arrays

As with all other variables, arrays also have to be defined and preferably initialized. The format for defining an array is:

```
<variable_type> <arrayName>[<# of cells>];
```

Where `variable_type` is the type of variable to be stored in the array (e.g., `int`, `float`, `char`) and `arrayName` is the name to be given to the array. The rules for naming arrays follow the same restrictions as the names for normal variables. Between the straight brackets next to the name of the array (i.e., `[<# of cells>]`) is the specification of the number of cells to be contained in the array. This is expressed as an integer value. For example, defining array `a` above to collect reactor outlet steam temperatures as floating point values, would be done as follows:

```
float a[86400];
```

By doing this, we have defined 86,400 floating point variables that are just like any other `float` variable, but are indexed for ease of manipulation. So, if we wanted, we could access, read and change the values of any of these variables independently, just as if they were normal variables. For example, we can make the following value assignment to the variable `a[12376]`:

```
a[12376] = 325.7;
```

We can do the same thing with integer arrays, double precision floating point arrays, character arrays, etc. Arrays can also hold pointers as well as other complex data types (that we haven't seen yet). We shall see these later.

Now that we know how to define arrays, let's learn how to initialize them. One easy way to do so for small arrays is to actually place the values within curly brackets as we define the array.

```
int b[10] = {34, 76, 91, 101, 2, 853, 36, 85, 99, 467};
```

The first value (`34`) will be assigned to the first cell (`b[0]`), the second value (`76`) to the second cell (`b[1]`), etc. Note that there are exactly 10 entries within the curly brackets. Now put these statements in the `main()` function of a new C program and print out two or three of these array cells.

```
printf("The value of b[3] is %d \n", b[3]);
printf("The value of b[9] is %d \n", b[9]);
printf("The value of b[5] is %d \n", b[5]);
```

Go ahead and do this. You will see that it will print out

```
The value of b[3] is 101
The value of b[9] is 467
The value of b[5] is 853
```

So, this begs the question: What happens if there are <u>fewer</u> values inside the curly brackets than the specified size of the array? For example:

```
int b[10] = {34, 76, 91, 101, 2, 853, 36};
```

Run the same printf code again. You will see that the results are:

```
The value of b[3] is 101
The value of b[9] is 0
The value of b[5] is 853
```

You guessed it. It assigns initial values to the cells beginning with `b[0]` until there are no more initial values inside the curly brackets. Then it sets to 0 the values of the remaining variables that do not have a corresponding initial value. Hence they are all initialized, just not all of them to a specific, non-zero value. So, for a large array (say, 86,400 cells), if we wanted to initialize all the array cells to 0 (indeed a good thing to do), all one would have to do is

```
float a[86400] = {0.0};
```

And all of them would be initialized to 0.0 (actually, to 0.000000). Try it now for three arbitrary cells:

```
printf("The value of a[30357] is %f \n", a[30357]);
printf("The value of a[972] is %f \n", a[972]);
printf("The value of a[5945] is %f \n", a[5945]);
```

You will see that the output confirms that the values of the cells that we arbitrarily selected are indeed 0.000000.

This leads to our next question: What happens if we provide <u>too many</u> values? That is, we have more values inside the curly brackets then the size of the array. For example,

```
int b[5] = {34, 76, 91, 101, 2, 853, 36, 85, 99, 467};
```

The compiler will become confused and give you warnings, but if you insist on running the program in spite of the warnings, it will actually work.

One can also initialize an array using a loop, setting a value to each of the cells individually. However, this is very expensive computationally and not typically necessary unless there is a specific set of values with which one would like to initialize the array, and those values are not 0. However, this is rare.

So, what happens if we don't initialize? It depends. Possibly nothing, or possibly bad things. Let's look at the bad things that could happen.

We declare another array named c of double precision floating point variables and not initialize it. Then use the `printf()` statements and see what prints out.

```
double c[10];
printf("The value of c[3] is %lf \n", c[3]);
printf("The value of c[9] is %lf \n", c[9]);
printf("The value of c[5] is %lf \n", c[5]);
```

What we get will probably be garbage, or just maybe 0.0. Try it. You must remember that all variables are by default "initialized" to whatever values remain in the bits located in the block of memory that was allocated to a variable from the last time that memory space was used. However, the initial values will be arbitrary, something you generally don't want.

One more point: we can simply use the initialization process to size the array automatically. If we leave the [ ] brackets empty, the compiler will size the array to exactly the number of initial values are inside the curly brackets. For example,

```
int d[] = {34, 76, 91, 101, 2, 853, 36};
```

The size of the array d will be automatically set to 7 cells. This, however, is impractical for all but small arrays.

Before learning how to use arrays within loops and how to pass arrays to user-defined functions that we might define and call, let's examine how arrays and pointers are related; very closely, as we shall see. This will help you better understand how arrays work internally.

---

3   Arrays, Pointers and Pointer Math

The reason we held off covering arrays until we had covered pointers is that array names are in fact pointers. The name of an array is a pointer that points to the first cell in the array. Given that the cells are all in contiguous memory and that they are all of the same size, the processor only needs to know the *offset* of a particular cell from the first cell to access it very efficiently. So, this is where the pointer math we saw in the last chapter plays an important role. Let's more deeply discuss the idea of pointers and arrays.

We declare the array c as above and initialize the first three cells to 10, 20 and 30. The others can be allowed to be initialized to 0 by default.

```
int c[10]= {10, 20, 30};
```

The name of the array c is a pointer to the variable in the first cell c[0]. Let's see whether this is true by adding the following statements to the code above:

```
printf("The address contained in c is %p \n", c);
printf("The address of c[0] is %p \n", &c[0]);
```

You will get the same address. This allows us to use pointer math to "move" the pointer along the array to access other cells and their values. (The pointer doesn't really "move" per se; it changes its value to the address of a different block of memory along the sequence of memory blocks associated with the array.) We said earlier in Chap. 6 that one could add integer values to pointer addresses, and that the address would become incremented by the integer value to be added times the block size (in bytes) for the relevant type of variable. To refresh your memory, if in the context of a 32-bit representation for an integer variable (i.e., 4 bytes), we want to add 4 to an arbitrary address of 3000 (its decimal equivalent), the answer would be not 3004, but rather 3016. This is 4 memory elements * 4 bytes each = 16 bytes.

This is particularly relevant in the context of an array because, as we know, arrays exist in contiguous memory, and all the cells contain variables of the same type, and thus, are of the same size. The addresses of all cells in an array are nothing more than *offsets* of the address of the first cell. So, for an integer array of 14 cells called arr:

```
&arr[0]  =  arr  +  0
&arr[1]  =  arr  +  1
&arr[2]  =  arr  +  2
        .
        .
        .
        .
&arr[13] =  arr  +  13
```

Note that the above is not C code, but rather traditional mathematical equations that assume that the address-of operator is a mathematical operation (which it's not) and arrays exist in mathematics (which do not as such).

Given the above, we can use the indirection operator ($*$) to access the value of cells in the array indirectly through the addresses as follows: (again, these are traditional math equations, not C code, and the equal sign = is <u>not</u> an assignment operation here.)

```
arr[5]  =  *(arr  +  5)
arr[13] =  *(arr  +  13)
```

Let's see if this is true in a C program now. Type in the following code (of course, inside a main () function) in a C program:

```
int arr[13] = {0, 10, 20, 30, 40, 50, 60, 70, 80, 90, 100, 110, 120};
printf("The content of the sixth cell is %d \n", arr[5]);
printf("The content of the sixth cell is %d \n", *(arr + 5));
```

The output should be:

```
The content of the sixth cell is 50
The content of the sixth cell is 50
```

This ability to move back and forth along the array by adding or subtracting offsets to the current address is what allows for the quick and efficient random access in arrays. As it turns out, pointer math is only relevant in the context of arrays, as no other data structure in C guarantees being in contiguous memory.

Please make sure you understand this relationship between arrays, pointers and pointer math. It will become important when we learn about passing arrays to user-defined functions.

4   Arrays and Loops

Arrays are highly synergistic with loops. As we mentioned earlier, the index of a cell can be represented by an integer variable that can be incremented (or decremented) systematically. If we use such a variable in an array inside a loop, we can populate each cell with values rather easily. For example, say we want to populate a 20-cell integer array where each successive cell is twice the value of the previous one. Assume the first one will have a value of 1. We can easily do this as follows:

```
int arr[20] = {0}, n;
for(n=0; n<20; n++)
    {
    arr[n] = arr[n-1] * 2;
    printf("The content of cell number %d is %d \n", n, arr[n]);
    }
```

Try it!

You got a bunch of garbage, right? That is because in the first iteration (when n=0), n-1 will be cell number -1, which is undefined, as array indices must always be positive integers. In spite of this, the C program dutifully tried to do as it was asked to do and used whatever was in the memory location just in front of the first cell of the array. Given that all other values depended on this initial value, it is not surprising that you got garbage. Once again, we must think like a computer!

So, to fix it, we also need to initialize the value of arr[0] but we must do it outside of the loop. Let's now run the following fixed code:

```
int arr[20] = {0}, n;
arr[0] = 1;
printf("The content of cell number %d is %d \n", 0, arr[0]);
for(n=1; n<20; n++)
    {
        arr[n] = arr[n-1] * 2;
        printf("The content of cell number %d is %d \n", n, arr[n]);
    }
```

You will see that this now works as intended! Note that we not only inserted the statement before the loop that set the value of arr[0] to 1, but we also started the loop from n=1, rather than n=0. Had we started the loop from n=0 again, we would have gotten the same garbage we got before because it still would have tried to access the contents of the memory location just in front of arr[0]. Notice that we also had to add one printf() statement before entering the loop that would print out the contents of arr[0], as it would not have printed out otherwise because the loop begins with arr[1].

Once we learn how to read from and write to external files, the use of loops and arrays will become much more meaningful. Nevertheless, let's practice some more, even if in relatively meaningless applications.

We next look at some of the operations we described in Sect. 2 above but could not show that it worked because we didn't yet know how to incorporate arrays in loops. Let's look at initialization.

```
int arr[20] = {0}, n;
for(n=0; n<20; n++)
    printf("The content of cell number %d is %d \n", n, arr[n]);
```

You will see from this code implementation that the initialization worked as intended. This is an easy way to initialize even very large arrays to 0.

Likewise, let's implement the following code to see what happens when an array is <u>not</u> initialized:

```
int arr[20], n;
for(n=0; n< 20; n++)
      printf("The content of cell %d is %d \n", n, arr[n]);
```

Each cell contains arbitrary numbers, right? Now let's see a partial initialization:

```
int arr[20] = {0, 10, 20, 30, 40, 50, 60, 70}, n;
for(n=0; n<20; n++)
      printf("The content of cell %d is %d \n", n, arr[n]);
```

Note how the first eight cells are correctly initialized, but the rest are set to 0. Please run this program to verify.

Lastly, let's over-initialize:

```
int arr[5] = {0, 10, 20, 30, 40, 50, 60, 70}, n;
for(n=0; n<5; n++)
      printf("The content of cell %d is %d \n", n, arr[n]);
```

This resulted in a compilation warning (not an error!), as the compiler could not reconcile the declaration and initialization of the array `arr[]`. Yet, it ran correctly nonetheless.

---

5   Passing Arrays to Functions

Next on the agenda is learning how to pass arrays to user-defined functions. We assume here that the array to be passed is local to the calling function. Passing arrays is useful if we need to pass several values, as it can be cumbersome to define each as a separate argument in the parameter list (however, remember that they do have to be of the same type!) Recall that array names are in fact pointers. So we are actually passing an array by reference, rather than by value. We do this by passing the array name only to the called function (without the brackets). This is, of course, the address of the first cell of the array. Naturally, this also includes identifying the kind of data type to which the pointer points. The user-defined function would already know the size of each cell in the array because the parameter list in its definition would indicate the type of variable to which the pointer (i.e., the array name) would point.

But this isn't all we need to pass. The calling function knows the size of the array being passed because the array was defined therein. However, the called function won't know how large the array is if we only were to pass to it the address of the first cell. So, we also need to let the called function know how large the array is. We do this by also passing an integer value corresponding to the number of cells in the array.

Now the called function knows where to begin (i.e., the address of the first cell), the type of data contained in the array (specified in the array name declaration in the parameter list), and how large the array is (from the integer passed). Say we declare array `arr[10]` in `main()` and initialize it to 0 as we did earlier. Then, it is passed to a user-defined function that will set the values of each array cell to double the value in the previous cell (as we did in the last section). Then, we print out the contents of each cell from `main()`. The full C program is as follows (don't forget the prototype!):

```c
#include <stdio.h>
#include <stdlib.h>

void double_it(int [], int);

int main()
{
    int arr[10] = {0}, n;
    for(n=0; n<10; n++)
        printf("The content of cell %d is initially %d \n", n, arr[n]);
    double_it(arr, 10);
    printf("\n\n");
    for(n=0; n<10; n++)
        printf("The content of cell %d is now %d \n", n, arr[n]);

    return 0;
}


void double_it(int a[], int i)
{
    int k = 0;
    a[0] = 1;
    for(k=1; k<i; k++)
        a[k] = a[k-1] * 2;
}
```

Note what we did here. We declared an array called `arr` in `main()`, initialized its cells all to 0, and put it in a loop to print out the initial contents of each cell. This is to confirm that initially, the array only held zero for the values of its cells. Then we called the user-defined function `double_it()` and passed to it the name of the array (`arr`) and its size (10). Since we are passing `arr` by reference to `double_it()`, we can expect that `double_it()` will be able to change the values of the cells of `arr[]` directly. This is the classic case of passing (calling) by reference. Then, we placed `arr[]` in a loop to print out the contents of each cell <u>after</u> `double_it()` did its thing. Of course, the values printed out for each cell in the second loop are each twice the value of the cell before it. Notice how we defined `double_it()`. It indicates that the first parameter (argument) is an array of integer variables, and the second is an integer. Moreover, just like we did in the similar example earlier, to avoid it multiplying 2*0 for every cell and getting 0, we initialized the value of `a[0]` to 1 (instead of the 0 originally contained therein), and then started the loop at `k=1` (instead of `k=0`).

Write this program and run it. You should get a sequence of ten printout statements stating that the initial values of each cell is 0. Then, immediately following it should be another ten statements indicating that the value of each cell is now twice the value of the previous one. This is correct.

Next, to show that arrays are indeed pointers, let's change the definition of the array in the parameter list to a pointer. (Everything else remains unchanged.)

```
#include <stdio.h>
#include <stdlib.h>

void double_it(int *, int);

int main()
{
    int arr[10] = {0}, n;
    for(n=0; n<10; n++)
        printf("The content of cell %d is initially %d \n", n, arr[n]);
    double_it(arr, 10);
    printf("\n\n");
    for(n=0; n<10; n++)
        printf("The content of cell %d is now %d \n", n, arr[n]);

    return 0;
}


void double_it(int * a, int i)
{
    int k = 0;
    a[0] = 1;
    for(k=1; k<i; k++)
        a[k] = a[k-1] * 2;
}
```

All we changed above was the prototype (int *, …) instead of (int [], …), and the parameter list in the definition of double_it() to (int * a, …) instead of (int a[], …). These changes are underlined and bold-faced above for ease of visibility. Nothing else was changed. The output is the same as for the previous version, and it is correct.

Please be sure to understand what we did here, as passing arrays to user-defined functions is quite common.

6   Character Arrays – Strings

We have delayed the discussion of a very important concept in computer programming – the *string* -- until now. This is because to truly understand strings, you first needed to learn about pointers and arrays. A *string* is a series of characters that when strung together represent a word, a sentence, a paragraph, or even a complete book. A string is actually an array of characters. However, strings have special treatment. We deal with strings in greater detail in Chap. 9, describing some special functions that allow us to manipulate strings rather easily. However, we would be remiss if we delayed the introduction of strings any longer.

Knowing that strings are arrays, we declare them just like arrays.

```
char str[20];
```

One of the differences between strings and "normal" arrays (those that don't hold characters) is that a *null terminator* (\0) is automatically placed at the end of the string to signify its end. This keeps the printf() function from printing out the entire array when the string is smaller than the array (as it typically is), and the rest of the cells in the array may contain garbage. While this is a good thing, the programmer does need to remember to leave at least one extra space in the character array for the null terminator. Therefore, the size of the character array always needs to be at least one cell larger than what you think you will need for the string.

While literal characters are enclosed in single quotation marks (e.g., `'a'`), literal strings are enclosed within double quotation marks (e.g., "`This is a literal string.`"). Strings can be read from the keyboard with `scanf()` as a string, and printed out with `printf()`. This is what we mean by strings getting special treatment, as normal arrays must be printed out one cell at a time.

Character arrays are initialized somewhat differently than normal arrays. Sure, we could do it the hard way:

```
char word[20];
word[0] = 'h';
word[1] = 'e';
word[2] = 'l';
word[3] = 'l';
word[4] = 'o';
word[5] ='\0';
```

Fortunately, there are much better ways of initializing strings. This is once again part of the special treatment we mentioned above.

One can initialize strings in (almost) the same way one would initialize a normal array:

```
char str[] = {"Welcome, ya'll!"};
```

However, we can do things that are not possible with normal arrays, such as:

```
char * str1 = "By gosh!";
```

One can even do this:

```
char * str2;
str2 = "Go Knights!!";
```

But one cannot do this:

```
char * str3;
str3 = {"Go Gators!!"};
```

Now let's examine input and output with strings to show how they get special treatment.

6.1   Inputting Strings with `scanf()`

Unlike normal arrays, strings can be read in as a one value. So, strings have their very own type specifier: `%s`. To read a string, the `scanf()` specification looks like this:

```
scanf("%s", word);
```

In the above statement, word is the name of the character array that will serve as the *string variable* that will hold the string to be entered from the keyboard. Note that we didn't put an & in front of word. This is <u>not</u> a mistake! The scanf() function doesn't need the & (which you now should recognize as the address-of operator) for a string because the string name is the name of an array, and therefore is already an address – that of the first cell in the array!

If a user intends to enter a single word from the keyboard, no quotation marks are used when entering the word. In fact, scanf() will assume that a quotation mark that might be included is a literal, and part of the string to be stored. However, you must know that when reading a string, scanf() stops reading as soon as it hits the first <u>whitespace</u>. So, if you've got this line of code:

```
scanf("%s", word);
```

And the user types on the keyboard:

```
reading a string
```

Then the string variable word will only acquire reading, and ignore the rest of the text after the whitespace. We should note that whitespaces are OK, however, when used within quotes – just not as part of inputs to scanf(). This is a limitation on entering strings from the keyboard when using scanf().

The way to enter more than one word with scanf() is to link the words with an underscore. Not ideal, no, but possible. In Chap. 9 we will see other input functions for strings and characters such as gets() and getchar() that operate differently than scanf().

6.2   Printing Strings with printf()

Using the same type specifier (%s), we can print out strings easily with printf() almost as if it was a normal variable.

For example:

```
printf("%s", word);
```

will print the content of string variable word to the display. Try it!

Various standard library functions can be used to manipulate strings. We will see this soon, in Chap. 9.

7   Multi-dimensional Arrays

Arrays can have more than one dimension; In fact they can have an arbitrary number of dimensions. We can indicate the number of dimensions when declaring it by using multiple brackets. For example:

```
int a[5][10];
int b[10][12][20];
```

The first array above (a) is two-dimensional, while array b is three-dimensional. The first set of brackets (in a) contains the row index while the second set of brackets represents the column index. While there is no limit on the number of dimensions, we will stick here to two- and three-dimensional arrays, as they are the most commonly used.

Multi-dimensional arrays can also be initialized in a similar way to one-dimensional ones. They are initialized one row at a time by placing the values to be initially assigned in each row in curly brackets: the first set of brackets equates to the first row; the second set to the second row, etc./.

```
int c[2][2] = {{1,2} {3,4}};
```

Initializes `c[0][0]=1; c[0][1]=2; c[1][0]=3;` and `c[1][1]=4`.
What, then, if we have an incomplete initialization? Such as:

```
int c[2][2] = {{1} {3,4}};
```

Well, then, the initialization follows the same general rules for initializing one-dimensional arrays, except now it is row by row as follows: `c[0][0]=1`, `c[0][1]=0`, `c[1][0]=3`, and `c[1][1]=4`.

Working with multi-dimensional arrays in loops requires nested loops. In other words, loops within loops. A two-deep nested loop works in the following fashion: the outer loop that we mentioned in Chap. 4 processes one row during each of its iterations. The inner loop then processes each column position in the row being processed within that iteration of the outer loop. When the inner loop finishes processing all the positions in the row, then the inner loop exits, and the outer loop goes to the next row, where it executes the inner loop again to process all the column positions of this next row.

See the example below for a two dimensional array.

```
int main()
{
int myarray[3][4] = {{0, 10, 20, 30}, {40, 50, 60, 70}, {80, 90, 100, 110} };
int i, j;
for (i=0; i<3; i++)
        for (j=0; j<4; j++)
                printf("The value of the array at row %d and column %d, "
                        " is %d \n", i, j, myarray[i][j]);

return 0;
}
```

By extension, a three-dimensional array will require three nested loops as seen in the following code:

```
int main()
{
int myarray[2][3][4] = {  {{0, 10, 20, 30}, {40, 50, 60, 70},
            {80, 90, 100, 110}},
        {{120, 130, 140, 150}, {160, 170, 180, 190}, {200, 210, 220, 230}} };
int i, j, k;
for (i=0; i<2; i++)
      for (j=0; j<3; j++)
            for (k=0; k<4; k++)
                    printf("The value of the array at row %d, column %d, and "
                        " height %d is %d \n", i, j, k, myarray[i][j][k]);
return 0;
}
```

Write the above programs, compile them and run them. The output of the two-dimensional array is:

```
The value of the array at row 0 and column 0 is 0
The value of the array at row 0 and column 1 is 10
The value of the array at row 0 and column 2 is 20
The value of the array at row 0 and column 3 is 30
The value of the array at row 1 and column 0 is 40
The value of the array at row 1 and column 1 is 50
The value of the array at row 1 and column 2 is 60
The value of the array at row 1 and column 3 is 70
The value of the array at row 2 and column 0 is 80
The value of the array at row 2 and column 1 is 90
The value of the array at row 2 and column 2 is 100
The value of the array at row 2 and column 3 is 110
```

The output of the three-dimensional array is.

```
The value of the array at row 0, column 0, and height 0 is 0
The value of the array at row 0, column 0, and height 1 is 10
The value of the array at row 0, column 0, and height 2 is 20
The value of the array at row 0, column 0, and height 3 is 30
The value of the array at row 0, column 1, and height 0 is 40
The value of the array at row 0, column 1, and height 1 is 50
The value of the array at row 0, column 1, and height 2 is 60
The value of the array at row 0, column 1, and height 3 is 70
The value of the array at row 0, column 2, and height 0 is 80
The value of the array at row 0, column 2, and height 1 is 90
The value of the array at row 0, column 2, and height 2 is 100
The value of the array at row 0, column 2, and height 3 is 110
The value of the array at row 1, column 0, and height 0 is 120
The value of the array at row 1, column 0, and height 1 is 130
The value of the array at row 1, column 0, and height 2 is 140
The value of the array at row 1, column 0, and height 3 is 150
The value of the array at row 1, column 1, and height 0 is 160
The value of the array at row 1, column 1, and height 1 is 170
The value of the array at row 1, column 1, and height 2 is 180
The value of the array at row 1, column 1, and height 3 is 190
The value of the array at row 1, column 2, and height 0 is 200
The value of the array at row 1, column 2, and height 1 is 210
The value of the array at row 1, column 2, and height 2 is 220
The value of the array at row 1, column 2, and height 3 is 230
```

Arrays can also hold addresses (pointers) in their cells. In fact, this is really useful for strings, as a one-dimensional array could be used to store several strings, which normally would take a two-dimensional string.

```
char * suit[4] = {"hearts", "diamonds", "spades", "clubs"};
```

The array `suit[]` is one-dimensional and holds four cells. Each cell holds a pointer. The `char` `*` says that the elements of the array are pointers to `char`, which, of course means they are arrays, …, and strings! Note how the component strings are initialized. To show this concept graphically:

Comment:

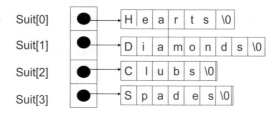

8   Summary and Conclusion

In this chapter, the learner has been introduced to arrays – an essential data structure in computer programming. An array is a data structure where several variables of the same type have the same name, and are only distinguished by an index following its name. The index, placed between straight brackets immediately after the name of the array, is an integer that denotes the place of that particular variable (i.e., cell) within the structure. Arrays are much more useful than simple variables when working with large amounts of data – or even when working with small amounts of data. An array, then, is a sequence of similarly-sized blocks of memory that are allocated in contiguous memory. Importantly, we have learned that an array name is a pointer to the first cell in the array. Understanding this concept can serve to facilitate the passing of arrays to user-defined functions, something that we also discussed and about which we did some practice exercises.

We also learned how to use arrays within simple loops. This feature brings to light the great useful-ness of arrays, where varying the index can permit the performance of the same action on each cell sequentially.

We also introduced the learner to strings – arrays of characters -- and how they are treated some-what differently than normal arrays. We also discussed how strings are initialized, how they are cap-tured from the keyboard and how they can be printed out to the display.

Lastly, we extended the concept of arrays to multi-dimensional arrays and did some exercises with these.

9   Problems

1) Create a 10-cell array containing the following integers in this order: 23, 43, 2, 48, 21, 17, 28, 19, 36 and 10. Write a program that takes in an integer input from the keyboard, between 0 and 50. The program returns "Yes, the number <number> is found in the array" if the integer entered is a member of the array; and "No, the number <num> is not in the array." if it is not. This introduces a very simple form of search, something we will see in more detail later in Chap. 12.

2) Write a program that does the same as problem #1 above except that rather than initializing it with specific values as in problem #1, populate the array with random numbers between 0 and 50 through a user-defined function.

3) Write a program that captures the ambient temperatures in your home over a 24 h period. The measurements are to be taken once per hour. Because we do not have access to a temperature recording device, simulate it by generating random numbers between 0 and 50 deg. C. and convert the values to deg. F. (Note that the random number will be an integer while the converted temperature will be a real number (`float` or `double`), so handle them properly to avoid mismatches of data types.) Then compute the average, maximum and minimum temperatures in deg. F, and print out a list of the hourly temperatures for a 24-h period, one hour per line. At the bottom of the list print out the average, maximum and minimum temperatures. You can do this all in `main()`.

4) Write a program to do the exact same thing as problem #3 above except write a user-defined function that accepts an already-populated array from `main()` that contains the 25 temperatures in deg. F and calculates the average, max and min temperatures. The output is to be done from the `main()` function.

5) Write a program that creates a 10x10 two-dimensional array containing integers where in each row, the value of one cell is that of the previous one multiplied by 2. Assume the first column of every row has the same value as the last column of the previous row. Print out each row in one line. Do this all in `main()`.

6) Write a program that maps each letter of the English alphabet to an integer between 1 and 26. Print out each letter of the alphabet next to the integer value starting from 1 – one letter/number combination per line of printout. This makes for a very simple look-up table A user should be able to enter an integer number and get back the corresponding character in the alphabet.

7) Write a program that asks a user to enter his/her name from the keyboard, first the first name and then the last name. It then prints out "`Hello <first name> <last name>!`"

Structures

8

We now know about arrays and how they can facilitate storing and manipulating large sets of similar data very efficiently. Now we face a conceptual application where we have to create a database that contains information about the students in a class. We would want their names, their student ID numbers, year in college, major, and overall GPA. We can try to do it on an array, but we will hit a roadblock: the name is a string, the ID is an integer (could also be a string, but let's assume not), the year in college is an integer, the major is a string and the GPA is a floating point number. Therefore, we cannot use arrays for this application because these pieces of information are not of the same data types, and, of course, we know that arrays require that all the data must be of the same type. Fortunately, C gives us a second type of data structure that can be used for this type of application. They are called *structures*. The name is unfortunate because we have seen sequential structures, selection structures, and repetition structures, so it can be confusing when we simply say *structures*. However, the context of the dialog should serve to disambiguate its meaning, just as it does with the over-used *.

1   Structures – A Brief Introduction

Structures work much differently than arrays. One structure only holds one set of data (i.e., one student's information), so we need several of these to cover the class. Furthermore, while the data in one structure are located in contiguous memory, two similar structures (i.e., the data for two students in the same class) are not necessarily placed in contiguous memory. The focus is not so much on how to store and retrieve data efficiently, but rather, to build exactly the group of data types that one needs to express the data needs of the application. In database systems, these data entities are called *records*, but we will simply call them structures here. C gives the programmer the ability to *design* a structure to fill the needs of the application.

We can design a structure through the `struct` keyword. This is best shown through an example.

Sticking to our application above, we want to build a structure that holds the information related to the students in a typical college class. We can do this as follows:

© Springer Nature Switzerland AG 2020
A. J. Gonzalez, *Computer Programming in C for Beginners*,
https://doi.org/10.1007/978-3-030-50750-3_8

```
struct student  {
    char name[20];
    int ID;
    int year;
    char major[30];
    float GPA;
};
```

The `struct` keyword identifies to the compiler that what follows is the <u>template</u> of a structure to store related but dissimilar data. Of course, `struct` is a reserved keyword in C, and cannot be used to label anything else in C.

The label next to `struct` is the *structure tag*, which is the name we want to give to this particular structure template. The structure tag is optional -- we don't have to name the structure -- it can be left *anonymous*. However, until we learn some other things, we shall assume that a structure tag is always to be included.

The items that appear to be variable definitions inside the curly brackets are called the *members* of the `struct` template. They do NOT represent variable definitions per se because this is only a template, but they are tightly integrated into the design of the structure. The members of a structure <u>instance</u> are individually accessible to the programmer to store data (of the appropriate type) and retrieve any data stored therein. The individual members can be treated as if they were normal as well as independent variables, like cells in an array.

You may wonder why we underlined the words <u>template</u> and <u>instance</u> in the discussion above. The answer is that what is created through the `struct` keyword is merely a *template* (aka, a *model)* of the structures we would like to have. It is <u>not</u> a variable. The reason this is done is that it would be very inefficient if any time we wanted to build a variable that looked like a certain structure, we would have to use the `struct` construct above to create each such "working structure", so to speak. So, C instead makes the structure defined through `struct` merely a reproducible template from which we can create actual working structures that look like that, and can be used as defined variables in a program. The process of creating these "working copies" of the template that become defined variables is called *instantiation*, or *making instances of*, the template. This is very much like building a class in object-oriented programming and then creating instance-level objects of the class, but we digress.

So, you ask, given that we have defined a structure template as we did above, how can we instantiate it to create working variables? Let's get into that next:

2   Instantiating Structure Variables

There are three ways to instantiate a structure – that is, to create instances that have actual defined variables.

2.1   Instantiating within the Body of the `struct` Definition

This is the easiest of the three ways to do it, but also the most limiting because if an instance is not created in the body of the structure definition, it must then be done later in other ways. To instantiate within the body of the template definition, the programmer needs to place the name(s) of the instance(s) between the closing curly bracket } and the semicolon that completes the `struct` body. (We should note that this is one of the very few cases in C where a semicolon follows the closing curly bracket in a statement.) More than one instance can be included, but they need to be separated by commas. For example (instantiated variables are in bold face type):

```
struct student  {
    char name[20];
    int ID;
    int year;
    char major[30];
    float GPA;
 } student1, student2, student3, student4;
```

In the above cases, we succeeded in instantiating four structure variables. However, we did so very inefficiently in that if we wanted to make 100 instances, the structure body would be very large indeed. So, while this works well, it is only good for a small number of instantiations.

Or, we can also instantiate arrays of structure instances. This is a way to combine the advantages of arrays and structures. For example, if we had 250 students in the class, we could do:

```
struct student  {
    char name[20];
    int ID;
    int year;
    char major[30];
    float GPA;
 } students[250];
```

This means that rather than having one individual structure instance for each student, we now easily define them as cells in an array. We will revisit this later when we learn how to access the members of the structure instance variables.

Oh, yes, we can also instantiate pointers that point to a structure instance that looks like the student structure. We can do that as:

```
struct student  {
    char name[20];
    int ID;
    int year;
    char major[30];
    float GPA;
 } * struct_ptr;
```

How to assign values to the members through pointers will be discussed later.

2.2   Instantiating Structure Variables Using the Structure Tag

The second way to instantiate structure variables is to use the structure tag. This means that we can easily instantiate new structure variables by using the keyword struct and the structure tag of an already-defined structure template that is not anonymous. This provides much greater flexibility because we can instantiate new variables anywhere in the program and as often as we want without having to do it within the structure template definition. Two important considerations here: the structure template has to be already defined, and it must have been assigned a structure tag. Anonymous structures (which are per se legal) cannot be used for this, as the compiler would not know what the structure instance would look like. For example, if the following structure was defined:

```
struct student  {
     char name[20];
     int ID;
     int year;
     char major[30];
     float GPA;
};
```

We could instantiate new variables later in the code by stating:

```
struct student john_smith;
```

just as if we had placed john_smith in the body of the template definition as described in Sect. 2.1. While more flexible than the first way to instantiate, this can also be somewhat cumbersome. Of course, the above two methods are not mutually exclusive, as we can create instances in the template definition as well as later through this method. Nevertheless, let's go on to describe the third way, which is our preferred way to instantiate structure variables.

2.3   Defining New Structure Data Types with `typedef`

Let's back up a bit and describe a very useful feature of C in the context of its strongly typed nature. C allows a programmer to define new data types. Mind you, we don't mean defining new variables of a certain type – we already know how to do that. We specifically mean defining a new type of data! The newly-defined data type can look however we want and it is henceforth treated in the same way as all other data types such as int, float, etc. New data types can be defined with the keyword typedef. Let us next look into the typedef operator, which is also a reserved keyword in C.

The typedef operator requires a name for the new data type being defined. The naming convention is the same as for variable names. Between the typedef keyword and the name of the new data type is the definition of the new type. The format is as follows:

```
typedef <data type definition> <data type name>;
```

For example, we can define a new data type called Var for a particular application program, that would be, for example, long unsigned int, through the following statement:

```
typedef long unsigned int Var;
```

However, this does little more than save us some typing. On the other hand, the availability of the struct data structure gives us some real opportunities here. We can define a new type of data that serves to store student information. We shall call this new data type Student. (The capital S is not a typo – it is intended to make it different from the structure tag student.) The format for this is:

```
typedef struct student   {
     char name[20];
     int ID;
     int year;
     char major[30];
     float GPA;
} Student;
```

Note that the definition of the new data type is found between the `typedef` keyword and the name of the new data type (`Student`). In this case, it happens to be a structure template. Now, every time we wish to instantiate new instances of the `student` structure template, we can simply define them as:

```
Student john_smith;
```

We can also declare.

```
Student course{250};
Student * student_ptr;
```

Keep in mind that the scope of the variables we have instantiated above is local. That is, they are allocated at compile time and once their scope ends, the memory they occupy is returned to the free memory stack for later re-use. This is OK for now, but we will want to define them as global later.

Incidentally, structure instance members can be initialized, similar to how we initialized arrays, using values inside curly brackets, but only when the structure is being instantiated. For example:

```
struct student john = {"Smith", 12345, 3, "Engineering", 3.47};
```

or

```
Student john = {"Smith", 12345, 3, "Engineering", 3.47};
```

Now that we know how to instantiate such variables, as well as pointers to these variables, let's now see how we can use them by initializing them and setting values for their members.

---

3   Member Access Operators: The Dot and the Arrow Operators

Two standard operators in C allow us to access the members of a structure instance. For example, let's say we want to assign the following values to the different members of an instance of structure `student` (not during initialization):

name: John Smith
ID: 1234567
year: 3
major: Computer Science
GPA: 3.75

Accessing the members of a structure require that we specify the name of the structure <u>instance</u> (not the structure tag!) and the name of the member. The *structure member operator*, more commonly known as the *dot operator*, works by using a dot to separate these two labels. The format of the dot operator is as follows:

```
<instance_name>.<member_name>
```

A member of a structure instance that is so identified can have its value read and/or set as if it was a "normal" variable, which of course, it actually is. Let's now put the above in code by incorporating the structure above inside the main () function of our next program. We will instantiate the structure student using the typedef operator and create an instance called john for short.

```
int main()
{
        typedef struct student   {
                char name[20];
                int ID;
                int year;
                char major[30];
                float GPA;
          } Student;

Student john;

john.ID = 1234567;
john.year = 3;
john.GPA = 3.47;

printf("Student ID is %d;   Student is in year %d ; and Student's GPA
     is %f \n", john.ID, john.year, john.GPA);   // same line as above

return 0;
}
```

Go ahead and do it (we won't do the strings just yet – there are things you will need to learn first in Chap. 9.) Now compile it and run it to see that it works.

Now to prove that the structure template named student is <u>not</u> an instance level variable and cannot be used to hold any data, write the following alternative code and let's see what happens:

```
int main()
{
        struct student   {
                char name[20];
                int ID;
                int year;
                char major[30];
                float GPA;
          };
```

```
student.ID = 1234567;
printf("Student  ID  is  %d;    Student  is  in  year  %d ;  and  Student's  GPA
is %f  \n", student.ID);  // same line

return 0;
}
```

Doesn't compile, does it? Aha! It says "error: 'student' undeclared". This is, of course, because the template (aka, its structure tag) is <u>not</u> a working variable and cannot be used other than for instantiating working variables.

One can also work with pointers to structure instances, rather than with the instances directly. While on the surface one would wonder why we would do that when we can just deal with structure instances directly, there is an important application of this in dynamically-allocated memory, when the structure instances don't have names but are instead pointed at by a pointer. We cover this in Chap. 11, so until then, just take our word for it.

The reason we must discuss it here is that the dot operator does not work with pointers to structure instances. So, we must use the *arrow operator* $->$. Officially called the *structure pointer operator*, it works similarly as the dot operator, so it is not that big a deal; but it is a different operator, so we need to learn how to use it.

Similarly to the dot operator, the format for the arrow operator is:

```
<instance_name_ptr> -> <member_name>
```

So, if we already have an instance of the structure student called john, we can declare a pointer to john called john_ptr as follows:

```
Student * john_ptr = &john;
```

We could set the value of john's ID, year and GPA through the pointer with the following statements in main():

```
john_ptr->ID = 12345;
john_ptr->year = 2;
john_ptr->GPA = 3.47;
```

with the calls to printf() as follows:

```
printf("John's ID is %d \n\n", john_ptr->ID);
printf("John's year is %d \n\n", john_ptr->year);
printf("John's GPA is %d \n\n", john_ptr->GPA);
```

The output will be:

```
John's ID is 12345
John's ID is 2
John's ID is 3.470000
```

Which, other than for the flood of zeroes after the 47, is correct. We'll deal with the extra zeroes later.

We will be working much more with the arrow operator when we get to dynamic memory allocation, but we leave this for now.

4   Passing Structures to Functions

Now we consider what to do to pass structures to user-defined functions. To explain this properly through an example, we will define a function called `printout()` that when passed a populated structure instance variable (i.e., one with values assigned to its members), it will print out its (non-string!) contents. A silly excuse for a user-defined function to be sure, but it will serve our purposes just fine.

```c
#include <stdio.h>
#include <stdlib.h>

void printout(Student);

int main()
  {
     typedef struct student  {
       char name[20];
       int ID;
       int year;
       char major[20];
       float GPA;
    }  Student;

  Student john;
  john.ID = 1234567;
  john.year = 3;
  john.GPA = 3.47;

  printout(john);

  return 0;
 }

void printout(Student one)
{
     printf("Student ID is %d; Student is in year %d; and Student's
           GPA = %f \n", one.ID, one.year, one.GPA); // same line
}
```

Type this in your editor, compile it and execute it. What? It doesn't compile? That is because we placed the definition of the structure data type `Student` inside of `main()`. This makes the data type `Student` local to `main()` and means that the definition for our function `printout()` was not able to recognize it when it references the parameter one being of type Student. So, it is important that from now on, we place the structure data type definition outside of main(), thereby making it global in scope (i.e., everything in the file can now see it). Let's now re-write the code as follows:

```
#include <stdio.h>
#include <stdlib.h>

typedef struct student  {
      char name[20];
      int ID;
      int year;
      char major[20];
      float GPA;
  } Student;

void printout(Student);
int main()
 {
    Student john;
    john.ID = 1234567;
    john.year = 3;
    john.GPA = 3.47;

    printout(john);
    return 0;
}

void printout(Student one)
 {
      printf("Student ID is %d ; Student is in year %d ; and Student's"
          "GPA = %f \n", one.ID, one.year, one.GPA);
 }
```

You will find that this now works. So, we managed to pass an entire structure variable of type Student, by value. This is one way to pass (and also return) structures to/from called functions.

Of course, we can also pass individual members just as if we're passing int and float variables like we did earlier in this course. For example (without reproducing the entire program here) we could pass a single member to some other user-defined function called function1() (not shown) as follows:

```
function1(john.ID);
```

We should emphasize here that we didn't use the function printout() in our example just above because it does not accept single members as it was defined, but rather, an entire structure. Therefore, that would not have worked. Instead, function function1() is a notional function (i.e., not actually defined nor shown here) that would be defined to accept individual member variables.

If we wanted to pass a structure instance by reference, we could do so by passing pointers to structure instances (i.e., their addresses). This means we would have to use the arrow operator in the user-defined function (but no big deal otherwise). For example,

```c
#include <stdio.h>
#include <stdlib.h>

typedef struct student  {
        char name[20];
        int ID;
        int year;
        char major[20];
        float GPA;
     } Student;

void printout(Student);
void reset(Student *);

int main()
{
    Student john;
    Student * john_ptr = &john;

    john_ptr->ID = 12345;
    john_ptr->year = 2;
    john_ptr->GPA = 3.47;

    printout(john);
    printf("\n");
    reset(john_ptr);
    printout(john);

    return 0;
}

void printout(Student one)
{
    printf("Student ID is %d; Student is in year %d; and Student GPA
      = %f \n", one.ID, one.year, one.GPA); // on same line
}

void reset(Student * two)
{
   two->ID = 67890;
   two->year = 5;
   two->GPA = 1.92;
}
```

The rather convoluted code initially assigns values to three of the members of john in main(), and prints out their values for verification by calling the function printout() from main(). Note that printout() is called by value, as it does not need to change anything in john. It then passes the address of john through the pointer john_ptr to the function reset() that changes the values of the (non-string) instance members of john. This call is done by reference, as reset() does need to make changes to the values of members in john. Then printout() is called again (by value!) from main() to verify that the values were indeed modified by reset(). This program illustrates passing structures instances by value (to printout()) and by reference (to reset()). The output should be as follows:

```
Student ID is 12345; Student is in year 2; and Student GPA = 3.470000
Student ID is 67890; Student is in year 5; and Student GPA = 1.920000
```

Implement the code above and see for yourself. Then modify the code to pass john to printout() by reference.

5   Structures, Arrays, and Loops

Structures and arrays go well together. The ability of an array to group large numbers of similar variables synergistically compensates for the major limitation of structures – the inability to do just that. Now that we defined a structure as a new data type, the array can group together structure instances, as they are all of the same data type.

Moreover, members of structure instances can contain arrays. Incidentally, structure instance members can also be other structures, but this is less common, so we will skip this for now and concentrate on arrays and pointers.

Say we want an array containing all the students in a class, for example, ENG 101. Our data type Student represents a structure of type student, as we saw in previous exercises. We have 250 students in the class, so we create an array called eng_101[250] to store information for all students. We begin with:

```
Student eng_101[250];
```

The definition above specifies that the array eng_101[] contains 250 instances of the data type Student, which of course, we know that it is a structure data type of the struct student template. So, we see that by placing them in an array, one can easily instantiate multiple struct instances in one fell swoop.

Now let's say that all the students in ENG 101 are in their first year of college, so we want to initialize the value of their member named year to 1. We can easily do this in a loop that goes through every member year of every cell in eng_101[] and sets its value to 1 as shown in the code below.

```
    typedef struct student   {
      char name[20];
      int ID;
      int year;
      char major[20];
      float GPA;
    } Student;

int main()
{
   Student eng_101[250];
   int n;

   for(n=0; n<250; n++) {
      eng_101[n].year = 1;
      printf("The value of cell %d is %d \n", n, eng_101[n].year);
      }

   return 0;
}
```

There will be a lot of printing to screen here, but you will see that it should print:

```
The value of cell 0 is 1
The value of cell 1 is 1
      .

      .

The value of cell 249 is 1
```

We chose the `year` member because it is the only one that could plausibly be the same for all students in the class. None of the other members could realistically have the same value for every student. That would mean typing in each one of those values, one by one. So, that is not practical to do until we learn how to read and write to/from external files (which will come soon enough).

This example also gives the learner the ability to see how one would handle members of structures placed in arrays. That is, using the array name and cell number as the name of the structure instance in front of the dot operator.

---

6   Summary and Conclusion

This chapter introduced a second important data structure in C called the `struct`. The major difference between structures and arrays is that `structs` can hold more than one type of data as variables, including pointers. One disadvantage to `structs` is that several such structure instances cannot be strung together as can cells in an array. Nevertheless, arrays and structures are very synergistic, as one can place structure instances in an array and in that way string several of them together. Likewise, the members of a structure instance can contain arrays.

The struct keyword is used to declare a template of the desired structure, from which instances can be created (instantiated). The original template cannot hold values, as it does not define an actual set of variables. Instances of the template must be generated, and these can hold data and be manipulated as variables. We discussed the three main ways to instantiate instance(s) of a struct in program: 1) listing the names of the instances at the end of the struct template definition; 2) Using the keyword struct followed by the structure tag and the name(s) of the instance(s) anywhere in the program after the template has been defined, and; 3) defining a new data type with typedef that is based on the defined struct template, and simply declaring new instances in the same way as one would define normal variables. The last is the one preferred here, but all three work just fine.

We also discussed how to initialize structure members upon instantiation as well as how to assign values to the members of a struct instance. The dot operator is used to directly assign values to the struct instance members, while the arrow operator is used to assign values indirectly through a pointer that points to an instance of struct. The arrow operator will become more important when we learn how to allocate memory dynamically (at run time).

Next, we learned that structure instances can be passed to user-defined functions, individually as well as part of arrays. Structure instances can be passed by value as well as by reference. The important thing to remember here is that the definition of the structure template must be defined as global, as is the type definition. Individual members of a structure instance can also be passed as if they were normal variables.

Finally, we saw the relationship between structures and arrays, and how the two data structures, which are fundamentally different, are so complementary. We also saw how to use structures in loops.

7   Problems

1) Write a program that contains a structure that can hold information about the eight (nine?) planets in the solar system. This information is *num* (an integer indicating the position of this planet in relation to distance to the sun (e.g., Mercury = 1, Earth = 3, Neptune = 7, etc.), *moons* (integer), *radius* in 1000 Km (integer) and *mass* in Kg/cubic Km (floating point). Create eight (nine if you want to includes Pluto) independent instances of this structure. Look up the correct values in the Internet and assign them to the corresponding members of these instances. No output is necessary, but you should verify its correctness by inserting some printf() statements that print out some of the values of the planets (you can skip the name, as it is a string).

2) Continue working with problem 1) above by placing the eight/nine instances in an array. Verify that they are accessible by inserting printf() statements to print out the values held by the instance members.

3) Continue working with problem 1) above by creating pointers to structure instances for each of the eight/nine planets. Set the values of the members of the structure instances indirectly through the pointers and the arrow operators. Use printf() statements to verify that the values were assigned properly.

Strings and Advanced I/O

9

This chapter is a combination of two topics, neither of which is enough to warrant one chapter by itself. Here we provide more details on two concepts that you have already seen: strings and input/output. We begin with strings.

1 Strings – A Deeper Treatment

We have already looked at strings, albeit on a superficial level. Now we dive into them at a deeper level, armed with the knowledge that a string is a character array, and therefore, a pointer to the first element of said array. We already discussed the initialization of string variables in Chap. 7, but it is good to review it here.

1.1 Initializing Strings

Given that strings are arrays, it should suggest that the operator we used for assigning number values to variables (=) wouldn't work with strings because they don't work with "normal" arrays. Interestingly, in spite of this, strings can be initialized using such operators. For example:

```
char str[] = {"Hi ya'll!"};
char * str1 = "By gosh!";
```

Surprisingly, both statements above work! The first one is clear in that it involves an array of characters because the type is `char`. We initialize it almost the same way we would for any other array, except now we have the quotation marks " " around the string literal, and the characters are not comma-delineated, as are the initial values of "normal" arrays. The second statement is somewhat more surprising because it creates a pointer to a character. It is counter-intuitive because it allows a pointer to be assigned something that does not look like an address, as we did previously for pointers. In both cases, the compiler knows to make it point to the first character of the quoted string. Alternatively, the combination of the two statements:

© Springer Nature Switzerland AG 2020
A. J. Gonzalez, *Computer Programming in C for Beginners*,
https://doi.org/10.1007/978-3-030-50750-3_9

```
char * str2;
str2 = "Go Knights!";
```

also works. In all of the above cases, we are initializing either an array, or pointers that point to characters. However, note that the following will <u>not</u> work (try it and see for yourself.)

```
char * str3;
str3 = {"Go Knights - all the way!"};
```

Adding the last line causes compilation to fail because the curly brackets { } only mean something in the context of array initialization.

Note that the assignment operator = works when assigning a value to a string, but <u>only</u> during initialization. If we write:

```
char str4[25] = {"My name is John."};
char str5[25];
str5 = str4;
```

This does not work (will not compile) because ultimately, strings are arrays and arrays cannot be assigned values in this fashion.

Instead, strings can only be manipulated through certain standard library functions whose prototypes are found in string.h. So, always be sure to include this .h file in all your programs.

```
#include <string.h>
```

Let's now see what these functions are and how to use them to set the value of the previously defined str5 from str4.

1.2   Setting Values to String Variables

Let's now replace the last statement in Sect. 1.1 above (str5 = str4;) with a standard C function called strcpy() that has two strings for arguments as follows:

```
strcpy(str5, str4);
```

strcpy() will assign (in reality, copy) the string in the second argument (str4) to the first argument (str5). Now, let's add the following line to the program:

```
printf("%s\n", str5);
```

It will print.

```
My name is John.
```

This is how strings are assigned to string variables, other than during initialization.

For more examples, type into your IDE editor the following code:

```
char str6[50];
strcpy(str6, "I am happy to be a C programmer!");
printf("%s\n", str6);
```

The program will print out

```
I am happy to be a C programmer!
```

In effect, `strcpy()` acts as the assignment operator = for strings.

1.3 The Length of a String

Next, we take a look at `strlen()`. This is an easy one. We'll use `str6` from our example above, so assume that `str6` has already been defined and contains the string `I am happy to be a C programmer!`. The function `strlen()` accepts a string (either a variable or a literal) and returns an integer value equal to the length of the string passed to it. That is the number of characters that the string contains. We can put it right inside a `printf()` statement. Now the statement.

```
printf("The length of string str6 is %d \n", strlen(str6));
```

will print out.

```
The length of string str6 is 32
```

Which, of course, is correct (count them!). Note that spaces are counted but the \0 NULL terminator is not.

1.4 Comparing Strings

Next let's work with a function that serves to compare strings for lexicographical order. It generally serves the same purpose that the equality operator (==) did for numbers and characters, except it provides more information than just **true** or **false**. This function is called the `strcmp()` function. Its arguments include two strings to be compared to each other. The function `strcmp()` returns a negative number when its first argument is lexicographically less than its second argument. It returns a positive number when the opposite is true, and 0 when the two strings are identical. We will use the strings `str` and `str1` that we have already defined and to which we have assigned values above.

Let's begin by comparing `str` (contains "Hi ya'll!"} to `str1` (contains "By gosh!") through the following statement:

```
strcmp(str1, str); // str has "Hi ya'll!" and str1 has "By gosh!"
```

Lexicographically, a 'B' comes before (i.e., is less than) an 'H', so `str1` would come before (would be less than) `str` because it begins with a 'B' (as in "**B**y gosh!"), while `str` begins with an 'H' (as in "**H**i ya'll!). Given that `str1` indeed is less than `str`, `strcmp()` will return a negative number. Let's verify that:

```
char str[] = {"Hi y'all!"};
char * str1 = "By gosh!";
int n;
n = strcmp(str1, str);
printf("The value returned by strcmp() is %d \n", n);
```

Sure enough, it prints out:

```
The value returned by strcmp() is -1.
```

Now let's change the order and make the comparison statement be:

```
strcmp(str, str1);
```

We won't show you the complete code for this (you should be able to figure it out yourself) but the output in this revised case is now:

```
The value returned by strcmp() is 1.
```

Of course, if we compare two identical strings using the following comparison.

```
strcmp(str1, str1);
```

The program will print out

```
The value returned by strcmp() is 0.
```

The value of this function comes when a comparison of two strings can lead to a selection of several statements to execute, as in a selection structure. For instance:

```
if(strcmp(str, str1) == 0)
   printf("The strings are identical");
else
   printf("The strings are not the same");
```

Of course, we can do much more with this, such as sort lists of strings by alphabetical order. But for now, let's move on.

1.5   Concatenating Strings

The word *concatenate* means to link things together. In our context here, it is interpreted as attaching one string to the end of another string. To do this in C, we use the function strcat(), which takes two argument strings. This function tacks on the second argument string to the end of the first argument (i.e., destination) string. In doing so, it will overwrite the NULL terminator (\0) of the first string. Furthermore, strcat() also performs an implicit assignment of the newly concatenated string to the destination string variable in its argument list. By doing this, the destination string variable now holds the newly-concatenated string. This is important to remember, as it means that the value of the string variable in the first argument is now modified from its original value. However, be sure that the size of the array of the first argument is large enough to accommodate the newly-concatenated string. That is why the sizes of the arrays are set to a relatively large number (40) in the code just below. For example,

```
char str7[40] = {"My name is "};
char str8[40] = {"John Smith"};
strcat(str7, str8);
printf("The new value of str7 is now: %s \n", str7);
```

The printed output will be:

```
The new value of str7 is now: My name is John Smith
```

Of course, if we reverse the order of the arguments of the `strcat()` function and print out `str8`, we get an awkward, Yoda-like statement:

```
The new value of str7 is now: John SmithMy name is
```

without the benefit of a space between `h` and `M`.

OK, enough for strings, as you now should know enough to perform relatively complex manipulations of strings. We now go on to discuss other ways to enter strings from the keyboard which are in some ways better than `scanf()`.

2   Other Input/Output Functions in C for Characters and Strings

We mentioned earlier that there are other input/output functions in C besides the `printf()` and the `scanf()`, specifically as they relate to strings. This is where we introduce them.

2.1   The `puts()` Function

The `puts()` function prints the string passed to it as an argument to the standard output (the screen display in our case), automatically followed by a newline. It returns an integer value, but this is in most cases useless.

Let's work with the `puts()` a little bit. Please write the following short program:

```
#include <stdio.h>
#include <stdlib.h>
#include <string.h>

int main()
{
    char str1[] = {"My favorite sport is football …"};
    printf("Hello world!\n");
    puts(str1);
    puts("… followed by football, and then football");

    return 0;
}
```

The output is, as you would expect:

```
Hello world!
My favorite sport is football …
… followed by football, and then football
```

Note how `puts()` placed the newline after it printed the string without us telling it explicitly to do so, as we had to do with `printf()`. However, it will not print numbers (unless inside the string), or print the values of variables, or evaluate expressions, as does `printf()`. Try placing the following statement after the second `puts()` but before the `return`:

```
puts(10);
```

And see how it returns a runtime error (although it does compile, albeit with a warning). `puts()` is strictly for printing strings; and for that, it is easier to use than `printf()` in many ways.

2.2   The `putchar()` Function

A second output function is the `putchar()`. As its name suggests, it will print out a character passed to it as an argument.

Try adding the following statement to the above program:

```
putchar('a');
```

You will see that it will print out `a` as requested. However, note that it does not include a newline, as did `puts()`. This is likely because, in most applications, it is unlikely that one will wish to print one character per line.

If one would like to use this function to print out a string, it would have to be placed in a loop and print out one character at a time. Sure, that can be done, but what is the point when we have `puts()` and `printf()` that can do it more easily (for the programmer).

2.3   The `gets()` Function

The `gets()` function is the input "mate", so to speak, to `puts()`. `gets()` is specifically useful when seeking strings from the user via the keyboard. It reads a string from the standard input stream (the keyboard) and stores it in the array passed to it as an argument. It stops when it encounters a newline, and appends the NULL terminator (`\0`) automatically to the end of the string.

The big advantage to `gets()` is that it can accept white spaces – something `scanf()` cannot do. To prove this, enter the following code into your program above (you may wish to comment out all other statements to avoid clutter):

```
char str2[20];
puts("Enter a string");
gets(str2);
puts(str2);
```

Now, compile, run and enter something that contains white spaces (e.g., My name is John Smith), and you'll see that it does not stop when it sees the whitespace, as would scanf(). This is its major advantage over scanf() when reading strings. However, it cannot read anything other than strings.

2.4   The getchar() Function

We discuss this function only for the sake of completeness. The getchar() function is the mate of putchar(). It is much less useful than gets(), as it only accepts a character from the keyboard, and does not assign it to any variable. Therefore, it takes no arguments. It returns the integer equivalent of the character entered as per the ASCII table, which one can then assign to a char variable. However, we have not discussed this table or the relationship between integers and characters. So we will not discuss it any further. However, if you are inextricably overcome with curiosity, try the following code:

```
char a;
puts("Enter one character");
a=getchar();
putchar(a);
```

Enter x (or any character) and it will print it right back.

The main takeaways from this section is that there are alternatives to printf() and scanf() that are easier to use for strings and characters. However, they do not work for evaluating variables or expressions, as does printf().

3   Optional Formatting Features of printf()

There are several features of printf() that we have not yet explored. The printf() function actually permits a certain level of format control by the programmer for its output. The actual complete format for printf() when specifying something to print is:

```
%[flags][width][.precision]type_specifier
```

Where the fields enclosed in straight brackets are optional. That's why we have been able to ignore them up to this point. We'll start with the type specifiers.

We have already learned how to use the %d, %f, %lf, %c, %p and %s type specifiers, respectively for int, float, double, and char types, plus pointers and strings. So, we won't repeat what you already (should) know. However, there are other type specifiers in C. You probably won't be using these at a beginner programmer level, but here are some of these other ones anyway (just in case).

For integer values:

- %i: signed decimal integer (same as d in printf(), but not for scanf())
- %u: unsigned decimal integer
- %o: unsigned octal integer
- %x or %X: unsigned hexadecimal integer (a-f or A-F)

- `%hi` **or** `%hu`: Modifies the integer specifier to mean short (the h). Allocates smaller blocks of memory space for storing integer variables to economize memory use when using low integer values.
- `%li` **or** `%lu`: Modifies the integer specifier to mean long (the l). Allocates twice as much memory as the default integer size for the individual computer when very large integers are being used.

For real number values, there are several other specifiers in addition to `f` and `lf`:

- `%E` **or** `%e`: Floating point number in scientific notation – e.g., 1.234567E+006 or 1.234567e+006
- `%G` **or** `%g`: Can do either floating point values or scientific notation, depending on some criteria with regards to the number itself.

We now describe and discuss the optional formatting features of the `printf()` function. These optional features are within the square brackets in the format above. We shall start with the `width`.

3.1   The `width` Specifier

If we simply print out an integer value with `%d`, the `printf()` function will merely print it out. However, if we want to make columns to spread out the numbers, possibly to fall under separate headings in a table, we can set the field width to what we want with this optional field specification. For example, if we want to make the column width five spaces, we can do so as follows:

```
int n = 55, m = 27;
printf("The values of n and m are %5d %5d \n", n, m);
```

The digit 5 between the `%` and the `d` indicates that we want a field of 5 characters (minimum!) width. Note that the printout will be as follows:

```
The values of n and m are    55    27
```

Likewise, we can increase the field to 10 by replacing the digit 5 by `10` in the specifier (`%10d`). This produces an output of:

```
The value of n and m are            55            27
```

This can facilitate the construction of tabular outputs (tables). For example, type in, compile and execute the following code (as part of a C program):

```
int n;
for(n=0; n<10; n++)
  printf("%15d%15d \n", n, n+10);
```

The output will look as follows:

```
        0               10
        1               11
        2               12
        3               13
        4               14
        5               15
        6               16
        7               17
        8               18
        9               19
```

Now you have the makings of a nicely-formatted table.

Next, try making the integer to be printed larger than the size of the field. You will see that it will enlarge the size of the field to fit it in. This is because remember that the `width` is the minimum size of the field! We won't show you that here - you can try it yourself.

The `width` specifier works differently for real numbers (`float` and `double`). If you recall when we printed out such real numbers in previous chapters and the number of digits after the decimal point was six (e.g., `12.000000`), which were way too many. That is the (normal) default `width` specifier for `float` and `double` values after the decimal point when real numbers are printed with `printf()`. This default depends on the specific compiler used, but most use six as the default. This default value now plays a role in the size of the field for real numbers. When one includes the whole numbers (before the decimal point) and the decimal point itself, the number of digits could well exceed the size of the specified field width `width`. As it does with integers, the size of the field expands beyond the minimum width specified, but the values can run on each other, making the output nearly unreadable. For example:

```
float x = 72.23, y = 106.81;
printf("The values for floating point are: %5f%5f \n", x, y);
```

The above statements specify a field width of 5 characters. However, the variable x already has 5 digits (the `72` plus the decimal point plus the `23` = 5 spaces). When the default 6 significant digits after the decimal point are added, the necessary width of the field is increased to 9 (the 72 plus the decimal point plus the default 6). This makes the printed output `72.230000`. It is worse for y as it will need a field that will be 10 characters wide to fit it in, with the output being `106.810000`. So, the complete output would now look like this:

```
The values for floating point are: 72.230000106.810000
```

Please write, compile and run this little program to see for yourself.

That output is rather hard to visualize properly for us humans, right? So, we can do two things. The obvious one is to increase the width of the field. If we increase it to 15 for each variable, no problem! Try it.

```
float x = 72.23, y = 106.81;
printf("The values for floating point are: %15f%15f \n", x, y);
```

The output is now:

```
The values for floating point are:        72.230000        106.810000
```

This is much nicer, right?

The problem is that we still have the meaningless (for this application) four digits after the last meaningful digit to the right of the decimal point. This can be fixed with the second of the two optional specification in `printf()` - the .precision.

3.2   The .precision Specifier

This second optional specifier allows us to limit (or increase!) the number of significant digits printed <u>after</u> the decimal point. It requires a period in front of it to identify it to the compiler, and it is placed <u>after</u> the `width` specifier. The use of the period makes it intuitive, as you are really specifying how many significant digits are to be printed after the decimal point. So sticking with the floating point values in our example (which is really the main reason this feature exists) and limiting the number of digits to two (2) as shown below:

```
float x = 72.23, y = 106.81;
printf("The values for floating point are: %15.2f%15.2f \n", x, y);
```

See below for the output. (We included the previous `printf()` in the first line, as it was in the using the prior format <u>without</u> the precision specification so we could easily compare). Now the output looks even better!

```
The values for floating point are:        72.230000        106.810000
The values for floating point are:            72.23            106.81
```

But what if we have an application that requires extreme precision? We use double precision variables and need to increase the precision to 10 digits after the decimal point.

```
double a = 47.963815834769, b = 216.345674621879;
printf("For double pres. Fl. Pt: %20.12lf%20.12lf \n", a, b);
```

Yields an output of

```
For double pres. Fl. Pt:      47.963815834769      216.345674621879
```

So, yes, as shown above, we can also increase the number of significant digits after the decimal point beyond the default 6 spaces.

Some more examples,

```
printf("%.2lf", 43.216495);
```

The line above will print `43.21` instead of `43.216495` because the precision specifier of `.2` dictates that only two significant figures are to be printed after the decimal point.

It works a bit different for integers. For integers, it specifies the number of digits to be printed. It pads the number with zeroes on the left of the number if the integer to be printed is smaller than the precision.

So we move right on to the flag specifier.

3.3   The flag Specifier

The flag specifier is the third optional specifier in printf(). It involves preceding the width specifier with one of several symbols (characters) that act as *flags* to signal to printf() that it must do certain things, as specified by the programmer. Because they are characters (actually, not all of them), they are not confused with the width specifier.

The minus sign '–' in front of the width specifier makes all the numbers left-justified, instead of right-justified, which is the default. Try modifying your existing code above with a – in front of the width specifier. You will see that the numbers change position inside the field, although the field size remains the same as originally specified.

A plus sign '+' forces the sign of the number to be shown, even if positive (e.g. 5 would be printed as +5).

A zero '0' (this is the exception to all the flags being characters) in front of the width specifier pads with zeroes instead of spaces (see "width"). So, try putting a 0 and take out the –. You will see a bunch of zeroes taking up the spaces which previously were empty. Not pretty, so it is unlikely that you will need this flag. For example,

```
printf("%+05d", 47);
```

would print +0047 instead of 47. Notice that the field width is 5, as specified by the width option. Also note that the above line actually uses two flags, the + and the 0.

We now put to bed the discussion about formatting with printf() by providing one last example/exercise. Please go ahead and type in the following in your editor inside main():

```
printf("The number is %4d\n", 123); // field wider than the number
printf("The number is %4d\n", 1234); // field same size as number
printf("The number is %4d\n", 12345); // number larger than field
printf("The number is %5d\n", 1234); // field wider than number
printf("The number is %8.6d\n", 1234); // integer > precision
printf("The number is %+8.6d\n", 1234); // puts the + sign
printf("The number is %+8.6f\n", 1234.); // float number
printf("The number is %+8.2f\n", 1.234); // float number
```

The output will be:

```
The number is  123
The number is 1234
The number is 12345
The number is  1234
The number is   001234
The number is  +001234
The number is +1234.000000
The number is    +1.23
```

Please take a close look at the spacing to confirm that the program worked correctly. Keep in mind that there is one blank space between is and % inside the quotes in each of the above printf() statements. This means that there will be at least one space between is and the field in the printed output. So, when you count the spaces to verify the specifications above, be sure to account for this space, as the field begins <u>after</u> this one blank space. The most interesting one is the fifth statement, where the width of the field is 8 and the precision for the integer is 6. The number only occupies four spaces (1234), but because it is an integer whose precision is six, the other two spaces are padded with zeroes in the output. However, not the entire width of 8 is padded with zeroes – just up to the precision. We encourage you to experiment further with statements such as those above, but leave it up to you.

3.4   Really Long Strings in printf()

One last thing before we leave the discussion on printf(). If you have a very long string literal in a printf() and you'd like to have it shown on multiple lines <u>in the printf() statement</u>, just close the string at the end of one line with a " and reopen it on the next line with another ", like so:

```
printf("This is a really, really, really, really, really, really, "
          "really long string\n");
```

OK, please experiment with these optional format specifiers to learn more about how they work.

4   Escape Characters

We now bring your attention to the symbol \n that we have been using within the printf() quotes to force a new line to print in the output. Now it is time to explain what it is and how it works.

Oftentimes when printing out a literal string, we would like to insert therein some characters that have a special meaning. We don't want printf() to just print out the character at face value, but instead, implement its special meaning or functionality. To do this, the programmer must tell the compiler that this character is not to be taken literally (even though it is inside the quotation marks in the printf()), but rather have it do whatever the special character does. We use *escape characters* to accomplish this. The escape character, as you may have already guessed, is the backslash \. The character that immediately follows it is the one with the special meaning that we would like to have do its thing. In this case, n causes a newline to be printed. So, when it sees an \n inside its string literal, the printf() function now knows that n is not really an n to be printed out literally, but rather, an indication that a newline is to be printed. Many other meaningful characters in C will also require an escape character in front of it. Some of the more common ones include \t for tab and the NULL terminator \0.

Interestingly enough, sometimes we may wish to do the converse – that is, actually print out a single or double quote, or even a backslash as part of our output. The escape character also helps us in that regard. For including a double quote in the output without causing printf() to think that it ends the string, we can use \". Likewise, for \' and \\.

Note that the % character also serves as an escape character by telling the compiler that what follows it is the data type specifier. However, % only has this special meaning in the context of printf() and not in the C language in general, as it is also used for integer division (mod). However, if we wish to print a literal % in a string in printf(), we use %%, rather than \%.

5   External File I/O

This is an important concept in programming, as writing to screen would be very limiting if it were the only form of output. One often needs to save data to a permanent form of storage that survives the end of the program, as well as reading from files that may contain much data. This can easily be done with variants of the functions `printf()` and `scanf()` that work very similarly to `printf()` and `scanf()`. These variants are called `fprintf()` and `fscanf()` (the f, of course, stands for file). The main difference between these variants and the corresponding print-to-screen originals is that the former need to be told exactly where the output is to be written. We begin first by showing you how to <u>write</u> to external files.

5.1   Writing to External Files

Say we have an integer array of 10 cells with arbitrary integer values.

```
int a[] = {10, 11, 12, 13, 14, 15, 16, 17, 18, 19};
```

We wish to preserve these data by writing them to an external file in the hard drive called `data_a.txt` which will be located in the same directory as the program. We can do this as follows:

First, we define a pointer of type `FILE`. This pointer will serve to indicate the location of the file to which we want to write the contents of array `a[]`.

```
FILE * fout;
```

`FILE` is a standard library variable type definition and is prototyped in `stdio.h`. `fout` is just the name we chose for the pointer that we just defined. We can call it any name we want as long as it is legal, but `fout` is typically used by convention.

Next, we open the file to which we want to write the output using the following statement:

```
fout = fopen("data_a.txt", "w");
```

The standard C function `fopen()` will create a file with the name specified in the first field within the parentheses. It returns an address in memory where this file is located. We proceed to assign that address to our just declared `FILE` pointer `fout`. Through this pointer is how we access this new file. The "w" inside the second set of quotes tells the compiler that this file is to be written to, thus the w. There are other such specifiers, such as "r" for reading from the file and "a" to append, among others. Simple enough, right? Well, not so fast.

What if the opening of this new file fails for some reason? It is usually for lack of memory, but could be other reasons, such as an illegal file name being specified. In this case, the function `fopen` will return an address of `NULL`. However, it won't indicate an error or stop execution – it will simply and quietly return `NULL`. This places the burden on the programmer to catch these failure-to-launch problems, so to speak, when they come up. Therefore, we should always test the output of `fopen()` for `NULL,` and alert the user and discontinue execution when this happens.

For expediency, we will assume here that `fopen()` will <u>not</u> return NULL. However, you should never, ever make this assumption in your programs! We'll discuss what to do about this a bit later in this chapter, but for now, this (faulty!) assumption holds.

The `fprintf()` function is almost identical to `printf()` except that it requires one more field: the address where the file that is to receive the output is located. This added field is the very first one within the parentheses of fprintf(), in front of the string specification field. The easy part is that all it needs is the name of the pointer to the file to which it is to write the output. fprintf() will take care of the rest automatically.

We now write the fprintf() function in a loop that will write each cell of the array a[] to this file. We put all the statements together below. The fclose() function closes the file. This is important if one wants to be sure that the file is not corrupted and/or it is to be used again later in the same program or by other programs before this program terminates. Most operating systems will automatically close the file after the program terminates if the program left it open, but the fclose() makes sure it is closed, closed correctly and promptly. It is good programming practice. So,

```
int a[] = {10, 11, 12, 13, 14, 15, 16, 17, 18, 19};
int n;
FILE * fout;
fout = fopen("data_a.txt", "w"); // We assume it does NOT return NULL
for(n=0; n<10; n++)
     fprintf(fout, "%d", a[n]);
fclose(fout);
```

Now leave the IDE and go to the operating system. Find the data_a.txt file that the program above just created and open it. You will see that the output written to the file looks like this:

```
10111213141516171819
```

This format makes it hard to read later when we would want to read in these data. A better approach would be to make the fprintf() function as follows (all other statements remain the same):

```
fprintf(fout, "%d ", a[n]); // note the space between the d and the "
```

Now the output looks like:

```
10 11 12 13 14 15 16 17 18 19
```

which is much easier to read later. Even better is if we put a newline (\n) to put one number in each line:

```
fprintf(fout, "%d\n", a[n]);
```

Now the file looks like this:

```
10
11
12
13
14
15
16
17
18
19
```

We can do both: place various numbers in one line and then have other lines. Say we have a second array:

```
int b[] = {20, 21, 22, 23, 24, 25, 26, 27, 28, 29};
```

Because we want to write two variables in each line, our code snippet would now look like this:

```
int a[] = {10, 11, 12, 13, 14, 15, 16, 17, 18, 19};
int b[] = {20, 21, 22, 23, 24, 25, 26, 27, 28, 29};
int n;
FILE * fout;
fout = fopen("data_a.txt", "w");
for(n=0; n<10; n++)
     fprintf(fout, "%d %d \n", a[n], b[n]);
fclose(fout);
```

Now the output looks like this

```
10 20
11 21
12 22
13 23
14 24
15 25
16 26
17 27
18 28
19 29
```

One last thing: when `fopen()` sees the "w" in its argument, it assumes that a file by the name included in the same argument list <u>does not exist</u> and must therefore be created. If perchance a file by this same name already happens to exist, `fopen()` will simply overwrite it, thereby permanently destroying any data therein. So, be careful when you specify the name of the file to be created for writing to.

OK, please practice with this, especially how you would write members of a structure to external files.

Actually, writing to file is relatively easy. Reading from files, however, is a bit trickier. One must first know how the data are formatted in the file to be read. Let's go there next.

5.2   Reading from External Files

As we saw for `fprintf()`, `fscanf()` likewise requires the extra field that will tell it from where to read the input data. Therefore, it also needs to have the pointer to the file. This added field also goes at the front of the parenthetical expression that makes the argument list. Keep in mind that when `fopen()` sees an "r" and a file name, the file must already exist and be in the proper directory. Otherwise, it will fail to open it and return `NULL`. Let's show by example:

For reading from files we define arrays c[10] and d[10], We will use these arrays to store the data that we will read from the file data_a.txt that we created in the previous section. So:

```
int c[10], d[10];
int n;
FILE * fin;
fin = fopen("data_a.txt", "r");
for(n=0; n<10; n++)
      fscanf(fin, "%d %d", &c[n], &d[n]);
fclose(fin);
for (n=0; n<10; n++)
      printf("%d %d \n", c[n], d[n]);
```

Some changes we made that should be noted are: 1) We left c[] and d[] un-initialized so that we don't confuse the (human) reader. In this case, we don't need to initialize these arrays because we will be inserting data into them soon after defining them. 2) We used a file pointer named fin to hold the address of the file to be read. Once again, this particular name is just convention. 3) We used "r" in the fopen() function to indicate that we will be reading from this file, and not writing or doing anything else. 4) The fscanf() is set to read the values that we wrote out to data_a.txt in the previous part of this exercise. It should read the values and place them in arrays c[] and d[]. 5) We added a printf() to print to screen the contents of c[] and d[] after they have been populated with the data read from the file to verify that it worked. 6) Let's not forget the pesky & in front of the variables on fscanf()! We are setting the values read to specific variables, even if these variables are part of an array. 7) Don't forget to fclose() the files!

One last thing. Let's include the writing and reading functions in the same program. Very few applications would warrant this, but we want to use this to show the importance of fclose(). We now combine the last two snippets of code into one program as follows:

```
int a[] = {10, 11, 12, 13, 14, 15, 16, 17, 18, 19};
int b[] = {20, 21, 22, 23, 24, 25, 26, 27, 28, 29};
int n;
FILE * fout;
fout = fopen("data_a.txt", "w");
for(n=0; n<10; n++)
   fprintf(fout, "%d %d\n", a[n], b[n]);
fclose(fout);
int c[15];
int d[15];
FILE * fin;
fin = fopen("data_a.txt", "r");
for(n=0; n<10; n++)
    fscanf(fin, "%d %d\n", &c[n], &d[n]);
for(n=0; n<10; n++)
    printf("%d %d\n", c[n], d[n]);
fclose(fin);
```

Place this code into a complete program, compile and execute it. You will see that it will work well, printing out

```
10 20
11 21
12 22
13 23
14 24
15 25
16 26
17 27
18 28
19 29
```

Now comment out `fclose(fout);` (the one in **bold-face font**). You will notice that the results will not be correct, resulting in a modicum of garbage being printed out. Yet, after the program finishes executing, check out the file `data_a.txt` just created by the program and you will see that file closed properly and contains the correct data. What happened was that `fopen()` had a problem when trying to open a file (to read it) that was not closed. This underscores the need to always close your files as soon as you're done with them.

5.3   What About That Thing Where `fopen()` Returns `NULL`?

Before concluding this chapter, we still need to discuss this issue a bit more. As we said earlier, if there is insufficient memory or the name of the function is illegal, the file won't open successfully. Rather than declaring a runtime error and suspending execution, `fopen()` just returns `NULL` for the address of the file it presumably opened. This is unfortunate, of course, but it has a pretty easy solution: we simply call `fopen()` within the test of a single conditional structure and compare the value it returns to `NULL`. See below:

```
FILE * fin;
if ((fin=fopen("results.dat", "r")) == NULL)
      {
          printf("file could not be opened;
          return 0;
      }
<.. everything you want to do ..>}
```

By including `return 0;`, the function ends its execution. If `main()`, then the program ends altogether. If not `main()`, then you will want to use `exit()`, which aborts the program. Case closed.

6   Summary and Conclusion

This chapter covered several important issues in computer programming. While not as fundamental as what we covered in the previous chapters, these concepts represent very important steps forward as you advance in your knowledge and seek to write more complex programs.

The ability to create and manipulate strings is one of these, as the use and manipulation of strings is an essential aspect of programming. Given your familiarization with pointers and arrays, strings became easier to understand, not only at a conceptual level, but also at a practical one. Strings are simply character arrays. However, they enjoy special treatment not extended to normal arrays. This includes assigning strings to string variables when being initialized upon definition, and how to receive them as inputs, as well as how to output them. We also introduced and discussed various standard library string manipulation functions prototyped in `string.h`.

Also introduced were four alternative input/output functions for characters and strings: `puts()`, `gets()`, `putchar()` and `getchar()`. These standard library functions can facilitate the input and output of strings.

We have been working with `printf()` since Chap. 1. We had learned to do some simple things with it, but here we found that it offers the programmer some other options for printing outputs in different formats. These can make it easier to print tables. These options include setting the minimum width of a field, specifying the number of digits to be printed after the decimal point and several flags that can specify variations in how the output is to be printed.

Lastly and importantly, we learned how to read from and write to external files. We did this with variants of the `printf()` and `scanf()` functions. The only (major) difference is that these variants need to know where the file to which the function will be writing to or reading from is located. This information is provided by declaring a pointer of type `FILE` and setting its value by executing the `fopen()` function.

Examples and exercises were provided for all of these concepts.

7   Problems

1) Write a program that takes the temperature data collected in a problem in the last chapter and writes it out to an external file.
2) Write a program that takes an already populated array of structures for students in a class, as was done in the last chapter (let's keep it to five students for ease of data input), and writes the data to an external file.
3) Write a program that creates a formatted set of evenly-spaced column headings for the student database of problem #2 above. This includes: First Name, Last Name, Student ID, Year of Study, Major and GPA.
4) Write a program that takes the external file written by the program of problem 2) and reads its data, storing it in another similar array of structures, and then prints its output to screen in a tabulated fashion, using the column headings done in problem #3 above.
5) Write a program that does the same thing as problem #4 above except that it prints the output directly after reading it, i.e., without saving it to a data structure after being read.
6) The idea of using completely random numbers for the temperatures of problems #3 and #4 is not really satisfactory. The numbers were kind of crazy and the formatting was probably very ugly, based on what you knew at the time. Now that we know more about formatting the output and we have a bit more programming experience, let's re-do the problem but with the following changes:
   (a) Let's generate numbers directly into degrees Fahrenheit.
   (b) Let's begin with a low temp of the day at midnight, peaking at noon and descending towards the minimum temp again by midnight.

     (i) The low temperature should be 65 deg. F ± 5 degrees, determined randomly.

    (ii) The max temperature should be 90 deg. F ± 10 degrees, determined randomly.

  (iii) The hourly temperatures should rise progressively from the low at midnight to the high at noon, then descend progressively from the high at noon to the low at the next midnight.

  (iv) The amount of change of the temp (both up and down) should be linear and equal to the difference between high and low temperatures, divided by 12 (hours).

(c) Let's format the output better so that it is cleaner and more pleasing to the eye.

Multi-file Programs

10

This chapter describes and discusses a feature of computer programming that becomes essential when building larger programs (anything over a few hundred lines of code): how to write programs whose source code is contained in more than one file. This is an important feature, as complex commercial application programs are generally much too large to be written all in one file. This can make editing and recompiling the program code very cumbersome. Furthermore, large programs are typically developed by more than one programmer, thereby making a one-file program unmanageable when several programmers are concurrently working on the same file, even if only copies of it. Lastly, placing functions that can be reused in other programs by the programmer (or anyone else) in separate files makes it easy to port them between programs. In this chapter, we discuss how to tie together multiple files that together compose one program. Code::Blocks and other similar IDEs make building multi-file programs rather easy to do. Let's start.

1 Programming Considerations When Building Multi-file Programs

Writing a program in several files becomes rather easy when using an IDE such as Code::Blocks. Of course, this can also be done when using a command line interface for compilation, but this will not be discussed here. How exactly to do this in Code::Blocks is described in detail as part of our first example below (Sect. 3 of this chapter), so we leave that for then. Instead, we begin our discussion of multi-file programs by introducing some important things to do when writing a program over multiple files. Some are rather obvious, but we mention them anyway. Others are not so obvious and require more discussion below. We start with the obvious ones.

1.1 The Obvious Ones

The first one is really obvious: there is to be only one definition of the `main()` function in the program. Thus, you must <u>not</u> have `main()` functions defined in more than one of the files. In fact, by extension, all user-defined functions should be defined only once, and that definition should be contained in only one of the files that make up the multi-file program. As a corollary, a second obvious consideration is that the definition of any user-defined function (including `main()`) must be <u>completely</u> defined in one file. That is, part of the definition of a user-defined function cannot be located in one file and the rest in another file. Again, these considerations should be obvious (but here they are, just in case). Other considerations are not so obvious and we introduce them next.

© Springer Nature Switzerland AG 2020
A. J. Gonzalez, *Computer Programming in C for Beginners*,
https://doi.org/10.1007/978-3-030-50750-3_10

1.2   Scope of Variables

We now discuss how variables are defined and declared in a multi-file program to control in what files they can and cannot be referenced.

Local, or `automatic` variables, as they are formally called in C, are not a problem because they are only recognized in the function where they are defined. Once that function exits, that variable no longer exists and the memory that was allocated to it is returned to the free memory stack. So, there is no problem with local (`automatic`) variables vis-à-vis programs in multiple files.

Global variables are a different story, however, as they can be directly referenced by several functions. So the question arises as to whether global variables defined in one file are "visible" (i.e., able to be referenced) by functions in other files that are part of the same program. The answer is not necessarily so (but can be). Let's expand upon this.

As we mentioned earlier, global variables are defined outside of any function. There is no need to further identify them as global. However, they are not to be re-defined anywhere else in the program, whether in the same file or in other files. A second definition would attempt to create and allocate memory for a variable that already exists. This would confuse the compiler. Convention calls for global variables to be defined at the top of the source file, right after the pre-processor directives.

However, these variables can and must be declared in any other file where they are to be recognized as being the same variable. This is done by preceding the declarations in the other files with the identifier `extern` (a reserved keyword), thereby indicating that the variable is not only global but also *external*. Otherwise, these global variables will not be recognized in those files where they are not so declared. Be sure you use the exact same name for the variable (also obvious)! Moreover, be sure to use the `extern` label for the global variables when declaring them in files other than the original where they are first defined, lest the statement be interpreted as a second definition of the variable.

What if the programmer were to expressly want a global variable to be recognized as such <u>only in the file where it is defined</u>? This could be useful when making files available to others for their use within the same large program, as one would not want to have someone else's functions modify the value of one's global variable. To do this, the identifier `static` is used in the definition of the global variable to make it global but not external; that is, only accessible to functions within the same file where it is defined. This declaration is done in the variable definitions in the (only) file where this global variable is to be recognized. This is called an *internal linkage*. We'll see examples of all this below.

One more thing we must mention before we leave the subject of static variables. Local (automatic) variables can also be made static. In fact, `static` local variables cease to be `automatic` and now become `static` variables. While this may initially be confusing based on what we know about local variables, it serves the purpose of making a local variable persistent in a user-defined function that may be called several times. Normally, when a called function exits, all local variables cease to exist. However, when the value of a variable must persist over the many calls to that function, a local variable is made static. This provides permanent storage within a function across several calls to that function. This has nothing to do with multi-file programs, but it is an interesting – and useful – application of the `static` label for a variable.

1.3   Scope of User-Defined Functions

The question here is whether user-defined functions are "visible" when defined in one file and called by a function in a different file. The answer is yes, they are -- but the programmer does need to do one thing to make this work: the file from where the function is called (but in which it is not defined) must include a prototype of the called function. This tells the compiler that the function is defined elsewhere, and for more immediate purposes, what parameters it is to take in and what type of value it is to return (if any). Once the prototype is included, the function is called in the normal way -- the same way as it would be called if the definition was in the same file. In fact, this is no different than when a function is called (say from `main()`) in a one-file program where the function is defined after the point where it is called. The prototype serves to tell the compiler that the function is defined elsewhere in the code, yet provides it with the return type and the list and type of parameters for its immediate use. Thus, this is generally not a problem.

User-defined functions can also be made `static` to limit their scope to the file where they are defined. In such cases, place the `static` keyword in front of the function header (preceding the *return_type*) in its definition.

2   Our Example Program

Our example application is a program that calculates the average of an array of 10 floating point numbers. This program includes a user-defined function called `average()` that when it is called and passed an array that contains the numbers to be averaged, will calculate and return the average of the numbers found in the passed array. Below is the code for that program. Please enter it into your Code::Blocks `main.c` file and execute it to be sure it runs correctly (while all in the same file) before we begin to modify it and place parts of it in another file. To make the program simpler for our purposes in this example, we assume that the `average()` function knows the size of the array is 10. Such hard-coding of what should in reality be a passed argument is <u>not</u> good programming practice, but we will forego this to simplify things. Otherwise, to make it general, one should pass the size of the array as an argument to `average()`.

```c
#include <stdio.h>
#include <stdlib.h>

float average(float []);

int main()
{
    float array[10] = {4.8, 12.98, 82.1, 5.98, 19.75, 24.9, 75.7, 3.45, 10.0, 28.11};
    float avg = 0.0;

    avg = average(array);
    printf("The average value of the array is %.2f \n", avg);

    return 0;
}

float average(float a[])
{
    int n;
    float sum = 0.0;
    for(n=0; n<10; n++)
        sum += a[n];
    return sum/10;
}
```

Note that the array `array` is considered a local variable in `main()` and is being passed (by reference) to the function `average()`. This program should work fine, giving an average value of `26.78`.

We will now extend this example into several cases to highlight the specific issues discussed above.

3   Case 1: Simple Split with Local Variables

Let's create a new text file called `main1.c` and put it in the same directory where the `main.c` file is located. You can do that with Wordpad, Notepad, or some other screen editor. Leave the file completely blank and save it to that directory.

Now go to Code::Blocks and click on the "Project" tab on the menu above the user interface. Then click on "Add Files" in the resulting drop-down menu. It will open a window that shows all the files in the directory where the program is located, including `main1.c` (and of course, `main.c`). Click on `main1.c` and you will see that it will now appear as a file in the main Code::Blocks editor screen. You have now added a second file to the program.

Next, cut out the complete definition of the `average()` function from your base, single-file code in `main.c` and paste it into `main1.c`. <u>Do nothing else</u> to either file. Compile and run the now two-file program. It works! This is because the function `average()` remains prototyped in `main.c` even though it is no longer defined in `main.c`. This serves to tell the compiler that this function is defined elsewhere in the program. Easy, right? Now let's complicate things a bit.

4   Case 2: More Complex Version Using Local Variables

Let's write a second function that calculates the standard deviation of the numbers in the array. Place it in `main1.c`. The function for calculating the standard deviation is as follows: (for expediency we again assume that this function will also know that the array has 10 cells.)

```
float std_dev(float b[], float av)
{
    int n;
    float cumm_diff = 0.0, s = 0.0;
    for(n=0; n<10; n++)
        cumm_diff += (av - b[n]) * (av - b[n]);
    s = sqrt(cumm_diff/10);
    return s;
}
```

Now add a call to `std_dev()` from the `main()` function, setting the returned value to a floating point variable named `sd`, and print out the value of that variable. Be sure to place it <u>after</u> the call to `average()`, otherwise `std_dev()` won't have the right value for `av` in its argument. The function `main()` should now look like the following, with the new statements in **bold face** font:

```
int main()
{
    float array[10] = {4.8, 12.98, 82.1, 5.98, 19.75, 24.9, 75.7, 3.45, 10.0, 28.11};
    float avg = 0.0;
    float sd = 0.0;

    avg = average(array);
    sd = std_dev(array, avg);
    printf("The standard deviation of the array is %.2f \n", sd);
    printf("The average value of the array is %.2f \n", avg);

    return 0;
}
```

You will see that we get several warnings. For one warning, we must add math.h to main1.c so that it knows about the sqrt() function. Interestingly enough, it is given as a warning and not an error. However, don't do this yet, as we have another problem to fix.

It is also confused because the std_dev() function is called but not prototyped in main.c, so it issues another warning about this. Nevertheless, because no errors were detected, this program can be executed. So, let's run it.

The output in our computer is:

```
The average value of the array is 26.78
The standard deviation of the array is 2139095040.00
```

It computes the average correctly, but returns some nonsense for the standard deviation – yet another indication of why one should never ignore warnings!

So, now include math.h in main1.c and a prototype for std_dev() in main.c and run it again. You will see that it will now work, giving a correct value of 27.28 for the standard deviation.

5   Case 3: Introducing Global Variables into the Equation

OK, we said earlier that working with local variables in multi-file programs is easy because there are "walls" beyond which these local variables are not recognized, and it doesn't matter in which files these functions are, as they are local anyway. So there are no conflicts. Now let's make the array a global variable and see if the second file can "see" it (and reference it). We now modify our code in main.c to look as follows:

```
#include <stdio.h>
#include <stdlib.h>

float average(); // no need to pass the array because it is now global
float std_dev(float); // no need to pass the array because it is now global.

float array[10] = {4.8, 12.98, 82.1, 5.98, 19.75, 24.9, 75.7, 3.45, 10.0,
28.11}; // array[] is now global because it is defined outside any function.
```

```
int main()
{
    float avg = 0.0, s = 0.0;
    avg = average();    // no longer need to pass array[]
    s = std_dev(avg);   // no longer need to pass array[]

    printf("The average value of the array is %.2f \n", avg);
    printf("The standard deviation of the array is %.2f \n", s);

    return 0;
}
```

We also need to modify the user-defined functions because they no longer to need to have the array passed to them, as it is now global. Normally, we would still have to pass the length of the array, but let us again assume for expediency that we know it to be 10 cells long. We also modified the two user-defined functions in main1.c to reflect that the array is now called array and not a and b. See the code below.

```
float average()
{
    int n;
    float sum = 0.0;
    for(n=0; n<10; n++)
        sum += array[n];
    return sum/10;
}


float std_dev(float av)
{
    int n;
    float cumm_diff = 0.0, s = 0.0;
    for(n=0; n<10; n++)
        cumm_diff += (av - array[n]) * (av - array[n]);
    s = sqrt(cumm_diff/10);
    return s;
}
```

The two user-defined functions (average() and std_dev()) should be able to see array because it is global, right? They actually don't because they are in a different file from where array[] is defined. This will produce an error, so we must take some corrective action.

We can do one of two things: first, because it is not needed in main.c, we can put the definition of this array in main1.c and remove it from main.c. This will work because the global array is defined in the file that needs it, and in our program, only one file needs it. Try it!

Alternatively, we can leave it in main.c as it was originally, and then declare it again as extern in main1.c. However, in this case, we only need to declare array in main1.c, not define it (i.e., give values to its cells). This declaration in main1.c must add the extern prefix to the declaration of array[] in main1.c. This tells the compiler that it is the same global variable defined in another file (serves as a sort of "prototype" for variables). So, add the statement extern array[]; to main1.c and it should work.

6   Case 4: Complicating the Issue with More Global Variables

Now let's add a global variable in `main1.c` and see whether it is seen in `main.c`. Leaving everything else the same, let's make `avg.` a global variable in `main1.c` and reference it in `main.c`. Keep in mind that the user-defined functions will again have to be modified somewhat because we no longer need to pass this variable (`avg`) to other functions. The code now looks like this:

```
main.c:
#include <stdio.h>
#include <stdlib.h>
#include <math.h>

void average(void);
float std_dev(void);

float array[10] = {4.8, 12.98, 82.1, 5.98, 19.75, 24.9, 75.7, 3.45, 10.0,
28.11};
extern float avg;

int main()
{
    float s = 0.0;

    average();
    printf("The average value of the array is %.2f \n", avg);
    s = std_dev();
    printf("The standard deviation of the array is %.2f \n", s);

    return 0;
}
```

```
main1.c:
#include <stdio.h>
#include <stdlib.h>
#include <math.h>

extern float array[];
float avg = 0.0;

void average()
{
    int n;
    float sum = 0.0;
    for(n=0; n<10; n++)
        sum += array[n];
    avg = sum/10; // avg is now a global variable; no need to return it.
}
```

```
float std_dev()
{
    int n;
    float cumm_diff = 0.0;
    for(n=0; n<10; n++)
        cumm_diff += (avg - array[n]) * (avg - array[n]);
    return sqrt(cumm_diff/10);
}
```

The same thing applies as it did for the prior case. The global variable `avg` is declared and defined in `main1.c` and then declared (but not defined!) as `extern` in `main.c` and it works.

So, we can see that `extern` serves to tell the compiler that a global external variable has been defined elsewhere.

7   Case 5: More Complex Still – Functions That Are Not Seen

Now let's say we want to define a function in one of these files but purposely want it to be recognized only in that file. To show this, we define another function called `output()` that, when called, will simply print out the floating point value being passed to it. We define it and place it in `main1.c` where `average()` and `std_dev()` are also defined. We must also add a prototype for `output()` in `main1.c`, as it is called in `main1.c` before it is defined.

```
void output(float var)
{
    printf("The value of the variable is %.2f \n", var);
}
```

We slightly modify the `average()` function to include a call to `output()`. This is now (changes in **bold**):

```
void average()
{
    int n;
    float sum = 0.0, mean = 0.0;
    for(n=0; n<10; n++)
        sum += array[n];
    mean = sum/10;
    avg = mean;
    output(mean);
}
```

It will work just fine because `output()` is defined in `main1.c`, the same file where it is called by `average()`. The output of this program will now be:

```
The value of the variable is 26.78
The average value of the array is 26.78
The standard deviation of the array is 27.28
```

Now let's move the definition of output() to main.c. This also works because the prototype for output() in main1.c tells the compiler that its definition is somewhere else in the program. We do not need a prototype of output() in main.c because the function is not called from main.c. However, if we comment out the prototype for output() in main1.c, and compile/run the program, it will produce a warning about an implicit declaration of output(). The program will run, but the output of output() will be garbage. This is because its definition is not seen in main1.c, where it is being called. Try it.

8   Case 6: The Use of static for Functions

One last case: using the static modifier in front of the definition of output() can keep output() from being called by a function located in a file other than the one where it is defined. Let's move the definition of output() to main.c and label it as static. Given that output() is called in main1.c, it will not be able to be seen in main1.c because it is static, thus returning an error. Try it!

In summary, Code::Blocks makes it easy to write multi-file programs. However, C makes it important that the files properly "make visible", so to speak, the global variables and functions as desired by the programmer.

9   Summary and Conclusion

This chapter introduced the learner to building large programs over several files. More importantly, we describe and discuss how to make sure user-defined functions and global variables transcend the possibly many files in a program and manage to be recognized across them. While the example we employed is far from being either a complex or a large program, it is effective in demonstrating the pitfalls of not doing what is required for making user-defined functions and global variables be recognized where they are supposed to be recognized.

First, we wrote and included the example program in a single file to be sure it was fundamentally correct. Then, we modified it in several ways to demonstrate the issues involved. This came to six cases, two of which had two variations.

Case 1 simply placed the program in two files – one (main.c) containing only the main() function while the other one (main1.c) containing one user-defined function that receives an array from the main() function and computes and returns the average of its values. The prototype for this user-defined function was already in the main.c file when it included the entire program, so we left the prototype in main.c. We then cut and pasted the user-defined function (average()) to main1.c. This worked fine. This case also included a discussion of how to add other files to the project in the Code::Blocks IDE.

Case 2 complicated the situation a bit by adding a second user-defined function, whose definition is in the second file (main1.c) but is called by main(), and its prototype is not in main.c. Of course, it does not work properly. Making this correction resolves the problem. This indicates the importance of prototyping functions in files where they are used but not defined.

Case 3 introduced global variables. In this case, we used the same program as in Case 2 except we made the array that contains the values to be averaged a global variable. It is declared and initialized in main.c. This global array is not initially seen by the user-defined functions in main1.c until we make some corrections, and then it is.

Case 4 introduced a second global variable in `main1.c`, but not in `main.c`.

Case 5 introduced a third user-defined function and placed its definition in `main1.c`, from where it is also called. This works. However, when we move the definition to `main.c`, and comment out the prototype for this function in `main1.c`, it no longer works.

Case 6 made the `output()` function static and tried to call it from a function located in a file other than where it is defined. This results in an error.

While this is not a comprehensive treatment of how to build programs across several files, it should suffice for beginning programmers.

10   Problems

It is rather senseless to provide problems for this chapter, as it does not involve any new concepts in computer programming. The topic of this chapter merely allows the learner to be able to build larger programs. Therefore, we suggest that you use programs written in one file, compiled, run and verified for either exercises or problems in previous chapters, and convert them into programs of two or more files.

Dynamically-Allocated Memory and Linked Lists

11

The topic of this chapter is probably the most interesting in this book. The idea of defining and using variables at run time, and linking these together through pointers into a chain is a very powerful concept. Unfortunately, it is not an easy one for beginner programmers to understand or to program. This will be your most challenging chapter thus far, and by far! So, buckle up and tighten the straps on your helmets because we're going for a rough ride. We'll seek to make this as clear as possible.

1 An Introduction to Defining Variables During Run Time

So far, we have defined variables at compile time, whether they were individual `int`'s or `float`'s, or more complex data types such as arrays or structures. Memory blocks for these variables were allocated by the compiler before execution. An advantage of this is that the programmer need not worry about how much and where the memory allocated to these variables is – she just refers to the variables by name when using them in the program. The compiler knows exactly how much memory to set aside when a variable of a specific type is defined. Moreover, when the program finished using these variables (i.e., their scope ends), the no-longer-necessary memory space is automatically returned to free memory for reuse.

The disadvantage to what we have been doing is that the programmer needs to specify before compilation how many and what kind of variables will be used in the program, as it cannot be changed at run time. This is more significant when declaring arrays, as the programmer must predict how large an array (i.e., how many cells) the program will require. If she guesses low, the program will run out of array space and either crash or overwrite whatever variable may be adjacent to the end of the array memory. If she guesses high, then memory is being wasted -- the lesser of the two evils to be sure, but a non-trivial consideration in big data applications or in memory limited applications such as embedded computing. So, then, what is one to do? To the rescue comes the concept of *dynamic memory allocation*.

Dynamic memory allocation means that memory can be allocated to variables by the program at run time, just when the memory is required, in exactly the amounts required. By memory, we mean that variables can be defined (in a different way, but achieving the same general objective) while the program is running. The advantage is that the programmer need not guess how much memory will be needed (e.g., the size of an array). The program will allocate exactly what is needed when it is needed – no more and no less. The main disadvantage is that now the programmer is responsible for managing the memory. That is, if the program can allocate memory at run time, the program must

© Springer Nature Switzerland AG 2020
A. J. Gonzalez, *Computer Programming in C for Beginners*,
https://doi.org/10.1007/978-3-030-50750-3_11

also de-allocate the memory at run time when no longer needed. This means that when a dynamically-created variable is no longer needed, the program itself (not the operating system) must free the memory and explicitly return it to free memory for reuse. This is easy to do, but not always easy to remember to do for beginning programmers.

One thing we should mention about dynamically-allocated variables. Because they are created during runtime, they are not given names and thus remain anonymous. The only way to get to them is via pointers. As long as there is at least one pointer pointing to the dynamically-allocated block of memory, it can be accessed and its values can be read and changed, just like any other variable defined the "normal" way. However, care must be taken by the programmer that these blocks remain pointed at by at least one pointer at all times. Otherwise, they become inaccessible, making them not only useless but also prohibiting their deletion and reuse of their memory. The latter can often result in what is called *memory leaks*. This happens when memory is being increasingly allocated but not "liberated" when a variable is no longer needed, because, well, access to it is lost. When enough of these lost blocks exist that consume irretrievable memory, the computer will inevitably run out of memory.

In this chapter, you will learn how to create dynamically-allocated variables and how to free the memory once the variable is no longer needed.

2   How to Allocate Memory Dynamically for Variables

C makes it easy to do this with some pre-defined, standard library functions. However, the programmer needs to know how they work. Generally, this feature is not used to define independent simple variables (i.e., not part of an array or a structure) such as integer or floating point variables. Such are best defined through the "normal" way. Rather, it is intended for user-defined data types (defined with `typedef`) that use the `struct` structures.

The basic function to allocate memory dynamically is called `malloc()` – stands for "memory allocation". Its single argument is the size, in bytes, of the memory block to be allocated. Well, you're probably thinking that this might present a problem. If we wanted to allocate memory for an `int` or `float`, we could figure out the size ahead of time and simply put the value in bytes inside the parentheses. However, we just said that such variables are not commonly allocated dynamically. So, you might ask, how can I know the size of a specific `struct`?

Fortunately, C helps us out here again. The pre-defined function `sizeof()` returns the size in bytes of the data type passed to it as an argument. So, we can simply embed the `sizeof()` function as the argument for `malloc()` and problem solved. `malloc()` then returns a pointer to the block of (contiguous!) memory of that size.

As for the case with `fopen()` in the last chapter, if `malloc()` fails to successfully allocate a block of memory of that size (for whatever reason, but typically for lack of memory space), it will return a pointer to `NULL`. So the programmer needs to always check for `NULL` when using `malloc()` as there is no error message of any kind generated.

OK, let's write some code. We will use code snippets that we assume are part of a properly written program (i.e., that includes pre-processor directives, prototypes, `main()`, etc.).

Let's begin by practicing with `sizeof()` to see what the size of an integer variable is on your computer.

```
printf("The size of an integer variable in this computer is %d bytes\n",
    sizeof(int));  // continuation of line immediately above
```

Depending on the computer used, the answer might (most likely) be:

```
The size of an integer variable in this computer is 4 bytes
```

We can do the same thing with floating point variables and it will also return 4. A double precision floating point is 8 bytes, while a character variable is 1 byte. Try these to confirm.

So, now that we know how `sizeof()` works, our next step is to define a structured data type. To be consistent, we shall use the `student` structure that we used in a previous chapter.

```c
typedef struct student  {
   char name[20];
   int ID;
   int year;
   char major[25];
   float GPA;
 } Student;


typedef Student * Student_ptr;
```

Notice what we did in the line just above. We defined a new pointer variable that points to a `Student` data type and called this new data type `Student_ptr`. That will make it easier for us to declare pointers to `Student` type data blocks. Just for kicks, put the `Student` data type inside `sizeof()` and print it out just to see how much memory this data type takes up (hint: 60 bytes.)

Of course, we place the above `typedef` definitions outside of `main()` (or any other function, for that matter) to make them global and thus visible to all functions that need to use it (in the same file!).

Now we want to allocate one block of memory for each student and populate their values. We only do it for two students here to make the example manageable, but you'll get the point.

```c
int main()
{
    Student_ptr smith_ptr, jones_ptr;

    if((smith_ptr = malloc(sizeof(Student))) == NULL)
        {
            printf("The allocation failed! The program will now end.");
            return 0;
        }

    strcpy(smith_ptr->name, "Conner Smith");
    smith_ptr->ID = 12345;
    smith_ptr->year = 1;
    strcpy(smith_ptr->major, "Computer Science");
    smith_ptr->GPA = 3.86;

    printf("The name of the student is %s \n", smith_ptr->name);
    printf("The student's ID is %d \n", smith_ptr->ID);
    printf("The student's year of study is %d\n", smith_ptr->year);
    printf("The student's major is %s \n", smith_ptr->major);
    printf("The student's overall GPA is %.2f \n", smith_ptr->GPA);
    printf("\n\n");
```

```
        return 0;
}
```

The output is too long to print here, but you will get the correct answer. To add students, we would do as follows, in addition to and below the code above (but before the `return 0;` statement):

```
if((jones_ptr = malloc(sizeof(Student))) == NULL)
        {
                printf("The allocation failed! The program will now end.");
                return 0;
        }
strcpy(jones_ptr->name, "Kierstin Jones");
jones_ptr->ID = 34567;
jones_ptr->year = 1;
strcpy(jones_ptr->major, "Computer Engineering");
jones_ptr->GPA = 3.78;

printf("The name of the student is %s \n", jones_ptr->name);
printf("The student's ID is %d \n", jones_ptr->ID);
printf("The student's year of study is %d \n", jones_ptr->year);
printf("The student's major is %s \n", jones_ptr->major);
printf("The student's overall GPA is %.2f \n", jones_ptr->GPA);
printf("\n\n");
```

Now it would print out the results of the students Conner Smith and Kierstin Jones.

Once again we must reiterate that this is not why dynamic memory allocation was devised, as the memory requirements for this two-student example application would otherwise be very small. Normally, we would create many such student records and link them together in a *linked list* of students (but that's for the next section).

Now let's try using the dot operators on this. As you should already know, or at can least guess, it will <u>not</u> work, but let's confirm this. So, we just work with one statement to prove the point. We now use this statement to replace the one that sets the value of `ID` in the dynamically-allocated variable pointed at by `jones_ptr`.

```
jones_ptr.ID = 34567;
```

As we suspected, this produced a compilation error. So, for sure, do not use dot operators for accessing dynamically-allocated structure instances through pointers.

Now that we know how to build these anonymous, dynamically-allocated variables, let's next build a data structure that encompasses many of these blocks of dynamically-allocated memory.

3   Linked Structures – A Brief Introduction

You now know how to dynamically create blocks of memory at run time and access them through pointers (the only way to do so). Remember that such blocks of memory are instantiations of structures of the `struct` type. It is just another way to instantiate variables from the `struct` template, except now we can do it dynamically at run time. Therefore, it is best to define the structure that we want this variable to look like, as a new data type using the `typedef` operation. From this point forward, this is the only way that we will use to define a variable type that will be instantiated dynamically.

As we saw in the last section, knowing how to dynamically allocate a block of memory as an instance of a `struct` template and assigning values to its members is rather straight-forward. We used two new functions that you just learned (`sizeof()` and `malloc()`) to instantiate a dynamic variable, assign values to its members using the arrow operator, and voila! -- you have a structured variable instance that was instantiated at run time, with values assigned to its members.

However, declaring a new pointer variable for each of these dynamically-created blocks is a problem in and of itself, as the program would have to somehow keep track of all these pointers. The trick is how to link together several variable instances that the program will have created so that it can keep them together in a sensible way, and be able to access any and each of these blocks individually later for reading, for writing or for deleting, without having to assign an individual pointer to each one of them.

One way to do that, of course, is to put the pointers in an array. That is, each cell holds a pointer that points to a dynamically allocated block of memory. However, that defeats the whole purpose of dynamically allocating variables at run time, without having to know how large an array you will need. So, that is not a practical solution.

The better way to do it is to link the instances together using pointers and form a *linked structure*. There are several variations of linked structures (e.g., linked stacks, linked queues, etc.), but the one we will treat here is the most general of them: the *linked list*.

To visualize a linked list, think of elephants in a circus where one elephant grabs the tail of the one in front of it with its trunk, and its tail is in turn grabbed by the elephant behind it, and so on. These elephants are linked together, tail to trunk, to tail to trunk, into one possibly long chain. A similar thing describes a linked list. One dynamically-allocated block contains a pointer member that is set to point to another such block, which in turn has its pointer member pointing to another such block, and so on. Also, to be able to access the list, there is one pointer pointing to the first block in the list called the *head pointer*. Additionally, the "tail" is the last block in the linked list and the *tail pointer* points to it. One or more members of the dynamically-allocated structure instance would contain the data to be held in that variable. Graphically and conceptually, a linked list that carries a sequence of five integers would look like this:

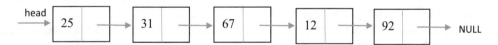

The pointer that points to the first block in the list (the `head` pointer) and the `tail` pointer (if one is used, which is typically not the case) are the only pointers that have to be defined in the "regular" way. All other pointers are members of the dynamically-allocated structure instances. The `head` pointer is a permanent pointer and it is the way to access the list. One can see that once we have accessed the first block on the linked list through the `head` pointer, we can access any other block by simply following the pointer sequence from one block to the next. If the `head` pointer was deleted, or if it was inadvertently redirected from the address of the first block, access to the list would be irretrievably lost, along with its contents.

This leads us to one of the most significant disadvantages of linked lists. There is no random access to the elements in this list. That is, in an array, one can directly access a specific cell by simply knowing its index number (the offset from the first element of the array). In that fashion, access to array cells is quick and efficient, as we saw during our discussion of arrays earlier. Unfortunately, access to members of a linked list is neither quick nor efficient because the memory blocks in a linked list are not in contiguous memory. Thus, the only way to access a particular "cell" (the formal name is *node*) is by searching for it linearly, starting from the `head` pointer. This is done by entering the list through its head and then following the links, one by one, making our way through the nodes until we find the desired node. This node can be desired because of its location in the list (e.g., occupies the 12th position in the list) or because it has some specific content that the program needs. A good metaphor for this is a treasure hunt, where clues will only get you to the site of the next clue, and so on for several clues until you finally reach the treasure.

4   How to Link Together Dynamically-Allocated Memory

So, what are these member links between nodes that we keep talking about? They are the pointers that point to the next node in the list and are aptly called *next pointers*.

As we said earlier, the basic form of any new variable type to be defined with the `typedef` operator is a `struct` structure. For a linked list, there is one more special requirement for this `struct`: that it be a *self-referencing structure*. This means that such a structure has one member (a pointer) that points to a variable type of the same type as the structure itself that holds it. Here is an example of a self-referencing structure.

```
typedef struct node {
        int number;
        struct node * next;
} Node;
```

In this structure, the data type `Node` is defined. An instantiation of it would have a first member, called the *data member* because it carries the data that this node is to hold. In the code just above, it is the integer member variable `number`. Of course, there can be more than one data member in a node, and there generally are. However, to keep things simple, let's just say that our example list has only very simple data needs – just the integer variable named `number` (you can name it anything you want as long as it is a legal name in C). The second member is a pointer that points to the same `struct node` data type (i.e., with a structure tag of `node`). This is the `next` pointer that we discussed above. It points to the next node in the list.

"But wait a minute!" you might say after you think about this a little (or a lot). How is this possible, since the structure `node` needs to be defined with this pointer in place, yet its definition includes pointing to a structure type that has not yet been defined? Ah, yes, great question, but C makes an exception and allows self-referencing structures to be defined just as shown above. We won't go into details as to how it does that; just know that they are legal, albeit counter-intuitive.

So, now we can have a node that contains a pointer variable that points to the same type of node. This `next` pointer is the tail of the elephant that points to the next node down the list. Unlike arrays, however, a linked list is not guaranteed to be in contiguous memory. That is, one node won't necessarily contiguously follow the previous one. Of course, the memory within one node will indeed be in contiguous memory – but not the nodes in the list. This is what makes access more difficult in linked lists, and involves a lot of "pointer chasing". The next pointer only has the address of where the next node lives in the computer's memory, and it can be anywhere in the data sector of the memory. The last point is irrelevant because the `next` pointer will find it wherever it is in memory. The point is, however, that the next node in most applications won't know where its previous node lives; so the list can only be traversed in one direction – head to tail (except for doubly-linked lists, but we will discuss those later).

Let's now write some code to build a linked list of five nodes, each of which contains only one data member – a random integer variable. We'll use the `struct` shown above. Naturally, we will have to do this in a `for` loop, as we need to build a list containing multiple nodes.

A linked list can be said to be empty when its `head` pointer points to NULL. Our first step below is to build the first node in the list and set values to its members.

```
#include <stdio.h>
#include <stdlib.h>
typedef struct node {
        int number;
        struct node * next;
} Node;

typedef Node * Nodeptr;
int main() {
    int n; // our counter variable. We'll need it later for the for loop.
    Nodeptr head = NULL; // We just created an empty linked list.
    if((head = malloc(sizeof(Node))) == NULL)
        return 0;
    // We have now created the first node and have set head to point to it
    head->number = 72; // Now we set the value of its only data member
    head->next = NULL; // This is the only node, so its next pointer => NULL

    return 0;
}
```

We have now built a linked list that contains only one node whose data value is 72. Graphically-speaking, we have done as shown below, where the box that looks a lot like a domino piece is the dynamically-allocated block of memory (the node):

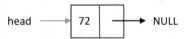

Now please insert a `printf()` or two at the end of the code above (but before `return 0;`) to confirm that the linked list exists and what value its only member has. Access this only node via the head pointer as below.

```
printf("The value of the data of this node is %d \n", head->number);
```

But this is rather easy. Now we have to add the other four nodes, which won't be as easy. You're probably thinking – "Aha! We could do it in a sequential structure because, after all, it is only four more nodes to add". Of course, we could, but that would not be fun -- nor would it be practical when you need to build a linked list with thousands of nodes in it. So, we will bite the bullet and do it in a loop.

The first thing we have to do is decide whether the subsequent nodes will be placed before or after the head node that we just added. In other words, are we building the list from front to back or from back to front? It doesn't really matter as one is just as easy to build as the other, but they are built differently, so we need to decide. Let's do it front to back (it is more intuitive), and then we can discuss the other way later.

To achieve this we will have to declare what we shall call here a *utility pointer*, which in this case will always be set to point to the last node in the list. We will label this pointer the `here` pointer. This pointer is not necessary because we could find the end of the list by going back to the first node through the head pointer, and then work our way towards the back of the list from there through the next pointers. However, in unidirectional linked lists such as this one, it can get computationally very expensive as the list grows larger and larger with each iteration. So, our `here` pointer will always point to the last node in the list and will save us the computational work of having to look for it starting from the `head` on every iteration.

We will also add a second utility pointer that will point to the new node being created in every iteration of our loop. This pointer will be called, aptly enough, the `newnode` pointer. So, let's add the following snippet to the code above, just above the `return   0;` statement that closes out the `main()` function. Note that it does not replace the earlier code that built the fist node, but rather builds from the second node on. That is why n starts from 1 and not from 0. We will explain later why we do it this way, but in the meantime, we show the entire program here.

```
#include <stdio.h>
#include <stdlib.h>
typedef struct node {
        int number;
        struct node * next;
} Node;

typedef Node * Nodeptr;

int main()
 {
    int n; // our counter variable.
    Nodeptr head = NULL; // We just created an empty linked list.
    Nodeptr here = NULL; // auxiliary pointer
    Nodeptr newnode = NULL; // another auxiliary pointer

    // Now to create the first node of the linked list:

    if((head = malloc(sizeof(Node))) == NULL)
        return 0;
    // We have just created the first node and have set head to point to it

    head->number = 72; // Now we set the value of its only data member
    head->next = NULL; // This is the only node, so its next pointer = NULL
    here = head; // The pointer here always points to the last node
                 // Because there is only one node, it is also the last node

    printf("The value of the number in this node is %d \n", head->number);
    // To verify that it works so far

    // Now to build the rest of the linked list:
```

```
for(n=1; n<5; n++) // note that it starts at 1, as the head node exists
    {
        if((newnode = malloc(sizeof(Node))) == NULL) // the node to be added
            return 0; // checks to ensure not NULL. Aborts program if NULL
        newnode->number = rand()%100; // assigns a value to the data member.
        newnode->next = NULL; // directs the next pointer to NULL - last one
        here->next = newnode; // now begins the pointer re-positioning
        here = newnode; // the here pointer moves along as the list is built
    }

    return 0;
}
```

Graphically speaking, this is what we do with the code above. It's hard to describe a loop with a single diagram but bear with us here. For adding the second node:

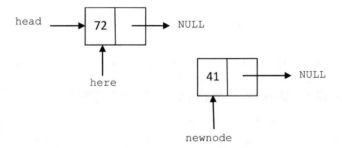

The above is what it looks like in the middle of the first loop iteration. Below is what it looks like at the end of the first iteration (and at the start of the second iteration).

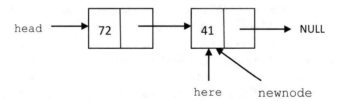

So, now we have two nodes in the list and here has been moved to point to the new last node: the newly-added one. newnode still points to the same node that was just added but will be reassigned to the subsequent new node in the second iteration.

Below is what the list will look like in the middle of the second iteration.

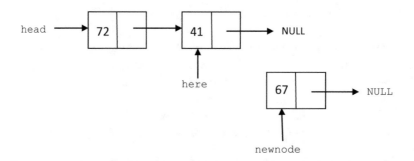

At the end of the second iteration, the linked list will now look like this:

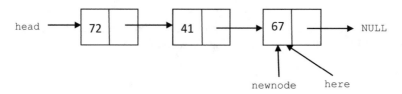

Each iteration of the `for` loop will add one node. At the end, the `next` pointer of the last node will remain pointing to `NULL`, so all will be well. Run the program to create such a linked list of five nodes. The conceptual graphical representation of the entire list is now.

OK, so why did we create the first node outside the loop? Well, there are several equally-valid ways to build a linked list, of course, but in the way we did it -- from front to back -- the `head` pointer is kept constantly pointing to the first node in the list, which doesn't change as the list grows. So, we created the first node outside and before the loop and set `head` to it so it does not need to change. We then used `here` to move down the list in the loop, always pointing to the last node, which changes in every iteration. Note that `here` was initially set to the `head` pointer.

Now that you know how to build a list from front to back, let's build one in the opposite direction: back-to-front. In this way of building a linked list, the last node will be added first and the first node will be added last. While the front-to-back program we wrote above keeps the head pointer constant and adds new nodes to the next pointer of the last node (indicated by the constantly moving `here` pointer), the back-to-front list builder will have to continually re-set the head pointer to the newest node added. We'll let you do this one by yourself as part of the problems at the end of the chapter, but here are some hints:

1) You will not need to create any nodes outside the loop, but you will need to define the `head` and `newnode` pointers before going into the loop. Initialize them all to `NULL`.

2) Next, you will write a `for` loop and inside it, write a statement that, in each iteration, redirects the `head` pointer to the new node being added <u>after</u> the new node's `next` pointer is redirected to the `head` pointer. Doing this <u>after</u> is important because if it is done <u>before</u>, the list will be lost forever.

These two programs that build linked lists may work well, but you won't be able to tell because there is no output function to tell us whether the list was created properly or not. Let's work on that next.

5 Traversing a Linked List

Moving through the list to visit each node is very important in linked lists. We call this action *traversing* a linked list. Traversing a list allows us to get to a specific node to either read its contents and/or to change them. It also allows the program to add new nodes in specific places (other than the front), as well as delete specific nodes. We could not do this without traversing the list. Moreover, to output the contents of a linked list, the program must also be able to *traverse* the list, one by one, and print the contents of a node before moving to the next node to do the same thing.

So, now we shall learn how to traverse a linked list. You have done a traversal of arrays already. That is, when you go through each cell, one by one, and do something with it (e.g., print out its content, change the contents, count them, etc.). It is easy to do in an array – just put a `for` loop to work and increment the index of the array by one using the loop counter variable as the `for` loop progresses. Traversal of a linked list is similar, although a bit more difficult to implement, as we must use traveling pointers.

A linked list traversal will normally start at the head of the list, as indicated by the `head` pointer (which is a constant). We will use an auxiliary pointer that starts at the head and moves from one node to the next. Our auxiliary pointer `aux` is moved by setting it to the value of the `next` pointer of whichever node it is in. Now let's write a simple user-defined function called `traverse()` that will receive a pointer to a type `Node` (the `head` pointer, of course) and traverse the linked list. Let's add the following code to the front-to-back linked list building program we wrote in the last section:

```
void traverse(Nodeptr head, int length)
{
        Nodeptr aux = head;
        int n;
        for(n=0; n<length; n++)    {
                printf("The value of node no. %d is %d \n", n, aux->number);
                aux = aux->next;   // moves the aux pointer along the list
        }
}
```

Don't forget to add the prototype for `traverse()` at the top of the file and call the function `traverse()` from `main()` with a second argument of 5. Note that the auxiliary pointer `aux` moves along the linked list by setting its value to `aux->next` at every iteration. Compile and execute the program now. It should work fine.

Nevertheless, what flaw do you see with this `traverse()` function? Well, it needs to know the length of the list so we can use the `for` loop to traverse it. Not a very practical thing. To fix this, the function needs to know that the traversal has reached the end of the list when the `aux` pointer happens to point to `NULL`. So, we will modify the function slightly to eliminate the need for passing the length of the list to it. We will now use a `while` loop rather than a `for`, and our end condition will be when the `aux` pointer points to `NULL`.   (Rather, the continuation criterion is whenever `aux` doesn't point to `NULL`.)

The revised `traverse()` function will now look like this:

```
void traverse(Nodeptr head)
{
      Nodeptr aux = head;
      int n = 0;
      while(aux != NULL)            {
            printf("The value of node no. %d is %d \n", n, aux->number);
            aux = aux->next;   // moves the aux pointer along the list
            n++; //Keeps count of the number of nodes visited - not essential
      }
}
```

Now it doesn't matter how long the list is - it will be traversed to its end – a much more general solution. That's good! Go ahead and implement this code to verify that the linked list you built was done correctly.

6   Inserting Nodes into an Existing Linked List

We now know how to build lists from scratch and how to traverse them. The next level up in difficulty is how to add and remove individual nodes to/from the list. One application of this could be a personal phonebook that you have built of all your friends and business associates that contains their email addresses and telephone numbers. As with the contact list we all have on our cell phones, we frequently add new contacts, and when we "unfriend" someone, the first thing we do is delete his/her entry from the contact list, as we may not want to be reminded of him/her. Let's do insertions into the linked list next. There are three kinds of insertions: 1) At the front of the list (rather easy); 2) At the end of the list (not quite as easy), and 3) Somewhere in the middle of the list (harder still). We begin with easy.

6.1   Inserting New Nodes at the Front of the Linked List

We assume that the linked list exists and can be accessed through the head pointer. So, we want to create a single new node, populate its data member(s), and insert this new node in front of the first (i.e., head) node. This means we will have to redirect head to point to the new first node.

The first thing to do is create the dynamically allocated new node and populate it with the appropriate value(s). This is done with the following snippet of code, which adds a function called insertnode() (it requires user input to know what values to assign to the data member(s) of the new node.)

```
void insertnode_head(Nodeptr * first)
{
  Nodeptr newentry = NULL;
  int n = 0;
  printf("Enter the value to be assigned to the new entry? \n");
  scanf("%d", &n);

  if((newentry = malloc(sizeof(Node))) == NULL)
```

```
        exit(0);

    newentry->number = n;
    newentry->next = *first;
    *first = newentry;
}
```

Note that we are passing a <u>double pointer</u> to `insertnode_head()`. We know this because `Nodeptr` is itself a pointer, yet we indicate that `first` is a pointer to a pointer data type that points to a `Node` data type. So, then, why did we use a double pointer when calling the `insertnode_head()` function? Well, this function requires that the `head` pointer of the list be redirected to point to the newest node added, which now becomes the new first node in the revised list. The problem is that the new value of the `head` pointer (i.e., where it points to) must be changed in the <u>main()</u> function, which is where the `head` pointer variable (which is local) is defined. To do this, we must pass the `head` pointer from `main()` by reference, which means we must pass a pointer to it. So, a pointer to a pointer is a double pointer. Don't forget that when we call `insertnode_head()`, we must pass it the address of `head` (i.e., `&head`), not just `head`.

Also, don't forget to write a prototype for `insertnode_head()` and call it from `main()`. Also, add a call to `traverse()` after `insertnode_head()` executes to be sure it worked well. More importantly, please make sure you understand what the code above does.

6.2   Inserting New Nodes at the Tail of the Linked List

Now we write a second function that places the new node in the *tail* (i.e., the last node) of the list. It is almost the same except we now have to find the last node. We have to do it by starting from the head and employ an auxiliary pointer that moves from node to node. This is best done in a separate user-defined function called `find_last(head)`, which is given the `head` pointer to the list and returns a pointer to the last node in the list. We also write another new user-defined function called `newentry_tail()` that will actually make the insertion. It will call `find_last()` to find out where the last node is. Here are these two functions. We leave it up to you as a problem in the end of the chapter to add the proper code to `main()` to make this work (hint: there isn't much to add). We recommend just adding these to the program we have been building up to this point in this chapter.

```
Nodeptr find_last(Nodeptr head)
  {
    Nodeptr travel = head;
    while(travel->next != NULL)
        travel = travel->next;
    return travel;
  }
void newentry_tail(Nodeptr head)
  {
    Nodeptr last = find_last(head);
    Nodeptr newnode = NULL;
    int n = 0;

    printf("What value do you want to assign to this new node? \n");
    scanf("%d", &n);
```

```
    if((newnode = malloc(sizeof(Node))) == NULL)
        {
            printf("malloc didn't work. Bye!\n");
            exit(0);
        }
    newnode->number = n;
    newnode->next = NULL;
    last->next = newnode;
    traverse(head);
}
```

Why did we NOT need to use a double pointer in this function? The answer is that, unlike `insertnode_head()`, this function does not need to change the value of the `head` pointer. Therefore, the original head pointer local variable in `main()` does not have to be passed by reference – only by value.

6.3   Inserting a New Node Somewhere in Between

Now let's work through the most difficult one of the three – the function that adds a new node <u>after</u> the node whose pointer is passed to the function.

It is important to fully specify where to insert the new node. Therefore, we need to write a function that will find the node <u>after which</u> we wish to make the insertion of the new node. For expediency, let's make – believe that we know the contents of the list, even though the contents of each node were determined randomly. From running this program so many times and watching its repeatable output (no seeding of the random number generator), we know that the list contains the following numbers:

72, 41, 67, 34, and 0 (these may be different in your computer, so don't panic if they are.)

We want to put the new node right after the 34, and it will contain the number 75. So, let's write the code. We will need an auxiliary function that when called, will return the address of the node after which the insertion is to take place. Therefore, it will need to know what value the node after which we want to insert contains. Let's call this function `find_loc()` and it will accept one argument, which will be the `head` pointer of the list where the insertion is to happen.

The function `find_loc()` will inquire from the user the value of the `number` member of the node after which we want to insert the new node. It will find this node and return a pointer to it. Of course, if it cannot find it, it would have to say "Sorry, couldn't find the node" and exit gracefully. But let's not worry about that for now. We will leave that up to you to do later in the problems at the end of this chapter. Note, however, that as it is written below, if one were to enter a non-existing value for `number` (i.e., it doesn't exist in any of the nodes in the list), the code below will indeed crash, because the way it is written, the `while` loop would never finish!

```
Nodeptr find_loc(Nodeptr head)
{
    Nodeptr aux = head;
    int key = 0;

    printf("What node value do you want to put the new node after? \n");
    scanf("%d", &key);   // user enters value of key to be found in list

    while(aux->number != key)  // searches for node that contains the key
```

```
        aux = aux->next;

    return aux;   // pointer that points node containing key
}
```

So, find_loc() will return the location <u>after which</u> to make the insertion. We next write the function that will make the insertion. It will be composed of three actions: 1) finding the location for the insertion; 2) creating and populating the new node with the appropriate value(s); and 3) re-directing the pointers after the insertion.

```
void newentry_here(Nodeptr head)
{
    Nodeptr here = find_loc(head); // action 1 - now it knows where to insert

    Nodeptr newnode = NULL;
    int n = 0;
    printf("What value to assign? \n");
    scanf("%d", &n);
    if((newnode = malloc(sizeof(Node))) == NULL)  // action 2 - created node
      {
        printf("malloc didn't work. Bye!\n");
        exit(0);
      }

    newnode->number = n;   // action 2 - set the values of the members
    newnode->next = here->next;   // action 3 - redirect pointers
    here->next = newnode; // action 3 - redirect pointers

    traverse(head);


}
```

Try it. Please be sure to give it a number that you know to be on the list. Otherwise, as mentioned above, it will crash (infinite loop).

This function assumes that the new node will <u>not</u> be inserted at the head of the list. This way, it will not be necessary to use double pointers. If, on the other hand, the intent is to make the function general to insert anywhere, then it will need to use double pointers for passing head by reference in case it has to be changed.

As a summarizing general comment, one could use the insert_head() or the newentry_tail() functions to build a linked list from beginning to end. One of them (depending on how one wants to build the list) would be called over and over as the list is being built. However, that was not the intent of the code written above. Rather, it was designed to enter new nodes arbitrarily as needed by a user. Lastly, it is not necessary to write three separate functions to insert nodes at different locations in a linked list (the head, the tail, or in between). One function could be written to do all three. We did it this way solely for instructional reasons.

7   Deleting Nodes from the List

The purpose of this function is to delete nodes from an existing list. This is seemingly easy now that you have all the required user-defined functions. You will need the find_loc() function to identify the node to be deleted. Once it finds the node you want to delete, just re-direct the pointers around the node to be deleted and you are done. Well, except for one important thing: a node never knows where the node in front of it is – only where the one after it is. To delete a node we need to know both: the one before and the one after. This is because the next pointer of the *before* node must be re-directed to point to the node *after* the deleted node. Because once we are pointing at the node to be deleted and cannot look backward, we will have to modify the find_loc() function to also be able to also point to the node before the one to be deleted. We can do this in two ways:

1) Define a "*trailing pointer*" that trails the auxiliary pointer by one node at every iteration. So, when the auxiliary pointer that looks for the node to delete finds it, the trailing pointer will be pointing to the node just before it. The two pointers move in tandem along the list, but only the first (lead) pointer will be used to identify the node to be deleted.
2) Instead of searching for the value of the nodes with the lead pointer, do it with its next pointer. So, when the node is found, the (only) pointer will be pointing to the node before the node to be deleted.

We leave this for you to do as a problem at the end of the chapter.

8   Doubly-Linked Lists

So far in this chapter we have been discussing what are called singly-linked lists. That is, a node only knows where the node immediately after it is, but not the one just before it. While this simplifies the building of linked lists, it does complicate a traversal of a list when we are looking for a specific node to delete, as we saw above. To remedy this situation (at least partly), we can build doubly-linked lists. Nodes in such lists have two pointers instead of just the next pointer. One pointer (the *prior* pointer) points to the node just ahead, and of course, the next pointer points to the one immediately after. This means that there is no such thing as the head or tail of the list, unless the list is to be ordered. They are generally not commonly used because they require more memory for the prior pointer, and do not, in general, provide a tremendous advantage over singly-linked lists. Therefore, all we will say about these in this course is that they do exist.

9   Summary and Conclusion

In this chapter, we covered the concept of dynamically-allocated memory and learned how to apply it. Additionally, we covered how to build linked lists, how to insert nodes in different locations in a list, and how to delete nodes from the list.

   This chapter puts together many of the things learned in the earlier chapters. Thus, it represents a leap in difficulty for a beginner programmer. However, after going through it conscientiously, we hope that you agree when we say that it isn't all that difficult after all. In it we learned how to build linked lists with dynamically-allocated memory. Memory for these variables is allocated at run time, rather than at compile time. This has the advantage that memory is allocated on a just-in-time basis, eliminating the guesswork on the part of the programmer as to how large does an array need to be for a specific application. This is the main advantage of linked lists. Beyond this, they are more flexible than arrays when items must be regularly and arbitrarily inserted into and deleted from an <u>ordered</u> list. To do this in an array would require "shoving along" the contents of possibly many cells to make room for an insertion in a particular location (remember, it is an ordered list). This could potentially be computationally expensive. When deleting, "holes" would be left in the array. Of course, such holes could be of help when the time for the insertions comes, but it is not a clean operation.

The main disadvantage of linked lists is that they are only accessible from their heads. This results in computationally-expensive traversals of the list when one wishes to find a specific node in the list. For this reason, random access (i.e., going to a specific node in one operation, as arrays can do) is not possible in linked lists. Furthermore, because of the need to have every node carry along a `next` pointer, they require more memory than arrays.

Doubly-linked lists resolve the first disadvantage at the expense of the second. Yes, they can go back and forth, making traversals easier. This can be meaningful when doing binary searches (covered in Chap. 12). Their downside is the cost of additional memory requirements for each node. However, they do not completely solve the problem of lack of random access, but will always require more memory.

10   Problems

1) Add the necessary statements to the `main()` function of the program of Sect. 6.2 above to make the program work as intended.
2) Add the termination check to the `while` loop in the `find_loc()` function of Sect. 6.3 above. Your additions should ensure that the program won't crash if the value entered by the user cannot be found in the linked list.
3) Write a program that builds a linked list from back to front. Confirm by using the `traverse()` function at every iteration of the list-building process.
4) Write a program that builds a linked list containing random integer numbers, and can delete nodes from the list. It should ask the user to indicate the value of the data member of the node it is to delete.
5) Write a program that builds a 50-node linked list where each node contains a randomly-generated integer between 0 and 100. The program will calculate the average of the values of all nodes and compute the standard deviation.
6) Now for the challenge: Build a linked list that contains the letters of the alphabet, one in each node. The head node should contain 'a', the second node should contain 'b', the third 'c', etc. Then write a function that takes this linked list and <u>physically</u> reverses it, where after its execution, the head node contains 'z', the second 'y', etc. By that we mean that it re-directs all the `next` pointers to point to the nodes in front of them, so that after execution, the last node will be the head and the head node will be the last. Verify it by traversing the list before and after the reversal using the `traverse()` function shown in this chapter.

Searching and Sorting

12

As we approach the end of this introduction to C, your education would not be complete without learning about two of the most important, as well as common, tasks in computing: searching and sorting. These are two basic yet very important functions in computing; especially searching. We start with searching and then treat sorting. Be aware that this is not to be an in-depth treatment of these topics, as you do not yet have the necessary background for a complete discussion of them. However, this introduction will set you up well for moving up to the more advanced algorithms in searching and sorting.

1   Searching – A Brief Introduction

To search is to look for something of value to us. It can be for something as simple as a misplaced document in a pile of papers, a piece of jewelry in a drawer, a bargain airfare to Paris on the Internet, or for something as complex as the meaning of life. Of course, computers can only help us in our search for a cheap airfare to Paris – certainly not for the meaning of life! On the other hand, computers do have the ability to store and manipulate enormous volumes of data, and many computing tasks involve finding and retrieving a particular data item in these large volumes of data. However, to look for something in particular (say, a specific data record) in a large data repository (aka a *database*) can be a computationally expensive process if the volume of data (aka, *search space*) is large enough and/or the data are extraordinarily complex. This is true even for the fastest modern computers. Therefore, while there are simple search techniques that are indeed simple, such searches are often not efficient enough for complex searches through very large databases. So, several techniques have been developed to make a search more efficient. These take advantage of some natural characteristics of the data being sought, or of the nature of the search. Some of these take advantage of how the data are organized and/or the goals of the search itself. They include: ordered vs. unordered; unique vs. multiple; internal vs. external; on-line vs. off-line; algorithmic vs. heuristic; etc. These are variations of the basic search process that can modify how we search a given data structure.

A search function comprises three basic actions

1) A way to inspect the contents of a specific data item to determine whether this is the desired data item or not. This is done by comparing the relevant information in the data item (its *key*) with what we are looking for (the *target key*).

© Springer Nature Switzerland AG 2020
A. J. Gonzalez, *Computer Programming in C for Beginners*,
https://doi.org/10.1007/978-3-030-50750-3_12

2) A way to move systematically through the search space, one data item at a time, until the entire search space has been examined.
3) What to do when the sought-for data item is found, or when the search fails.

While the above are seemingly simple, implementing them is often not so simple (of course in this book we strive to keep things (relatively) simple).

Sometimes what we might want to seek is not a specific piece of information in an ocean of data, but rather a path through a graph (e.g., a route through a road network), a winning tactic in chess, or a particular diagnostic/repair solution in a *solution space*. These types of searches, for the most part, are much more complex and lie in the realm of *Artificial Intelligence* (AI). We leave that for your future education in AI, graph theory, algorithm design and analysis, machine vision, and such. In this chapter, we focus strictly on searching through an existing data structure for a specific piece of data.

2   The Sequential Search

The simplest and most basic of search techniques – at least conceptually, if not always in practice -- is the *sequential search*. In a sequential search, the search process goes through the data structure in a sequential basis, data item by data item, from the beginning to the end of the data structure, until either the desired item (the *target key*) is found and announced, or the entire structure has been searched and the desired item was not found. The latter is called a *failed search*. The order in which the data structure is searched corresponds to the natural construction of the data structure - typically from the beginning to the end, however, that may be defined in that data structure. For arrays, it would start at cell #0; for linked lists, it would start with the `head` node (that pointed at by the `head` pointer).

To make things easy, our data structure of choice here will be a linear, one-dimensional structure such as a one-dimensional array or a singly-linked list. By the way, while we have not discussed searches per se in prior chapters, some of the problems in the back of the chapters actually involved some searching. By doing those problems, you have already done basic searches.

Building a search function first requires having access to the data structure to be searched -- either the head node of a linked list or the name of the array. After all, you can't search a space that you can't access. The sequential search function is rather easy to program for simple searches. If searching through an array, build a `for` loop that increments the array index by one at every iteration, as it inspects the contents of each cell in turn. A second exit criterion should be placed inside the loop body that breaks out of the loop if/when the sought-after item is found. If/when found, the search should return the cell number where the data item was found. On the other hand, if the loop exits naturally, then it indicates a failed search, and it should be so noted.

If we are to search a linked list, we again build a loop, except with a `while` loop that has a terminating condition of reaching the end of the linked list (`NULL`). In this case, the program would move an auxiliary pointer (let's call it `aux`) through the list, starting at the `head` and ending when it points to `NULL`. At each step of the way (each iteration of the loop), `aux` will access the data member(s) of the node and compare specific things found therein to the target key, which is really what we want to find. If it is found in the node, success is declared and access to the "winning" node is established and maintained through a pointer (possibly `aux` itself) for possible further action (e.g., modification, deletion, accessing and/or printing other members of that node, etc.). If the target key is not found, then the program should proclaim a failed search and move on.

This is pretty easy and you should already know how to do this. Nevertheless, let's talk about details. We begin with a sequential search through an array.

2.1   Sequential Search of an Array for the First Appearance of a Key

First, we have to build an array. We'll build one containing random integers, only because they are easy to build. The array will be of 100 cells with the numbers being between 0 and 20. Thus, we are very likely to get some repeated numbers ... on purpose. The following program will build the array and allow us to verify its correctness. Write, compile, run and verify it.

```c
#include <stdio.h>
#include <stdlib.h>
#include <time.h>

int main()
{
    srand(time(NULL));
      int arr[100];
      int n;

      for(n=0; n<100; n++)
        {
          arr[n] = rand()%20;
          printf("Cell number %d with a value of %d\n", n, arr[n]);
        }

      return 0;
}
```

Next, let's write a user-defined function called search() that when passed that array (the search space) and the target key (the data item sought), it will return an integer indicating the number of the cell where the item was first found. For the sake of simplicity, we shall assume that the search function knows that the array will have 100 cells.

```c
int search(int a[], int key)
  {
      int k;
      for (k=0; k<100; k++)
        {
            if (a[k] == key)
                return k;
        }
      printf("The search has failed \n");
      return -1; // we return -1 to indicate a failed search.
  }
```

The program will require some lines of code to be added to main() that request the key from the user and then call search(), passing to it the array arr and the target key. It also needs lines of code that determine what to do with the result returned by search(). We leave that up to you to do as an exercise.

2.2   Sequential Search of an Array for Multiple Appearances of a Key

The next complication is how to handle the situation when more than one cell that have the target key are to be identified, rather than just the first one to be encountered. It is a little more difficult, but it offers some teachable moments.

The main thing to keep in mind is that a user-defined function can only return one item – in this case, one number. In our first version of the `search()` function, this was not a problem, as we only sought the first cell where the target key was found. Given that we cannot return more than one number, we'll have to do something else. One option – the lazy way! – is to use global variables whose values are set within the `search()` function. However, that also has problems, such as how many variables will we need to declare? Well, we don't know how many times the same number will appear randomly in the 100 cells. We could instead declare a global array and assign values to it progressively as the cell numbers where our key appears are progressively identified. But let's not do that.

Rather, we do it through calling the function by reference, but somewhat differently than we did in earlier chapters. We realize that this may make no sense at first glance, but recall that when a user-defined function returns something, it does so by value – that is, it only returns a value. Returning the address of a local array declared in `search()` would not work because once `search()` exits, that block of memory goes out of scope and would no longer exist as a variable. Yes, its values may persist for a while, but only until overwritten by some other activity in the program. So, we plan to not return anything in the normal way user-defined functions return values. Instead, what if the calling function passed some data structure to the user-defined function by reference that is initially empty? It would serve only to collect the output of the user-defined function when that output cannot be simply returned.

In line with this thinking, our approach will be that when `search()` is called from `main()`, we pass a second array defined in `main()` that will contain the cell numbers where the key was found by `search()`. This, of course, means that this second array would initially be blank (i.e., zeroes), and that we would have to know how large to make it ahead of time, but one step at a time. Let's look at some code next.

Replace the entire first part of the program above with the code below (except for the pre-processor directives).

```
int search(int [], int [], int);
int main()
  {
    srand(time(NULL));
    int arr1[100], arr2[20] = {0};
    int m, n, p;
    for(n=0; n<100; n++) // builds the array
      {
        arr1[n] = rand()%20;
        printf("Cell number %d with a value of %d\n", n, arr1[n]);
      }
    printf("What integer between 0 and 19 would you like "
           "to find? \n");
    scanf("%d", &p);
    m = search(arr1, arr2, p); // also passing arr2, which has zeroes
    if(m==0) // m is the number of times the target key was found
        {
```

```
                printf("The search failed! \n");   // if zero times, fail
                return 0;

        }
     printf("\n\n");
     printf("The cells where your desired number were found are: ");
     for(n=0; n<m; n++)
            printf(" %d,", arr2[n]);

      return 0;
}


int search(int a[], int b[], int key)
 {
    int k, i=0;
    for (k=0; k<100; k++)
      {
         if (a[k] == key)
           {
                b[i] = k;
                i++;
           }
         else
                continue;
      }
    return i;
 }
```

Now let's examine what we did. We discuss search() first – please follow carefully! The user-defined function search() is passed the additional array b[], where it will place all the cell numbers where the desired key was found in a[], which is really arr1[] in main(). Because it is passed by reference, setting the value of b[] in search() directly sets the values of arr2[] in main(), which is what we want to do. The search() function goes through the entire array arr1[], as it did in the previous version of this program. However, rather than stopping when it finds the first cell that contains the key and returns its cell number, it simply adds the cell number to arr2[] via array b[]. It keeps a separate counter i to be able to let main() know how many instances it found. The function main() will need to know this so it doesn't have to print out the contents of the entire array arr2[] when only the first few may be relevant. When search() finishes searching through a[] (in reality array arr1), it stops, returns the count i of cells that contained the target key, and exits. When control comes back to main() after search() exits, arr2[] already has all the values it needs. The function main() receives the count of how many cells in arr2[] have meaningful values (i), and sets about printing those out. If the count i is 0, main() interprets this as meaning that it didn't find any instances of the key in arr1[]. Please write the program, compile and run it. Verify that it works. Then, please try to understand what we did here.

Next we will do something similar, except with a linked list.

2.3   Sequential Search of a Linked List

We are hoping by now that we do not need to be as explicit in the description of this search function as we were in the previous two versions. First, we will need to build the linked list. Let's do the same thing – 100 nodes, each of which contains a random integer between 0 and 20. See the code below:

```
#include <stdio.h>
#include <stdlib.h>
#include <time.h>

typedef struct node  {
    int number;
    struct node * next;
}  Node;
typedef Node * Nodeptr;
int search_ll(Nodeptr, int);

int main()
  {
    int n, k, t;
    srand(time(NULL));
    Nodeptr head=NULL, aux=NULL, newnode=NULL;
    if ((head = malloc(sizeof(Node))) == NULL)
      {
        printf("Allocation failed.  Bye!");
        exit(0);
      }
    head->number = rand()%20;
    head->next = NULL;
    aux = head;

    for(n=1; n<100; n++)
      {
        if ((newnode = malloc(sizeof(Node))) == NULL)
          {
            printf("Allocation1 failed.  Bye!");
            exit(0);
          }
        newnode->number = rand()%20;
        newnode->next = NULL;
        aux->next = newnode;
        aux = newnode;
        printf("The value for node %d is: %d\n", n, newnode->number);
      }
    printf("\n\n");
    printf("What number do you want to find? \n");
    scanf("%d", &k);
    t = search_ll(head, k);
    if(t == -1)
      {
```

```
        printf("The search failed! \n");
        return 0;
      }
    else
        printf("The key was found in node # %d \n", t);

    return 0;
  }

int search_ll(Nodeptr top, int key)
  {
    Nodeptr aux1 = top;
    int m;
    for (m=0; m<100; m++)
      {
        if(aux1->number == key)
            return m;
        aux1=aux1->next;
      }
    return -1;
  }
```

Please write this program, compile it and run it. Verify the results through the printouts. Now let's discuss the code.

The main() function builds the linked list. You should already know how to do that from Chap. 11, but some review won't hurt. Similarly to what we did in the array-based search program, it requests a key from the user, and calls the search_ll() function, passing it the head and the target key to be sought. It receives the number of the first node encountered that contains the target key. Then it prints out the results. If the search_ll() function returns a – 1, this is indicative of a failed search, and it is so announced. Now for the search_ll() function:

The search is done in a for loop. This works only because the size of the linked list is known *apriori*. This is not often the case, so a more general approach would have been to search the linked list inside a while loop, checking for a pointer to NULL to signify the end of the list. We leave that for you to do as a chapter problem. The auxiliary pointer aux1 will be declared and initialized to head. This is the pointer that the program uses to traverse the linked list.

The comparison is made inside an if statement. If successful, the number of the iteration is returned and the function exits. Otherwise, it continues and updates aux1, as this is necessary to make it move down the list, accessing the subsequent node in each iteration.

Going through the entire loop implies the search failed, so search_ll() returns a – 1 and exits.

The main() function picks up the value of the cell number returned by search_ll() and announces it via a printf() statement. If the value returned by search_ll() is −1, then it announces that the search failed and ends. We should note that returning the node number in a linked list is not that useful, as the program would have to go back to the head node and move an auxiliary pointer so many times until the right node is found. That would amount to doing the search all over again! It would be better to simply return the auxiliary pointer aux1, which is already pointing to the node of interest. This would require no further work by the calling function.

As a problem at the end of the chapter, we ask that you modify this program to inform the numbers of nodes that contained the target key, as we did for the second array-based search. You could also set the values of an array of pointers in main() that represent the nodes that contained the target key.

We have been discussing searching lists that are unordered. That is, the contents have been added and deleted arbitrarily, in no special order. On the other hand, ordered lists are actually easier to search. Let's discuss that first, then continue to learning how to order a list.

2.4   Thoughts on Advanced Search Techniques

As we mentioned above, searching through an unordered list is more computationally expensive than searching through an ordered list. This is because the program can enter an ordered list at places other than the beginning, and immediately be able to determine on which part of the list contains the target key, if present in the list. This is what people did back in the days of printed telephone books: start in the middle and see exactly where in the alphabetically-ordered book the target is. If the target key was less than that, then one would further search the pages on the left side. Otherwise, one would continue searching only those pages on the right side. In either case, one could *prune* the search space by approximately half because one was certain that the target key would not be in the pruned part. That could significantly reduce the search space. Moreover, one could do that again and again, very quickly finding the right page, and then the right line. This is a popular search technique in computing, called the *binary search*. In this type of search, the program always begins to search in the middle of the un-pruned part of the list. It then determines which half of the list to prune away. It continues the search by going to the middle of the "active" part of the list. In only two steps, three-quarters of the list has been pruned away! Thus, binary searches are very efficient. Most algorithmic implementations use *recursion* to implement the concept. Recursion is an advanced computing technique that defines a function in terms of itself (yes, this is indeed possible). The function is called again and again by virtue of this embedded self-call, but with simpler and simpler problems (i.e., a smaller and smaller search space). Because recursion is beyond the scope of this book, we do not cover binary searches here any further.

Other more advanced search mechanisms not discussed here involve binary trees – not very difficult to understand – one just needs to have some pre-requisite knowledge to understand them.

3   Sorting a List

Sorting a list means rearranging the elements of that list in some sort of order – alphabetical order, numerical order (increasing or decreasing), temporal order – so that they can be read in that order. It is a common task in computing because ordered lists are much easier to search than unsorted. So, a list that is often searched could benefit from investing the computational cost once to get it sorted, and thereafter make the search operations more efficient. This could be worthwhile in the long run.

There are several classes of sorting algorithms: 1) Simple but relatively inefficient ones; 2) Complex but efficient ones; 3) Somewhere in between, and 4) graph-based sorting algorithms that are efficient and relatively simple to write but require somewhat advanced data structures. The complex ones, the graph-based ones and even the medium ones require knowledge of concepts and techniques not covered here because they are beyond the scope of a beginner programmer course. So we are forced to limit our discussion to the simple but inefficient algorithms. The types of lists we plan to sort here will be simple enough and small enough that their inefficiencies will not matter.

Sorting algorithms can be implemented in either linked lists or in contiguous (i.e., array-based) lists. However, they are much easier to implement in contiguous lists, as random movement from one cell to any other can be done instantaneously, and regions to be sorted can be much more easily identified. Because of this, we will only use arrays to hold the lists to be sorted in this discussion.

We will introduce two such simple but relatively inefficient algorithms: *SelectionSort* and *BubbleSort*. We begin with SelectionSort.

3.1   SelectionSort Algorithm

SelectionSort is easy to understand. It creates a *sorted* and an *unsorted* region in an array. The sorted region is initially empty (or only contains cell #0, as a list of one is by definition sorted) and the unsorted region encompasses the entire list (or from cell position 1 to the end). We will assume that the sorted region begins at cell #0 and grows to the right, but it can actually start from the other end as well and grow to the left. Nevertheless, because there is always a 0 cell at the beginning, it is convention that the sorted region will grow left to right. So:

Initially: [sorted region, unsorted region]

SelectionSort searches the unsorted region for the smallest valued element therein (assuming an increasing order sort is desired). Once found, it swaps its location with that of the first element of the unsorted region, and that element now becomes part of the sorted region. It continues to do this repeatedly so that the sorted region grows by one cell and the unsorted region shrinks by one cell during each iteration. This continues until the unsorted region becomes empty, and the entire list is sorted. See the example below. Each row is the result of one iteration of the sorting loop. Red indicates the sorted region while black indicates the unsorted region.

Note that on each row, the lowest black number is exchanged with the black number in the cell in the unsorted region that is immediately adjacent to the sorted region. This cell now becomes part of the sorted region.

1	6	4	7	3	2	5
1	2	4	7	3	6	5
1	2	3	7	4	6	5
1	2	3	4	7	6	5
1	2	3	4	5	6	7
1	2	3	4	5	6	7

The code for the SelectionSort algorithm is rather simple. It is as follows:

```
for(i=0; i<n; i++)   {
      small = i;
      for(j=i+1; j<n; j++)
            if(x[j] < x[small])
                  small = j;
      swap(x, i, small);
   }
```

Where the swap(arg1, arg2, arg3) function swaps the position of its first argument with that of its second argument in the array.

Let's now implement the code on the following array.

```
int a[] = {4, 1, 9, 5, 7, 3, 8, 0, 6, 2};
```

The integer n represents the size of the array, but for simplicity, we will assume that the user-defined functions swap() and printout() already "know" that the array is of size 10 cells.

```
// This is the SelectionSort Algorithm
#include <stdio.h>
#include <stdlib.h>

void swap(int [], int, int);
void printout(int []);

int main()
{
    int a[] = {4, 1, 9, 5, 7, 3, 8, 0, 6, 2};
    int i,j,small;

    printout(a);
    printf("\n\n");

    for(i=0; i<10; i++)   {
        small = i;
        for(j=i+1; j<10; j++) {
            if(a[j] < a[small])
                small = j;
        }
        swap(a, i, small);
    }
    printout(a);
    printf("\n\n");

    return 0;
}

void swap(int a[], int x, int y)
{
    int temp = 0;
    temp = a[x];
    a[x] = a[y];
    a[y] = temp;
}
```

```
void printout(int a[])
{
    int n;
    for(n=0; n<10; n++)
        printf(" %d ", a[n]);
}
```

The output will be:

```
4  1  9  5  7  3  8  0  6  2
0  1  2  3  4  5  6  7  8  9
```

To appreciate more intimately how the algorithm works, let's add a call to `printout()` in the outer loop to see how the array progresses from unsorted to sorted at every iteration.

Leaving all else unchanged, we insert a `printout()` and a `printf()` in the outer `for` loop as follows (in bold-face font):

```
for(i=0; i<10; i++)   {
        small = i;
        for(j=i+1; j<10; j++)
            if(a[j] < a[small])
                small = j;
        swap(a, i, small);
        printout(a);
        printf("\n");
```

The output is now:

```
4  1  9  5  7  3  8  0  6  2
0  1  9  5  7  3  8  4  6  2
0  1  9  5  7  3  8  4  6  2
0  1  2  5  7  3  8  4  6  9
0  1  2  3  7  5  8  4  6  9
0  1  2  3  4  5  8  7  6  9
0  1  2  3  4  5  8  7  6  9
0  1  2  3  4  5  6  7  8  9
0  1  2  3  4  5  6  7  8  9
0  1  2  3  4  5  6  7  8  9
0  1  2  3  4  5  6  7  8  9

0  1  2  3  4  5  6  7  8  9
```

One can see how the sorted region grows left to right until the entire list is sorted. In this case, the last three iterations of the outer loop result in identical outputs because the list is already sorted (by coincidence). Note that the algorithm doesn't recognize this, and just continues on its merry way as prescribed in the code.

Now let's look at another popular sorting algorithm.

3.2   BubbleSort Algorithm

The BubbleSort algorithm is one of the most popular sorting programs. It also works with a sorted and an unsorted region and only does local swaps. It compares the contents of two adjacent cells. If they are in the right order, then it does nothing and continues. However, if they are in reverse order, it swaps its contents. It basically picks up the largest element found and by comparing it to its adjacent neighbor, drags it to the end until it either meets a larger value or it reaches the end.

2	6	4	7	3	1	5
2	6	4	7	3	1	5
2	6	4	7	3	1	5
2	4	6	7	3	1	5
2	4	6	7	3	1	5
2	4	6	7	3	1	5
2	4	6	3	7	1	5
2	4	6	3	7	1	5
2	4	6	3	1	7	5
2	4	6	3	1	7	5
2	4	6	3	1	5	7
2	4	6	3	1	5	7

Let's focus our attention aon the table above. In each row, the two blue-colored numbers next to each other are compared to one another to determine whether they are in the correct order, but only with respect to each other. If they are, then the processor does nothing and moves on to the cell to the right and compares those two numbers – the right-most one of the two compared in the previous iteration, and then the new one to its right. If they are not in the right order, their positions are swapped before the processor moves on as above. This is done until the right-most one in the array is included in the comparison. Then the same process occurs again and again until the list is completely sorted. This table only shows the first iteration of the outer loop and the very beginning of the second one on the last row.

The C implementation of the BubbleSort algorithm is as follows: (obtained from CProgramming. com): a [ ] is the array that contains the list and n is the size of the array a.)

```
for(x=0; x<n; x++)    {
   for(y=0; y<n-1; y++)   {
       if(a[y] > a[y+1])
              swap(a, y, y+1);
          }
      }
```

Note that in the above snippet, the swap is done in the inner loop if the contents of the two cells being compared are in reverse order. In the SelectionSort, the swap was done in the outer loop.

Let's now implement this code above and execute the program with the array:

```
a[] = {2, 6, 8, 4, 7, 9, 3, 1, 5, 0};
```

We make the same assumption about the size of the array being known to be 10 for simplification. So, we replace n in the snippet above by 10.

```
#include <stdio.h>
#include <stdlib.h>

void swap(int [], int, int);
void printout(int []);
int main()
{
    int a[] = {2, 6, 8, 4, 7, 9, 3, 1, 5, 0};
    int x,y;

    printout(a);
    printf("\n\n");

    for(x=0; x<10; x++)    {
        for(y=0; y<10-1; y++)   {
            if(a[y] > a[y+1])
               swap(a, y, y+1);
        }
    }
    printf("\n");
    printout(a);
    printf("\n\n");

    return 0;
}

void swap(int a[], int i, int j)
{
    int temp = 0;
    temp = a[i];
    a[i] = a[j];
    a[j] = temp;
}

void printout(int a[])
{
    int n;
    for(n=0; n<10; n++)
        printf(" %d ", a[n]);
}
```

Sure enough, the output will be{

```
2 6 8 4 7 9 3 1 5 0
0 1 2 3 4 5 6 7 8 9
```

A nice animation of the Bubble-Sort algorithm can be found in https://www.quora.com/
In-laymans-terms-what-is-the-difference-between-a-bubble-sort-and-an-insert-sort

3.3   Thoughts on Advanced Sorting Algorithms

As we discussed for searching algorithms, several efficient and advanced sorting algorithms exist. The more complex and efficient ones also are typically implemented with recursion (MergeSort). Moreover, there are several that rely on trees (TreeSort) and others on heaps (HeapSort). Again, these are outside the scope of this book.

4   Summary and Conclusion

This chapter introduced the learner to two very important tasks in computing: how to search a data repository for something specific, and how to put a list of items in some type of order. Although the types of searching and sorting programs that we introduced are rather simple, they nevertheless expose the learner to these important concepts. More significantly, however, they provide an opportunity for the learner to put into practice many of the concepts learned in the first eleven chapters. More practice is never a bad thing.

5   Problems

1) Write a program that searches a linked list to determine the multiple nodes where the desired key is found. Build a list of 100 nodes with random numbers between 0 and 20. We only need to identify and save the node numbers for this problem.
2) Modify the problem above to find the nodes in the linked list that contain the key (multiple ones), but rather than just identifying the node numbers, it is to produce a set of pointers (an array of pointers) that point to each of these nodes for easy access.
3) Write a program that will search for strings in a list. The list should be called `beatles` and whose contents include "`john`", "`paul`", "`george`" and "`ringo`". Build a search function that will search the list for to see whether a user-provided name was one of the Beatles or not. Start with

   ```
   char * beatles[4] = {"john", "paul", "george", "ringo"};
   ```

   Then write the search function to search this array and see whether "`george`" and "`ringo`" are in that list. Then check to see whether "`mick`" and "`bruce`" are on that list.
4) Add the appropriate output statements to progressively inspect the progress of the BubbleSort as we did above for the SelectionSort. Sort the following list in increasing order.

   ```
   array[] = {2, 6, 8, 4, 7, 9, 3, 1, 5, 0};
   ```

5) Sort the following list in <u>descending</u> order with the SelectionSort algorithm.

   ```
   array[] = {2, 6, 8, 4, 7, 9, 3, 1, 5, 0};
   ```

6) Do the same as problem #5 except with the BubbleSort algorithm.
7) Rewrite the `search_ll()` function of Sect. 2.3 to use a `while` loop instead of a `for` loop. This will make it more general in that it won't be necessary to know the size of the linked list to be searched.

Glossary

Abstraction The process of labeling a set of low level instructions with one label to avoid having to re-state the possibly long set of instructions repeatedly.

Address-of Operator Returns the address in memory where its argument variable is located.

Arrays Indexed data structures that can hold multiple different variables of the same name and data type.

Arrow operator Operator able to access the value of a structure member variable to permit operations on this value. Used when a pointer to the structure instance is used.

ASCII Table Published table that maps characters to 8-bit integer values. This permits characters to be represented as 0's and 1's. These integers are nominally non-computable, but can actually be computed in C.

Bit Electronic element that can hold a binary level of voltage interpreted as a 0 or a 1.

Boolean operators Operators that evaluate the truth value of an expression and return 1 if true and 0 if false (not true).

Byte A string of eight sequentially-located bits.

Code::Blocks Open source IDE used in this book.

Conditional structures Also called selection structures. These are means to redirect the flow of execution depending on the result of some test.

Comment line Statements in the source code that are not considered for compilation by the compiler. They are used only to inform a human reader of the source code.

Compilation errors Errors in programs related to incorrect syntax in the source code statement. In effect, the compiler does not understand the statement and cannot compile it. Normally detected by the compiler and typically prohibit the compilation of the source code.

Compilation The process of translating source code statements into machine language instructions. This is done by compilers.

Computer memory A long string of binary elements called *bits*, each of which can hold either a 0 or a 1. A computer's memory is equipped with an indexing system (beyond the scope of this book) that allows any location in this long string to be found efficiently.

Computer program The process of putting together a set of *instructions* in a correct and meaningful sequence for the computer to execute, to achieve some desired result.

Data type A way to classify a variable so that the compiler will allocate sufficient memory to hold a specific type of variable.

Dot operator Operator able to access the value of a structure member variable to permit operations on this value. Used when the name of the structure instance is used directly

Double Pointers Pointers that hold the address of other pointers.

© Springer Nature Switzerland AG 2020
A. J. Gonzalez, *Computer Programming in C for Beginners*,
https://doi.org/10.1007/978-3-030-50750-3

Dynamic Memory Allocation A process through which memory blocks are allocated to variables during run time, rather than by the compiler prior to execution.

Executable program A file that contains the compiled and linked program in machine language, ready to execute. It is typically indicated by an .exe extension.

High-level programming languages Provide the syntax rules for quasi-English text statements that represent one or more of the instructions that make the instructions more easily understood and applied by humans. The statements must be translated into machine language to be understood by the computer processor.

Increment/decrement operators Operators that increment or decrement the value of an integer variable by 1.

Indirection operator Returns the value held by a variable whose address is contained in a pointer that is the argument of this operator.

Infinite loop A condition where a repetition structure will never cease executing the loop code because the conditions for loop cessation will never be attained.

Instructions operations that act on data to achieve some objective.

Instruction set instructions that can be executed by a processor and thereby included in a program.

Integrated Development Environment (IDE) A system that facilitates the building, debugging, compiling, linking and execution of programs by a programmer by providing tools to assist in this process.

Linked lists A data structure that can hold lists (of anything) using dynamically-allocated memory.

Logic Errors Errors in programs that compile and terminate properly but provide an incorrect answer. In effect, the program does what the programmer tells it to do, but that is not exactly what the programmer intended to do.

Loops Also called *Repetition Structurse*. These are means to redirect the flow of computation so that a block of instructions (statements) are executed repeatedly as long as some condition(s) hold true.

Machine language Instructions and data expressed as a long series of 0's and 1's.

Pointers Variables that hold the memory addresses of other variable, functions or files.

Pre-processor Directives C statements that are executed before the source code is compiled. These are used to modify the source code or to add the contents of other files to the source code.

Random number generator A standard function in C that generates a (pseudo-) random number. This is useful for many applications.

Repetition Structure Also called loops. These are means to redirect the flow of computation so that a block of instructions (statements) are executed repeatedly as long as some condition(s) hold true.

Reserved Keywords A set of 37 labels that have intrinsic meaning in C and thus cannot be used as names of variables or functions in C.

Run Time errors Errors in programs that compile successfully but some flaw in the program arises during run time that causes it to not terminate normally. Typically results in a program crash. If effect, the program executes the programmer's intent as expressed in the source code, but at least one flaw prohibits the completion of the program.

Searching The process of looking for a specific item (the *target key*) in a possibly large data structure or database.

Selection Structures Also called conditional structures. These are means to redirect the flow of execution depending on the result of some test.

Sorting The process of placing items in some pre-determined order, such as alphabetically, descending numerical order, etc.

Source Code An ordered sequence of high-level language statements authored by the programmer that composes the computer program.

String A character array that is treated somewhat specially by the C language. It can be used to hold words, sentences, paragraphs, etc.

Structures Data structures that can hold variables of many different data types in one grouping.

Variables Locations in main memory that can hold values of data to be easily retrieved and updated later.

Index

A

Abstraction, 65, 66
Adding nodes to linked list, 169
Address-of operator, 84, 91, 93–95, 102, 108
Anonymous structures, 116
Array cell, 99, 100, 104, 161
Arrays, 62, 90, 95, 97–114, 117, 123–125, 127, 128, 131,
　　132, 139–142, 144, 149–153, 155, 157, 158, 161,
　　162, 167, 172, 173, 176–179, 181–186, 188
Arrays and pointers, 101, 123
Arrays of strings, 107
Arrow operator, 117–120, 122, 125, 161
ASCII Table, 18, 133
Assignment operator, 16, 17, 23, 26, 74, 85, 102,
　　128, 129
automatic variables, 68, 77, 148

B

Binary search, 173, 182
Bits, 15, 18–21, 29, 43, 47, 53, 55, 59, 73, 75–77, 86, 88,
　　91, 94, 95, 101, 116, 131, 137, 139, 141, 143,
　　144, 150, 155, 167
Block of code, 8, 37, 38, 40–42, 44, 47
Boolean operators, 27–29, 37, 40
break statement, 42–45, 48, 51, 55, 61
BubbleSort algorithm, 186, 188
Bytes, 18, 21, 84, 91–93, 101, 158, 159

C

Call-by-reference, 79, 88–90, 95, 96
Call-by-value, 79, 88
Called function, 66, 70–73, 75, 77, 79, 88–90, 95, 104,
　　121, 148
Calling a function, 67
Calling function, 65–81, 87–90, 95, 96, 104, 178
char, 16, 18, 83, 84, 91, 93, 111, 127, 133
Character arrays, 99, 106–108, 127, 144
Code::Blocks, vi, 2–7, 10, 13, 16, 17, 147, 149, 150, 155
Comment lines, 6, 8–10, 17
Compilation, 1, 5, 7, 8, 11, 19, 32, 53, 67, 73, 98, 104,
　　128, 147, 157

Compilation errors, 2, 10, 13, 21, 26, 51, 74, 160
Computer instructions, 1
Computer memory, 15, 98
Computer program, 1, 15, 58, 67
Conditional statement, 36, 37
Conditional structure, 35, 37, 143
const, 16, 32, 33
Constants in C, 9, 32–34, 76, 166, 167
Contiguous memory, 98, 101, 102, 111, 113, 158, 162
Continuation criterion, 49, 50, 52, 58, 167
continue statement, 50–52
Controlling expression, 43, 45
Counter-controlled loops, 47, 60, 61
Counter variables, 47, 49–53, 55, 61, 167

D

Data members of node, 162, 163, 168, 173, 176
Data structures, 33, 98, 99, 102, 111, 113, 116, 124, 125,
　　144, 160, 175, 176, 178, 182
Declaring variables, 15
#define, 8, 9, 32, 33
Defining a function, 67, 68, 89
Defining data types, 18, 116, 125
Defining variables, 9, 18, 157
Deleting nodes from linked list, 172
Direct referencing, 83
Dot operator, 118, 119, 124, 125, 160
double, 16, 18, 21, 69, 92, 98, 100, 105, 106, 112, 133,
　　135, 136
Double pointers, 93–96, 169–171
Double selection structures, 39–42, 45
Doubly-linked lists, 163, 172, 173
do-while loop, 47, 57, 58, 62, 63
Dynamically-allocated memory, 119, 157–173

E

Entry condition loop, 48, 49, 57
Equality operator, 17, 129
Escape characters, 138
Executable files, 1, 19
Exit condition loop, 48, 57

© Springer Nature Switzerland AG 2020
A. J. Gonzalez, *Computer Programming in C for Beginners*,
https://doi.org/10.1007/978-3-030-50750-3

Exit criterion, 48–50, 55, 176
Exit-control variable, 48, 49
External file I/O, 139–143
extern variables, 148, 152, 154

F
fclose(), 142
FILE data type, 139
flag specifier in printf(), 137, 138
float, 16, 18, 21, 22, 83, 97, 99, 112, 116, 121, 133,
    135–137, 158
fopen(), 139, 141–144, 158
for loops, 47, 49–56, 60–63, 163, 166, 167, 176, 181,
    185, 188
fprintf(), 139–141
fscanf(), 139, 141, 142
Function arguments, 67–69, 72, 73, 75, 87, 88, 90, 104,
    129–131, 133, 149, 150, 158, 167, 170, 184
Function parameters, 68–71, 73, 104, 121, 149
Function prototypes, 7, 70

G
getchar(), 108, 133, 144
gets(), 108, 132, 133, 144
Global variables, 7, 74, 76, 77, 79, 90, 148,
    151–155, 178

H
Header files, 7, 8
head pointer, 161–164, 166–170, 176
High-level programming languages, v, 1, 16

I
if-then statements, 36
#include, 8, 14
Increment/decrement operators, 26, 27, 53, 55, 84
Indirect referencing, 83
Indirection operator, 85, 93, 95, 102
Infinite loops, 48, 53, 55, 57, 171
Initializing arrays, 98–101
Initializing strings, 107, 127, 128
Instruction set, 1
int, 17, 18
Integer division, 24, 25, 138
Integrated development environment (IDE), vi, 2, 10, 13,
    16, 49, 59, 61, 63, 69, 128, 140, 147, 155
Internal linkage, 148

L
Linked list nodes, 168, 171, 172, 176, 188
Linked lists, 87, 157–173, 176, 179–182, 188
Local variables, 77–79, 88–90, 148, 150, 151, 170
Logic errors, 2, 12, 13, 19, 22, 39
Loop, 26, 47
Loop body, 47, 48, 50–57, 61, 176
Loop iteration, 61, 62, 165

M
Machine language, 1, 10, 66, 76
main.c, 5, 17, 149–156
main() function, 6–11, 16, 17, 19, 20, 37, 42, 44, 45,
    60, 61, 65–78, 80, 81, 84, 89–91, 96, 99, 102,
    104, 105, 112, 118–121, 123, 137, 143, 147, 149,
    150, 155, 158, 159, 164, 167, 169, 170, 173,
    177–179, 181
malloc(), 158, 161
Mathematical operators, 33
Mod division, 25, 45, 60
Multi-dimensional arrays, 108–111
Multi-file programs, 18, 76, 79, 147–156
Multiple selection structures, 40–43, 45

N
Nested loops, 62, 63, 109
newline control character, 12
next pointer, 162, 164, 166, 167, 172, 173
NULL, 87, 130, 132, 139, 141, 143, 158, 163, 166, 167,
    176, 181
Null terminator, 106, 107, 129, 130, 132, 138

O
Operators in C, 16, 117
Ordered search, 175, 182

P
Passing arrays, 102, 104–106
Passing by reference, 96
Passing by value, 75
Passing structures to functions, 120–123
Passing to functions, 66, 75, 79, 88, 104–106, 111,
    120–123
Pointer, 83–96
Pointer arithmetic, 90
Pointer math, 90–93, 101–102
Pointer variables, 83–96, 159, 161, 162, 169
Post-increment/decrement operator, 26
precision specifier in printf(), 136–137
Pre-increment/decrement operator, 26, 27
Pre-processor directives, 8–9, 32, 33, 59–61, 69, 71, 75,
    148, 158, 178
printf() function, 12, 14, 15, 19–22, 26, 27, 29–31, 38,
    39, 41, 44, 50, 52, 54, 56, 57, 61–63, 67, 73, 74, 85,
    94, 95, 100, 103, 106–108, 119, 125, 129, 131–139,
    142, 144, 163, 181, 185
Programmer-defined functions, 68
Programming structures, 35, 36, 45, 111
Pseudo-statements, 7, 9
putchar(), 132, 133, 144
puts(), 131–132, 144

R
The rand() function, 59–61
Random numbers in C, 58–60, 63
Random access, 98, 102, 161, 173

Referencing a variable, 75
Repetition structures, 26, 35, 42, 47–64, 113
Reserved keywords, 7, 16, 32, 36, 39, 42, 49, 56, 68, 69,
        87, 114, 116, 148
Returning a value, 66, 69, 74, 75
return statement, 17, 42, 69, 87
Run-time errors, 13, 31, 67, 73

S
scanf() function, 30, 31, 67, 86, 107–108, 132,
        133, 139, 144
Scope of variables, 75–79, 148
Search space, 175–177, 182
Searching a list, 182
SelectionSort algorithm, 183–185, 188
Selection structures, 35–45, 47, 48, 51, 52, 55, 61, 63,
        113, 130
Self-referencing structure, 162
Sentinel-controlled loops, 48, 55, 57, 61, 63
Sentinel variable, 56–58
Sequential search, 176–182
Sequential structures, 35, 113, 163
Short-circuit evaluation, 28
Signed integer, 24, 53
Single selection structures, 36–40, 45, 55
sizeof(), 158, 159, 161
Sorting a list, 182–188
Source code, 1, 2, 5–10, 13, 17, 19, 32, 37, 43, 71, 76, 147
Source file, 1, 2, 5, 10, 17, 68, 148
srand() function, 59
Stack address, 77
Static functions, 155
Static variables, 79, 148
strcat(), 130, 131
strcmp(), 129, 130
strcpy(), 128, 129
Strings, 106–108, 127–133
strlen(), 129

struct, 16, 113–116, 123–125, 158, 160–163
Structure instance, 114–120, 122, 123, 125, 160, 161
Structure member operators, 118
Structure members, 125
Structures, 113–125
Structure tag, 114–116, 118, 119, 125, 162
Structure template, 114–118, 125
Structures and arrays, 123–125
switch structure, 35, 42–45, 52, 80

T
tail pointer, 161
Target key, 175–179, 181, 182
Test condition, 35, 36, 38, 39, 41, 47, 55
Traversing a linked list, 167–168
Type specifier, 19, 21, 23, 87, 107, 108, 133, 138
typedef, 16, 116–118, 125, 158, 159, 161, 162

U
Unordered search, 175, 182
Unsigned integer, 24
User-defined functions, 42, 68–71, 74–76, 79–81, 83, 84,
        87, 95, 96, 101, 102, 104–106, 111, 120, 121,
        125, 147–149, 152, 153, 155, 156, 167, 169, 172,
        177–179, 184

V
Variables, 15–34
Variables, address of, 85, 87, 90, 91 85, 87, 90, 91, 93,
        95

W
while loops, 47, 55–58, 60–63, 167, 170, 173, 176,
        181, 188
width specifier in printf(), 134–136

Printed in the United States
by Baker & Taylor Publisher Services